Conversations with William Kennedy

Literary Conversations Series

Peggy Whitman Prenshaw
General Editor

Conversations
with William Kennedy

Edited by
Neila C. Seshachari

University Press of Mississippi
Jackson

Books by William Kennedy

The Ink Truck. New York: Dial Press, 1969.
Legs. New York: Coward McCann & Geoghegan, 1975.
Billy Phelan's Greatest Game. New York; Viking Press, 1978.
Ironweed. New York: Viking Press, 1983.
O Albany! Improbable City of Political Wizards, Fearless Ethnics, Spectacular Aristo-crats, Splendid Nobodies and Underrated Scoundrels. Albany, NY: Washington Park Press, 1983. New York: Viking Press, 1983.
Charlie Malarkey and the Belly Button Machine, by William Kennedy and Brendan Kennedy. Children's Book. New York: The Atlantic Monthly Press, 1987.
Quinn's Book. New York: Viking Penguin, 1988.
Very Old Bones. New York: Viking Press, 1992.
Riding the Yellow Trolley Car. New York: Viking Press, 1993.
Charlie Malarkey and the Singing Moose, by William Kennedy and Brendan Kennedy. Children's Book. New York: Viking Press, 1994.
The Flaming Corsage. New York: Viking Press, 1996.

Copyright © 1997 by University Press of Mississippi
All rights reserved
Manufactured in the United States of America

00 99 98 97   4 3 2 1

The paper in this book meets the guidelines for permanence and durability of the Committee on Production Guidelines for Book Longevity of the Council on Library Resources.

Library of Congress Cataloging-in-Publication Data

Kennedy, William, 1928–
    Conversations with William Kennedy / edited by Neila C.
Seshachari.
        p.   cm.—(Literary conversations series)
    Includes index.
    ISBN 1-57806-011-7 (alk. paper).—ISBN 1-57806-012-5 (pbk. :
alk. paper)
    1. Kennedy, William, 1928–   —Interviews. 2. Authors,
American—20th century—Interviews. I. Seshachari, Neila C.
II. Title. III. Series.
PS3561.E428Z466   1997
813'.54—dc21
    [B]   97-10794
                                                   CIP

British Library Cataloging-in-Publication data available

Contents

Introduction

Most scholars recognize William Kennedy as an outstanding voice in contemporary American letters. Kennedy is not just the scholar's writer, however, or a "writer's writer," as he has sometimes been called. As an outstanding novelist, prize-winning journalist, screenwriter, collaborator in two children's storybooks, and more recently as playwright, he has stamped his writerly personality on so many artistic ventures that his name is readily recognized for one reason or another.

Movie fans know Kennedy as the author of the novel and script writer of the movie *Ironweed* starring Meryl Streep and Jack Nicholson. Writers admire him as one who started the New York State Writers Institute in Albany with part of the money that came with his MacArthur Award and which has become his permanent legacy to the writing community, since the state of New York now supports it. Literary readers love the humor and sweep of his wondrous cycle of novels about Albany. Television viewers remember seeing Kennedy with Diane Sawyer in CBS "Sixty Minutes" on Sunday, 23 December 1984, or perhaps watching him on the television program, "William Kennedy's Albany" (October 1995) on PBS. Residents of Albany and its environs now think of Kennedy as the playwright whose *Grand View* played to full houses when it premiered in Albany in May 1996. Novelist, journalist, screenwriter, and playwright, Kennedy has emerged as a man for all seasons. It is hard to believe that until 1983, not many outside Albany and New York State knew his name.

William Kennedy's meteoric rise to fame in 1983 and his continuing popularity since are the stuff of drama and folklore. From being a relatively obscure writer of three novels, he was catapulted into literary prominence with the publication of *Ironweed* (Viking 1983), which received both the National Book Critics Circle Award and the Pulitzer Prize. That same year, he received the much coveted MacArthur "genius" award and his three previous novels were reissued. Kennedy sold the screen rights to *Ironweed, Legs,* and *Billy Phelan's Greatest Game* and Francis Ford Coppola asked him to collaborate on the screenplay of *The Cotton Club.* Albany declared "A City-Wide Celebration of Albany and William Kennedy," 6–9 September 1984. Governor

Mario Cuomo honored him with the prestigious New York State Governor's Arts Award that same year and declared that "Albany [had] found its Homer" in William Kennedy. And the editors of *Syracuse Herald American's Stars* Magazine declared, "Kennedy is Upstate New York's reigning man of letters. He has ridden the trajectory of Albany's multifarious history to heights of literary success and—finally—to financial reward."

It is not surprising that William Kennedy was overwhelmed by all that attention—his wife Dana recalls that after receiving his MacArthur Award of $264,000 tax free over five years, he would go about the house in high spirits muttering, "How sweet it is!" but in spite of his euphoria, he never lost his bearing. Kennedy is a conscientious writer who works hard at developing his craft—in writing fiction, nonfiction, plays, and screenplays. He is a meticulous scholar of history yet prodigal in viewing it through his magical vision. He is mystical and irreverent simultaneously. He is funny, deep, and outrageous. And he is gregarious and speaks like a book.

Little wonder then that he should be popular in his hometown, Albany, and home state, New York, as well as in Puerto Rico, his home for six years, where he was featured in a number of interviews and newspaper articles even prior to the publication of *Ironweed*, and before he received his MacArthur Award and Pulitzer Prize. Kennedy cooperates readily with interviewers. He talks with light-hearted candor about his own development as a writer, as well as his personal fascination with Albany's history and politics. His interviews ripple with humor and searching comments on his own early hard times, his literary influences, his "religious experience of literature," his belief in his own subconscious, his reliance on the mystical elements in life, or any other aspect of his writing career.

The following selections include, among others, four interviews or interview-based articles before Kennedy received the MacArthur "genius" award in January 1983, and four more published before the announcement of the Pulitzer Prize in April 1984. Although some commonality is to be expected in all, the interviews themselves can be categorized into broad divisions. The earliest ones, which are often interview-based journalistic articles, focus on his career change from journalist to novelist and the relative merit or burden of being trained in journalism for one who has become a career novelist. Coinciding with the MacArthur big-money cash award and the publication of *Ironweed*, and a reprinting of *Legs,* and *Billy Phelan's Greatest Game,* interviews and articles tend to identify Kennedy as an icon of folklore—very much like the celebrated bootlegger and gangster Jack (Legs) Diamond, but of a different sort—a mythic, hometown hero himself, who leaves his home in quest of himself for seven years and comes back home to discover that Albany and its history embody all the stimulus he needs for his writing life. Alongside these interviews, there are those that probe his writing techniques and his place in the legacy of (Irish) American literature. Most interviews mention Kennedy's painstaking craftsmanship and his seriousness as a writer. The later interviews naturally include Kennedy's forays into the film world and the theatre. Some probe the influence of his religious Irish Catholic upbringing on his writing. No matter what the emphasis of the hour, the interviews, taken together, mirror the psychic growth of a first-rate writer's mind and the development of his craft. Collectively, these interviews will enable readers to piece together landmarks in Kennedy's development from journalist to writer, to screenwriter and playwright, as well as follow the major events in his writing life.

William Kennedy's sudden entrance into literary limelight may give the impression that he came in from the cold, but nothing could be farther from the truth. His literary apprenticeship started at a young age. At Christian Brothers Academy, he wrote for *The Sentry,* the school newspaper. He was editor of *Siena News* and an associate editor of *Beverwyck* magazine, both publications of Siena College. After graduating in 1949 with a bachelor's degree in English, he became a sportswriter and columnist for the *Post Star* in Glens Falls, New York. Drafted into the U.S. Army in 1950, he continued to send, from his posting in Germany, riproaringly embarrassing articles about the sorry state of the U.S. army to the *Post Star* until the army prudently transferred him to serve as sports editor of *Ivy Leaves,* the Fourth Division's weekly newspaper, thus keeping the young enthusiast too busy to indulge in military bashing. The army even sent him to cover the 1952 Olympic Games in Helsinki for the military publication. And back home in Albany after his release, he worked for three-and-a-half years for the *Times-Union.*

William Kennedy's success as a novelist has eclipsed his achievements as a journalist. Of his journalistic stint in Albany's premier newspaper, Kennedy has said, "The *Times-Union* was exactly the right place for me. The job let me live in and learn about my own city. The editors, before long, let me write the way I wanted. And so between 1952 and 1956, I covered everything worth covering, except heavy politics. . . . I left the paper in 1956 because I was bored and repeating myself." Recalling his years in Puerto Rico, he tells Tom Smith, "In 1956 I went to San Juan for the first time, then to Miami in '57, and back to San Juan later in '57 until 1963. In the summer of 1959 we

[William J. Dorvillier as editor, Andrew Viglucci as city editor] started *The San Juan Star,* an English language daily in the bilingual community, and it's still going. . . . I had a good time for two years and then I quit, which was my swan song as a full-time journalist. I realized that after those years as managing editor, which is as high as I ever aspired, I wanted to return to fiction. The [managing] editor's job was an offer I couldn't refuse—starting a newspaper from scratch and helping it grow in two years to 20,000 circulation, and be very influential. The editor won a Pulitzer Prize that first year for our editorial campaign against the church." In 1965, after his return to Albany, Kennedy himself was nominated for the Pulitzer Prize for his Albany slum articles in the *Times-Union.* Even though he didn't win the coveted prize, he received three other journalistic awards for his series on integration and slums in Albany in 1966–67.

Musing about his journalistic days, he says to Dan Cryer in 1996, "It was magical to be a newspaperman and also to be a writer. . . . I really wanted the world that I was reporting on to be the raw material for my life as a writer. But it took me a while to see how to use it. And what you have to do is just absorb it and then let it become part of your memory and your imagination and then evoke it when it's necessary." He admits to working "part-time as a journalist even to this rainy July day in the early summer of 1992," when he was writing a piece on Damon Runyon, his first hero and role model, for *Riding the Yellow Trolley Car,* which is a collection of Kennedy's selected nonfiction covering his entire career, "the earliest story" dating to 1954. "This book, in a way, is a writer's oblique autobiography (of his taste, if nothing else)," he writes in its introductory chapter, "The Beginning of the Book." "It is the tracking of a style."

It is not surprising that journalism vs. novel writing should come up as a key question in many of his interviews. The theme of his very first full-length interview, "The Portrait of a Writer as a Writer" in 1969, was in the form of a question: Can journalist and novelist co-exist happily within one person to the mutual satisfaction of both? Or was Hemingway really right all the time, that newspapering is the nemesis of creative writers? Kennedy scoffs at the notion that journalists can't also write great fiction. He is even more emphatic in his answer twenty-five years later. "Of course they can," he says to Don Williams, "otherwise how do you account for García Márquez, Ernest Hemingway, Theodore Dreiser, John O'Hara, Stephen Crane. There's a drive, I think, when you want to be a writer, that, if you've got it in you, nothing is going to stop it."

Kennedy's investigative forays as a journalist into Albany's seamy side of life—its shabby politics, clashes between immigrant and patrician societies, and its littered nooks harboring the homeless—eventually led to the writing of his successful nonfiction book, *O Albany! Improbable City of Political Wizards, Fearless Ethnics, Spectacular Aristocrats, Splendid Nobodies, and Underrated Scoundrels* (1983), which was reissued in paperback by Viking in 1996, with the publication of *The Flaming Corsage.* Kennedy's championship of his native city and his intrepid humor and candor in dealing with its shabby politics shine forth in the book. In the first chapter titled "Albany as a State of Mind," he begins: "I write this book not as a booster of Albany which I am, nor as an apologist for the city, which I sometimes am, but rather as a person whose imagination has become fused with a single place, and in that place finds all the elements that a man ever needs for the life of the soul." He concludes with a certitude and a promise: "It is the task of *this and other books I have written, and hope to write,* to peer into the heart of this always-shifting past, to be there when it ceases to be what it was, when it becomes what it must become under scrutiny, when it turns so magically, so inevitably, from then into now" (Italics mine).

To read *O Albany!* and understand its politics, social structure, and historical contexts—such as Prohibition, the 1901 United Traction, the 1913 flood, the cholera epidemics, the Delavan Hotel fire, gangsterism, organized crime, the kidnapping of Dan O'Connell's nephew in 1933, to name the most famous—is to witness the raw material which Kennedy sifts and churns through his imagination to transform into hauntingly memorable literature. "I am not a sociologist. I'm not a historian. I'm a novelist, and I can do anything I want with it [Albany and its history]," he tells Dan Cryer in 1996. The characters and events in the novels are connected not only to Albany's history, but to one another's destinies. A minor character in one novel may become the protagonist of another. A number of characters walk in and out of their creator's work at critical times to become part of a cat's cradle of relationships between two extended families—the Phelans/Quinns, and the Daughertys—along with their entourage of friends and enemies. It must be mentioned, however, that all of his novels stand on their own, even though a Kennedy fan may take special delight in following the destinies of different characters who know one another and inhabit his Albany.

Kennedy is perennially fascinated with Albany, a city of unscrupulous politicians, hoodlums, of gambling dens, and ethnic neighborhoods, by his own admission. It is "as various as the American psyche," he tells Joseph

Barbato in 1983, and in a June 1996 interview, he tells Robert Friedman, "I possess Albany, it possesses me." Additionally, Kennedy tells *Fiction International* that he needs "a sense of a specific world that is definable, like the Jazz Age, or the Depression, so that if I want to set a book in that time I know the thrust a character will have. I want to know how an era affects the life of Albany. . . . By knowing what would be possible in this age or outlandish in this age, I can make the intuitive leaps you need to make in terms of character psychology." And he tells Dan Cryer, 'You start with the real world, and you have a character somewhere moving in that world and then it's the intersection of history with that character that catapults you into the creation of the novel."

Kennedy's seven years away from Albany were crowded years devoted to journalism and writing, during which he married the erstwhile Broadway dancer Dana Sosa in a whirlwind courtship, fathered two of his three children, and turned himself into "a half-time newsman and full-time novelist (aspiring)." When he came back to Albany for good in 1963, he still had no published novel to show and tell, but he did not give up his self-affirmed vocation of novelist.

Of those longing days, he recounts how he couldn't call himself a writer even though he had written twenty or thirty short stories and a couple of novels, because nobody had published him. As he told Rudy Nelson, "[P]ublic acceptance was the only way you were anointed [as a writer]. But then many people do anoint themselves and one day decide, as I also did, as so many writers have to do, that you want to be a writer—the same as deciding you want to be a priest or a brain surgeon—and you work your way toward it."

Having baptized himself a writer, he came to regard writing as a religious experience. "Not because of its holiness," he says in his famous "Hopwood Lecture," "for as a profession it is more profane than sacred, but because of its enmeshment with the Catholic Church's supernatural virtues of faith, hope, and charity—as I had learned them." And he proceeds to explain himself with characteristic humor and irony. "Charity, of course, is what the writer supports himself with while he is finishing his novel. Hope is the virtue by which he firmly trusts that someday, somewhere, somebody will publish his novel. But it is in the virtue of faith that the writer grounds himself (or herself) in the true religious experience of literature; and faith was defined early on for me as a firm belief in the revealed *truths*—truths of God as religion would have it; truths of the writing life, as I would have it." Kennedy has continued to pursue the shimmering, shifting truths of the writing life as he sees them and has carved out his unique niche in American letters.

An event of great consequences to his literary aspirations was a novel writing class that Kennedy took in 1960 at the University of Puerto Rico in Rio Piedras from Saul Bellow, who had by then published five successful novels (*Dangling Man, The Victim, The Adventures of Augie March, Seize the Day,* and *Henderson the Rain King*) but was seventeen years away from his Nobel Prize. The young apprentice writer and the instructor struck a warm friendship but lost touch with each other for over two decades until Kennedy was assigned to do a story on Bellow in 1982. As Kennedy has revealed in a number of interviews, he was profoundly influenced by Below. He told Tom Smith in 1993, "Bellow said something that I never forgot, which was the idea that you should be prodigal. He said, just think about it, the billions of sperm that are expended in any given act of sex, but it only needs one to make a life." That and Bellow's remark that character is "the single most important element in determining a writer's worth." Bellow helped Kennedy get an agent for his newly completed novel manuscript about Albany, "The Angels and the Sparrows," which has never been published, but which Kennedy has transformed into *Very Old Bones.*

It was years before Kennedy realized that "The Angels and the Sparrows" was too bleak and somber. In 1969, he told Penny Maldonado, "I suppose it was a young man's unfinished education in literature. You mistake somberness for seriousness. You reject being funny. . . . Yet as a newspaperman I was always trying to see the funny side. . . . What I was unable to do was translate my comic feeling into literature. It was also an ignorance I had toward the power of comedy. I was unaware of the heights that comedy could go to. *Miss Lonelyhearts* is an example of a very comic novel that's also a serious one. It took me a long time to learn how to stop being ponderous."

His long apprenticeship as a novelist and the inexplicable slowness of his literary recognition baffled Kennedy. He voices this puzzling predicament poignantly in his *Paris Review* interview: "You know, I had had enormous success in everything I'd done in life, up until the time I decided to be a writer. I was a good student; I was a good soldier. I got a hole-in-one one day on the golf course. I bowled 299, just like Billy Phelan. I was a very good newspaperman. Anything I wanted to do in journalism, it seemed to work; it just fell into place. So I didn't understand why I was so successful as a journalist and zilch as a novelist and short-story writer."

Kennedy's first published novel, *The Ink Truck,* came in 1969. He wrote it deliberately in a surrealistic mode, he says, as a reaction to the journalistic realism that he was compelled to follow as a journalist. *The Ink Truck* was an "ambitious book in language." And it did not go unnoticed. In a brief interview for *Library Journal's* "First Novelists: Twenty-Five New Writers Discuss Their First Published Novels," he said, "My novel, *The Ink Truck,* is an effort to deny spiritual death access to the work area. . . . It is first a manic story, second a set of imposed and yet undiscovered meanings. It is, perhaps, a metaphor for commitment, a survival handbook for failures, a study in resistance, a comedy of metaphysical lust, a report on the full pursuit of disaster. . . . It is my hope that it will stand as an analgesic inspiration to all weird men of good will and rotten luck everywhere."[1] Many of the themes and ideas of his later novels can be found in embryo in this statement on his first novel.

Kennedy calls his novels the Albany Cycle. They all take place in Albany, even though the events span different historical times. In *The Ink Truck,* Albany as the locale is *implied* rather than specifically stated. The author's note, which Kennedy added when the novel was reprinted in 1984, says, "[T]his is not a book about an anonymous city, but about Albany, N.Y., and a few of its dynamics during two centuries." Kennedy's next three novels, *Legs,* which is the fictionalized account of the life and times of the historical bootlegger and gangster, Jack Diamond, and *Billy Phelan's Greatest Game* and *Ironweed,* set in the Depression era and which feature a son and father respectively as protagonists, are all set in twentieth-century Albany. *Quinn's Book* begins with the cosmic rage and cataclysm of Albany's notorious floods in 1849 and runs a decade and a half's gamut of Albany's, and America's, crowded history—kidnapings and murders, horse races, the human traffic of the Underground Railroad, battles between Irish immigrants and patrician Dutch dynasties, grand conspiracies, extravagant theatrical productions, vicious draft riots, and Civil War conflicts. *Very Old Bones,* though set in the twentieth century, spins a backward leap into 1887 and 1882 and follows the tragic aftermath of belief in Irish witchcraft. *The Flaming Corsage,* which highlights a murder mystery as its crux, begins in 1884 and ends in 1912, unfolding its events in a spellbinding narrative that is intriguingly nonlinear. To the question "Is there a grand design to the cycle?" he tells Robert Friedman in 1996, not at all. The cycle, in fact, "grew from the inside out—an

---

[1] Irene Stockvis, "First Novelists: Twenty-Five New Writers—Fall 1969—Discuss Their First Published Novels," *Library Journal* 94(1 October 1969): 3475.

organic growth, like a plant, like a tree, like a wheat field. One begets the other."

Kennedy's interest in Albany's history is all-consuming. "I've felt I wanted to understand where everything was in 1880, in 1884," he tells Barbara Fischkin in a 1983 interview. "I had a dream one night that I went back to 1884 or 1886 with a tape recorder. The tape recorder was about as big as this table, here. And it was in the back of a wagon, a horse and wagon. There was no electricity." So meticulously does Kennedy detail Albany's historical events which form the props to his utterly fictional narratives that he wants his sources at his fingertips: local history books of Albany city and county; and especially very old issues—from 1883 through 1921—of the daily newspaper, the Albany *Argus,* which he has stacked high in the basement of his sprawling home. A sense of place is paramount in a Kennedy novel. "If you leave out place, you leave out one of the principal ingredients of fiction," he says to Kay Bonetti. But it is not just place that he looks to put in his books—he knows it is more important to picture the *density of life* that infuses a place with vitality. Early in his novel-writing career, he felt distraught when he realized that he was leaving out the density of life in a given place. "I kept reading Faulkner's *The Sound and the Fury* over and over, trying to understand how he'd done it," he says in the *Paris Review* interview.

But Kennedy readily agrees that "you can exist without a place, as Kafka and Beckett will prove. You can just create the life of the mind and be extraordinary," if you have the power of language. To Kay Bonetti's comment that "there is a point of view, among some writers that language is all there is, that characters are purely 'linguistic constructs,'" Kennedy replies, "I would agree more than you think with that. Language is the *sine qua non.*"

A writer can exist without a place, too, if his or her novels are about ideas and philosophies, as in the case of Saul Bellow, Kennedy notes in *Weber Studies.* His own world, however, is "the world of event and speculation, and language but certainly not the expatiation of ideas or philosophical attitudes."

Kennedy's world is also the world of the Irish immigrants in Albany's history. It is inevitable that his Irish Catholic heritage should get linked with his literary achievements. When asked about the Irish-American literary tradition, Kennedy tells Peter J. Quinn in 1985, "When we talk about Irish-American writers . . . we are talking about an evolution. . . . God knows where I am in all of this, in this evolution, but I *know* all that has come before. . . . After Jack Kennedy, anything was possible. Goddammit, *we've* been President, and you can't hold us back anymore." He would, however, never even contemplate writing a novel about Ireland. That would be fraud. He is American. He tells Yale University undergraduate Melissa Biggs in 1988, "I don't think of myself as a hyphenated writer, the Irish-American. I think of myself as a writer who's using these materials of Irish American life to partly form an existence." Today, closer to the end of the millennium, when multiculturalism and ethnicity are in high demand in literary America, Kennedy muses in our 1996 interview that it is perhaps fated that critics would consider him an Irish-American writer, but he feels that he is also simply an American writer, who taps his American experiences to create fiction.

Kennedy continues to experiment boldly with linguistic constructs, nonlinear narratives, mystical overtones, polyphonic voices, surrealistic sweeps. At times his narratives soar on the magical realism of his imagination. He believes too that in transforming one's experience into a work of art, a writer also transforms one's "chosen art form, the novel, a micromillimeter or two." Asked whether he consciously attempts to transform the art form *every time* he writes a new novel, he said to me that it would be a happy accident if one could do that every time. But "the mandate for every writer is not to imitate yourself or anybody else." Thus it would never do to repeat a successful formula—the second novel would be as stale as yesterday's newspaper.

Early on in his career, in serious pursuit of style and invention, Kennedy not only "read and discussed the works of Sherwood Anderson, Hemingway, Dos Passos, Steinbeck, Caldwell, Fitzgerald, Mailer, Algren, Katherine Anne Porter, Flannery O'Connor, James Jones, Irwin Shaw, and Thomas Wolfe," but tried to emulate them. With characteristic humor, he confesses in "The Hopwood Lecture," "At first I was such an amateur I couldn't even imitate them, but in the year or two after I left the army I managed to write dialogue that sounded very like Hemingway and John O'Hara. I could describe the contents of a kitchen refrigerator just like Thomas Wolfe, I could use intelligent obscenity just like Mailer, I could keep a sentence running around the block, just like Faulkner. But where was Kennedy?" In 1989, he tells *Paris Review,* "as soon as you abandon your overt efforts at Style, that's where you begin to find your own voice. Then it becomes a matter of editing out what doesn't belong—a subordinate clause that says, 'That's Kafka,' or 'That's Melville,' whoever it might be. If you don't get rid of that, every time you reread that sentence you think: petty larceny." Needless to say, Kennedy's style has become distinctively Kennedian.

This collection of interviews reveals in various ways William Kennedy's high seriousness in pursuing the craft of fiction. Character, language, humor, mysticism, surrealism, narrative structure of the novel—he has pursued them all vigorously, as well as talked about them at length. "The secret things that we don't understand—these are what is truly fascinating. That's why fiction is so important to me," he tells Scott Christianson of *The Washington Park Spirit* as early as 1974. He is fascinated with Márquez for his mythical South-American town of Macondo and his exploration of the vast reaches of absurdity. "It is this sense of a second part to life, which rationality has no grasp on, that I feel I know," he tells his interviewer. "It exists! I know it exists and that is why I use surrealism in my work." At another time, Kennedy muses to Bonetti: "I don't think you can talk about the life of the soul if you don't talk about surrealistic, metaphysical elements. . . . [T]hat mystical element . . . exists in everybody's life." He acknowledges his fondness and reverence for (Mexican) Juan Rulfo, (Peruvian) Mario Vargas-Llosa, and (Colombian) García Márquez, and "Cuban writers," all of whom use magical elements in their fiction. At another time he writes, "And mystery is not only great sport, it's also, as [film director] Luis Buñuel cleverly pointed out, the basic element in all works of art." Writers know that "this isn't a flaw in their makeup, but a happy gift of a particular kind, like being born double-jointed." And he says to Rudy Nelson, "Mystery is important in creating fiction. In creating anything. . . . The high drama of imagined worlds becomes a Rosetta Stone—the key that unlocks the very real mysteries and complexities of our daily lives; and so fiction at its best has extraordinary significance for all of us." Similarly, he tells Edward C. Reilly, "The mystical part is just the element of dream in everybody's life, the element of the improbable that is always with us." And in a 1987 speech, he writes, "[T]he core of the kind of writing I've come to value: first dreaming, and then executing, the improbable, and on good days, the impossible."

If William Kennedy consciously eased himself out of full-time journalism in order to pursue novel writing, he seems to have been drawn most naturally into the film world in 1983 after the publication of *Ironweed, Legs,* and *Billy Phelan's Greatest Game.* Francis Ford Coppola, who read *Legs* with great fascination, called Kennedy in June 1983 and invited him to serve as dialogue writer for his movie, *The Cotton Club,* which was about the gangster-run Harlem nightclub of the 1920s and '30s. Kennedy has described himself as a "film freak" who had tried for years to get screenwriting assignments. The call from Coppola opened the doors to a new dimension in his writing life.

"Then came the film option for *Billy Phelan*—I am writing the script now," he tells Joseph Barbato. "*Legs* had already been optioned, for about a year, but they had never thought of me as the writer. I'll be writing that script next." Gene Kirkwood was going to produce, and Mickey Rourke was committed to star in it. Suddenly, Kennedy was being asked to write filmscripts. "Working with Coppola has been an exotic episode in my life," he says. "Great fun—that's the main thing. I've learned how to write a movie, I'll tell you that." About his scriptwriting of *Ironweed,* Kennedy says to Patrick Farrelly, "What I am trying to do is create a cinematic work of art, not something that will be the same as the book." And aware that film versions of famous novels have often resulted in bitter recriminations, Kennedy adds, "The book needs to be transferred to the screen in a way that sustains it as a work of art." But the film, in spite of its top billing with Meryl Streep and Jack Nicholson, was not as much of a box office success as the book was. Kennedy is ambivalent toward a career in film. He has defined writing novels with film in mind as a "sin." In a 1992 interview, he told his friend Tom Smith, "Movies are great fun and journalism is wonderful, but all these are composite operations that have to deal with approval by other people, even approval of yourself to deal with the other people. You have to wonder how movies ever get made, once you get into the movie business, because it is so ridiculous as a life pursuit." But Kennedy has been lured into screenwriting again. In January 1997, Universal Pictures optioned *The Flaming Corsage,* with Kennedy writing the screenplay.

Kennedy's latest novel, *The Flaming Corsage* (Viking 1996), elicits high praise in *Time* magazine from R.Z. Sheppard, who calls it "his best novel yet" and one that contains "more dramatic events, bright dialogue and strong characters than most novels twice its size" of just over 200 pages. Most critics agree that it is Kennedy's best novel since *Ironweed.* Yet some critics continue to write that Kennedy depicts a man's world to the detriment of the feminine or female world. We discussed this issue in our interview. Charging him with depicting only "Madonnas or prostitutes" is tantamount to "literary slander," he says. He doesn't understand why certain kinds of critics continue to think that way. "I have never answered a critic in my life," he adds, "that I know of."

Now at the pinnacle of his career, Kennedy continues to ponder his craft and dream up new narrative techniques for each new novel. He also finds himself referred to as a playwright, especially in his hometown. *Grand View,* which broke all records in Albany in May 1996, is his first produced full-length play. Another play, "The Sparrows," based on some episodes in *Very Old Bones,* has "problems," he tells me, of being "novelistic." He thinks of both plays as "works in progress." "The Sparrows" is the full-length version of a one-act play titled "Dinner at the Phelans," that was published in *Weber Studies: An Interdisciplinary Humanities Journal,* the journal I edit, in 1993. "I have always had long-standing respect for the theatre," he says. "This is a new world for me." To Dan Cryer, he says, "I've learned a lot about play-writing and I feel up to the challenge. . . . Not that I am going to change professions or anything. . . . The novel is the supreme form as far as I am concerned." And hours after I record his interview, he tells me that he has hit upon a (different) narrative structure for a new novel brewing in his mind.

Two questions that pop up in recent interviews are whether he is likely to write about other places—like Puerto Rico or Cuba, for example—and whether he will now write about contemporary Albany. He tells Martin Preib, "To write about the present time, to me, would be kind of autobiographical, or else purely journalistic, venture. . . . I just think I have a pluperfect imagi-nation. It's already 'had.' " And to Robert Friedman, he says, "Even if I write about Cuba, it would be part of the [Albany] cycle. Why would I want to write about anything else?"

A phenomenon that would pique his readers' interests is Kennedy's epi-phanic discovery of a new writer in his literary world. Just before the reissu-ance of *An Albany Trio* (*Legs, Billy Phelan's Greatest Game,* and *Ironweed*) in 1996, "I decided that Quinn [who appears as a child in *Ironweed* and as a minor character in *Very Old Bones*] was the writer [of the cycle] when I wrote the introduction last February," he tells Robert Friedman. This writer, obvi-ously Kennedy's surrogate, is the grandson of the colorful Maud Fallon and swashbuckling Daniel Quinn who is the protagonist of *Quinn's Book* and is named after the grandfather. How will this revelation impact the endless nar-rative possibilities of the cycle, now that the fictive writer—also the *implied* writer—of the cycle has stealthily entered the fictional world of his own creation?

To read this collection of interviews is to witness the growth of this re-markable writer from journalist to novelist, also to screenwriter and play-wright, hear William Kennedy outline and fill out his own "self portrait," and see him define himself and his craft through his own words and commen-taries. Reading Kennedy's interviews is a dialogic process—a two-way phe-nomenon, oftentimes as magical as his writing. Readers may find themselves pulled silently into these dialogues, so that they cease to be passive readers or observers and begin to hear their own voices participating in these conversations. This should surprise no one—polyphonic voices are regular fare in Kennediana.

As is customary with the Literary Conversations series, these interviews are arranged chronologically and reprinted as originally published, except where reprint rights could be secured only if factual misstatements were corrected or omitted.

No work of this nature is a singular act. Many people, by word or deed, have helped me in this venture. I would like to thank many: my husband and colleague, Candadai Seshachari, who first suggested I do this book, since I laughed so heartily and lost myself so hopelessly in reading Kennedy's works; all the writers, editors, and publishers who gave their permissions for reprinting quickly and those who ended up chatting with me because they had set aside this small business of signing permission letters for later; at Weber State University Stewart Library, Maridee Brown, Kathryn L. Payne, and Carol Hansen, all of whom helped me every time I asked them; also Betty Kusnierz, assistant to the Provost; Anne Stascavage, production editor at University Press of Mississippi; Weber State University, which gave me a grant that released me from teaching one course and supported my visit to Albany to interview William Kennedy.

I wish to specially acknowledge two, without whose assistance this book would not come to be. Seetha A-Srinivasan, Editor-in-Chief and Associate Director of University Press of Mississippi, who made thoughtful editorial suggestions and prodded me gently and artfully to the finish line. William Kennedy, without doubt the celebrated figure in this enterprise and now a personal friend, whose cooperation and help made the project seem as easy as it was enjoyable.

NCS
January 1997
Ogden, Utah

Chronology

1928 William Joseph Kennedy, an only child, is born in Albany, New York, on 16 January to William Joseph, Sr., and Mary Elizabeth McDonald Kennedy

1933 Begins to attend Public School 20

1936 An altar boy at Sacred Heart Church

1941–45 Attends Christian Brothers Academy and works on his high school newspaper, *The Sentry*

1945–49 Earns B.A. degree in English at Siena College, Loudonville, NY; becomes executive editor of the campus newspaper, *Siena News,* and associate editor of the campus magazine, *Beverwyck.*

1949 Starts working for Glens Falls (NY) *Post Star* as sports writer and columnist.

1950 Drafted into army, serves in Germany as a sports editor of 4th Infantry Division's weekly newspaper, *Ivy Leaves*

1952 Discharged from army, hired as reporter for Albany *Times-Union*

1956 Accepts job as reporter/columnist for new paper, *Puerto Rico World Journal* (San Juan), becomes assistant managing editor; paper folds in nine months.
Kennedy meets Broadway dancer Dana Sosa (Ana Daisy Segarra) on 27 December

1957 Whirlwind courtship of Dana; they marry 31 January.
Takes reporting job with *Miami Herald,* but quits in seven months to devote full time to fiction writing in Puerto Rico.

1958 Dana Elizabeth born 7 January
Becomes San Juan stringer for Time-Life

1959 Becomes the founding managing editor of *San Juan Star,* new paper
Katherine Anne born 4 June.

1960   *San Juan Star* editor (William J. Dorvillier) wins Pulitzer Prize
        for paper's editorials on church-state controversy.
        Kennedy enrolls in Saul Bellow's writing workshop at University
        of Puerto Rico, Rio Piedras, while working on "The Angels and
        the Sparrows," his unpublished novel

1961   Resigns full-time position at the *San Juan Star* to devote unim-
        peded time to novel

1963   Returns to Albany to take care of ailing father, begins reporting
        again for *Times-Union* and writes series on Albany neighborhoods
        that becomes the raw materials for *O Albany!*

1965   Wins NAACP, Newspaper Guild, NY State Publishers awards
        Nominated for Pulitzer for *Times-Union* investigative reporting
        on slums, racial integration of city

1969   First novel, *The Ink Truck,* published by Dial Press

1970   Brendan Christopher born 3 July

1971   Book editor of *Look* magazine

1972–75 Reviewer for *Life, New Republic, Saturday Review,* and *New York
        Times,* et al

1974–82 Part-time lecturer, State University of New York at Albany

1975   *Legs* published by Coward, McCann and Geoghegan

1978   *Billy Phelan's Greatest Game* published by Viking

1980–92 L.H.D. from eight universities and colleges, including Siena, his
        alma mater

1982–83 Visiting professor, English Department, Cornell University

1983   Receives John D. and Catherine T. MacArthur Foundation "ge-
        nius" award of $264,000 on 14 January
        Establishes N.Y. State Writers Institute at Albany with part of
        MacArthur money
        Ironweed published by Viking
        Legs, and *Billy Phelan's Greatest Game* are simultaneously pub-
        lished as Penguin paperbacks, the beginning of Kennedy's Albany
        Cycle of novels
        Receives tenure and full professorship at State University of New
        York—Albany
        Viking and Washington Park Press jointly publish *O Albany! Im-*

probable City of Political Wizards, Fearless Ethnics, Spectacular Aristocrats, Splendid Nobodies, and Underrated Scoundrels

1984   Receives National Book Critics Circle Award for *Ironweed*
Receives Pulitzer Prize for *Ironweed* on 16 April, day grandson, Casey Michael Rafferty is born
Governor Mario Cuomo and NY State Legislature make New York Writers Institute a state supported agency with Kennedy as director
Albany declares "A City-Wide Celebration of Albany and William Kennedy," 6–9 September
Francis Coppola's *The Cotton Club* film (with William Kennedy and Francis Coppola collaborating as script writers) has world premiere in Albany
New York State Governor's Award in the Arts
Frank O'Connor Literary Award
Columbus Foundation Award for *O Albany!*
Buys rooming house on Dove Street, Albany, where Jack Legs Diamond was murdered 18 December 1931

1986   *Charlie Malarkey and the Belly-Button Machine,* a children's book written with son Brendan, published by Atlantic Monthly Press
Creative Arts Award Citation, Brandeis University, Waltham, MA

1987   *Ironweed* film directed by Hector Babenco, script by Kennedy, has world premiere in Albany

1988   *Quinn's Book* published by Viking

1992   *Very Old Bones* published by Viking

1993   *Riding the Yellow Trolley Car* published by Viking
Elected to the American Academy of Arts and Letters
Completes draft of the three-act play, *The Sparrows,* based on *Very Old Bones*
Completes draft of three-act play, "The Sparrows"
Elected Commander of the Order of Arts and Letters, France

1994   *Charlie Malarkey and the Singing Moose,* a children's book written with son Brendan, published by Viking

1996   *The Flaming Corsage* published by Viking
One-volume omnibus edition of *An Albany Trio* (*Ironweed, Billy Phelan's Greatest Game* and *Legs*) published by Viking

Grand View, Kennedy's two-act play, premieres in Albany at Capital Repertory Theater to packed houses

1997   Universal Pictures options *The Flaming Corsage,* with Kennedy writing screenplay

Conversations with William Kennedy

Portrait of a Writer as a Writer

Penny Maldonado / 1969

Published in Sunday *San Juan Star Magazine* 12 October 1969: 4–5.
Reprinted by permission.

William Kennedy was vacationing in Puerto Rico when the following interview was conducted. A one-time resident of San Juan, Kennedy spent several weeks here in that prepublication limbo known to first novelists. The novel in question is Kennedy's *The Ink Truck* (Dial Press), which makes its official debut in bookstores this week.

While in San Juan, Kennedy simultaneously studied material related to John "Legs" Diamond, the subject of his second novel now in the planning stage, while interviewing local subjects in his capacity as feature writer-film critic-Sunday essayist for the Albany *Times-Union.*

Albany-born Kennedy was the first managing editor of the *San Juan STAR.* He met his wife, the former Dana Sosa, during his San Juan stint. The Kennedys reside with their two daughters in Albany, N.Y. In 1966–67, Kennedy was the recipient of three top journalistic awards for his series on integration and slums in Albany.

The Kennedy by-line appears regularly in the *National Observer.* to which he contributes literary profile pieces on such writers as Bernard Malamud, Saul Bellow, Arthur Miller, John Cheever, Norman Mailer and Allen Ginsberg, as well as book reviews. The theme of the interview that follows might be put in the form of a question: Can journalist and novelist co-exist happily within one man to the mutual satisfaction of both? Or was Hemingway really right all the time, that newspapering is the nemesis of creative writers?

A friend's apartment in Old San Juan was William Kennedy's own choice of location for the interview. While on vacation here he would re-visit it repeatedly. It was obvious, observing his manner during the interview, that he feels comfortable, easy and expansive in that setting of thick old chairs, books, magazines, paintings and memorabilia.

Kennedy stretched out in a chair with his feet on a hassock for most of the interview. Occasionally he would break this pose to emphasize a point, sitting forward suddenly and shooting his fingers out to stress a point. Casually

1

attired, at the moment of supreme comfort he shucked off first one loafer, then the other.

His friends remark how much Kennedy looks like a writer. It is attributed to his keen, very Irish face, the features remindful of poets past. His hair is auburn and so are his eyes. The eyes are most often set in an expression of wonder, sometimes lit by a quick smile that goes right to them, sometimes darkened by visions of doom. A strikingly Irish combination.

He is a natural funny man, as well as a superior user of words. Even in *tete-a-tetes* he molds suave sentences that knit together, become rich, absorbing, inspired paragraphs. It is obvious how much he relishes words. His listener waits in rapt silence as he performs paragraphs.

The interview was punctuated by visitors coming to see Kennedy, friends who go back to his newspaper days in San Juan. Several hours of questions and answers came to a natural conclusion when the bonds of friendship began to tug on William Kennedy's attention.

The Ink Truck, your first novel, is "ostensibly about a newspaper strike." How did you go from there to Legs Diamond?

Kennedy: The material has intrigued me for 20 years. I had wanted to do a political novel on Albany because it's a great town for that. I would take Albany at its peak times, its peak crises. I began to polarize between politics and crime. Then Diamond came in. I saw that Diamond would have to have his own novel—I have no interest in the sprawling journalistic novel incorporating everything. I focused in on Diamond and had the beginning of a novel in six weeks. At the same time I sold *The Ink Truck* to Dial Press.

Legs is my tentative title for the new book. I've been reading in criminal psychology, researching all summer. I started in Albany where Diamond was killed. At the *Times-Union* morgue I found a few heavily pilfered clips and obits and pieced together what I could and on the basis of that began to write a novel.

Everyone's written on Diamond—but their pieces are all cockeyed. This is what really intrigued me, growing up. No one speaks badly of him. Everybody's sort of awed by him, as if he were Jack Kennedy. Diamond was responsible for more killings probably in New York City than any other killer. Why the myth?

For a second time you've drawn on your capacities as a newspaperman in mining the material for a novel, this time through your research work.

Kennedy: It's difficult to be specific about the facts on Diamond. He was fantastically good copy for the newspapermen of his day. There was just a fantastic interest in the guy. He moved from New York City into the Catskills, where he absorbed the local bootleggers. They tried to kill him. Every day in 1930–31 there were stories about him. Franklin D. Roosevelt was governor of the state at the time. Diamond was tried twice and acquitted. The night after the final acquittal they gave a party for him and after the party they killed him. Nobody knows who.

When I first started *Legs,* I thought of writing the novel in the form of a movie script. I want it to be a screwy novel—unconventional in terms of structure. What I hope to do is re-enact the myth: Why are people so fantastically for Diamond? Why is Diamond our hero?

Could you elaborate on the germinal process that led to the writing of The Ink Truck.

Kennedy: It started off as a short story based on a real paper strike, written from notes I took during the strike. It was written as a wild, almost surrealistic thing six inches off the ground. No one will recognize anything about any particular strike.

The books is basically a hero trek. It starts off with a manic kind of exuberance, coming into its own with a climax in the first 60 pages. Then I take off with the hero, Bailey, a columnist on a newspaper. The rest of the novel is entirely a focus on what happens to Bailey as a result of his actions in the first 60 pages.

It's just like the classic pattern—he goes into an ascent, into the labyrinth of his mind and undergoes a series of deep personal changes. I really shouldn't be so ponderous about it. It's a comic novel. But like all good comic stuff, it's serious. I had been working on a novel about Puerto Rico but that first short story, the germ of *The Ink Truck,* just wouldn't go away. It stayed with me as an Idea and I kept it in the book.

It was a different type of writing for me. Screwy and comic and very bizarre. Bailey symbolizes resistance and protest, a kind of commitment to an impossible goal. Bailey is a guildsman. But the Guild in the novel is an absolutely lost cause. It's the whole idea of why a man sticks to a thing; an obsession, but not a sick obsession. It's the kind of obsession that makes life meaningful; without it you'd just drift. It's any kind of resistance to an overwhelming establishment.

How long did it take you to complete the novel?

Kennedy: Counting from short story to final manuscript, four years—with two years of that given to writing, really hard writing every day. It's almost impossible for anyone to write a real novel in less than a year and a half or two, because you don't really know your material right away. I re-wrote an awful lot. At one point I took out about 96 pages. I wrote the book maybe five times.

In novel-writing the idea of output is not quantitatively relevant, anyway. It's to put down and understand why you put down. You're writing to find out why you're writing what you're writing. I used to think that if I couldn't get something out, I had a writer's block. What I learned is that I have to trust my sub-conscious. This what journalists find out. The journalist is inundated with material. He has to let the material settle to see what he's got. But on a daily newspaper he has to do it as fast as possible.

You've followed two roads with a degree of success in both areas. Which came first, journalism or fiction, and how has one affected the other?

Kennedy: Fiction was first. In my freshman year at college a pal and I started a novel called "Brownstone Will Do." We took the title from Bartlett's Quotations. I wrote short stories largely in imitation of Damon Runyon. After the Army I became a sports writer and did reporting. I was going in both directions simultaneously by then. I didn't know what I wanted to be. I was absolutely in love with journalism. If I had a hero in those days it was Runyon. He was both a writer—and the highest paid journalist in the world.

I wrote about 30 stories in that period, none of them ever published. The only time I ever came close was with a rejection slip I got from *Atlantic Monthly.* It said: 'You write with a facility that has held our attention.' It was great; it kept me writing for the next 10 years. At one point I went to work for the *Miami-Herald,* a major influence since Miami was really a very good news town then with Puerto Ricans and Cubans providing good stories. It was really red-hot journalism. That was the place to be.

But somehow it wasn't enough. So I started to write a novel. It was an evolutionary thing. Having failed to publish a short story I decided to go on and fail to publish a novel. I always had the naive confidence that I would make a breakthrough someday.

In the ensuing years you've done everything from editing to free-lancing. When did you realize that you couldn't balance these two consuming passions?

Kennedy: I was an editor for two years. After a year of it I wrote a memo to myself—'You can't do both things. You can't be an editor and a fiction-writer. I was working a full day, coming home and writing until late at night. The novel that I wrote in that period was the one that solidified my belief that I was a novelist. Saul Bellow saw it and liked it and I picked up his agent, I had finally written something meaningful.

One publisher liked it but felt that it was too much unrelieved bleakness. Too down beat. It was the recounting of the death of a family, with only a few light moments to relieve the somberness. I suppose it was a hangover from a young man's unfinished education in literature. You mistake somberness for seriousness. You reject being funny. It was kind of an outline of my family of two generations back, or as I imagined them. What struck me was the tragedy of their lives; what I ignored or forgot was the light moments that everybody lives. One editor wrote that it was as if life was viewed through 'a black veil of doom.'

Yet as a newspaperman I was always trying to see the funny side. There was always levity and wit. You tried to bust the balloons of the publicity-hungry. What I was unable to do was translate my comic feeling into literature. It was also an ignorance I had toward the power of comedy. I was unaware of the heights that comedy could go to. *Miss Lonelyhearts,* is an example of a very comic novel that's also a serious one. It took me a long time to learn how to stop being ponderous.

The rejections from publishers never persuaded you that journalism might just be the better road?

Kennedy: All my life I've wanted to live as a writer, where you give your own assignments. I didn't want to be tied down to the journalistic schedule. You have to have freedom to think. And no adulation from the public can equal the feeling you get when you've got something hot off the typewriter. Of course anybody with any kind of creative mind can experience this.

Every journalist worth his salt read everything written by Hemingway. His notion was that journalism will kill whatever you have as a writer, because journalism is not trying to go into analytical motivation. It's dealing with surface logic. Mailer says that a journalist has got to spit it out and he doesn't have time to understand what he's writing about. I think he's being a little condescending, but it is the inability to give prolonged thought to what you're doing that prevents the journalist from getting into the undercurrents of his own work.

Does this hold true for the new journalists—Mailer, for example, and Gay Talese, and Breslin, that whole bunch?

Kennedy: I think the writers involved in journalism now are just great. Your good writers have always done some sort of journalism—like Camus, Faulkner, Stephen Crane, Ambrose Bierce—their journalism stands out in their day because they were able to equate the abstract with the event.

Mailer is so popular now because he's infinitely able to make everyday events so fantastically memorable. I think this is a great development. In addition to making journalists of novelists, it's also making your daily journalists think more like novelists, and what's resulting is your personal journalism, the journalism of Breslin and Tom Wolfe and Hamill and Talese.

I don't know why journalism became untrustworthy. Personal journalism went out of vogue in the thirties. The journalists became very organized and the news services became very important. It became progressively undermining of good writing, of individualistic writing. A good news story was one that had no adjectives and only 12 words to a paragraph. Now we've had a renaissance.

You still look upon yourself as a journalist, don't you?

Kennedy: I left full-time editing, but I've always retained a part of journalism in some way. I wouldn't want to be in any other profession.

You've come around full-circle in a sense, haven't you, by going back to Albany, the scene of your beginnings in the trade?

Kennedy: When I went back what I wanted was to find out about Albany. What was happening there. I took on a part-time job; I was assigned a neighborhood series of 26 articles that ran like forever. I did every neighborhood, getting people 85 and 90 years old to tell me about the origins of their neighborhoods, delving into the history. It was right up my alley. This gradually got me into the poverty thing. I did the muckraking and that was the journalistic highpoint of my career. A piece on the poverty program led into a piece on slumlords, which led to a piece on integration. For the first time I felt that my journalism was really doing something. The committed journalists were all beginning to blossom at that time, and it's still going on.

And literary criticism, when was that introduced?

Kennedy: When I got back to the States I was starved for someone to talk to about books. I had left them all back in Puerto Rico. I had to establish a whole new network. So to establish the link I did pieces for the *National Observer*—on Saul Bellow, Arthur Miller, Cheever, Baldwin, Auchincloss, Malamud. Whenever I could find somebody in striking distance. Expenses didn't matter a damn; it was to pick their brains.

All such interviews arrive at the point where the subject is asked about his writing habits and what books mean most to him, etc. Without giving away any specially kept secrets, could you give us a picture of how the writer functions?

Kennedy: In the old days I wrote at night. Now I've begun to discover with the luxury of freedom that the morning is the best part of the day. I've had things solved so many times in the morning after trying for hours at other times. I have a little office in my house that's a good sanctuary. I type because writing in longhand would slow me down.

Discipline is something you confront early as a writer. In the beginning I longed to go to the movies. Anything to get out from under the eternal gazing at my novel. I would gather that any guy who continues seriously for three years gets over the discipline problem. It's the most important thing in your life. You have to sit there and figure out what your head is doing. This is always very hard to achieve. Later on you worry less about what's on the paper. The young writer wants it to be perfectly inspirational and in line with his style.

The main thing is to remember what Sandburg said, that nobody ever gets anything without that rich, soft wanting.

Are there any books in your life that are affecting your thinking or your writing in any way?

Kennedy: I mentioned that I was reading in criminal psychology for the Diamond book. I'm also studying the *Tibetan Book of the Dead,* with a preface by Carl Jung. Jung rang a bell. I have a feeling that this will have something to bear on the new novel. Freud is where things were; Jung seems to be where things are going. The sense of mysticism that he brings to the personality, rather than the kind of determinist quality that you get out of Freud.

I don't like to read fiction anymore. Nothing intrigues me. I keep reading the same things over and over again—Camus, Nathanael West, Kafka, Jorge Luis Borges is another of my loves. To me he's very much in keeping with my feeling about Jung—the mysticism, the surrealism. The journalistic novels and the ethnic novels are dead. Farrell, Dreiser, Baldwin—you just don't want to read that anymore.

At one time we wanted literature to be tidy. Now we want untidy literature. Borges, as far as I'm concerned, is the greatest artist alive. He represents the breakout into where the best fiction will probably go: non-chronological, non-cohesive, quasi-mystical. The sense of fact is very big on the best-seller list, but I think that *Couples,* and *Airport* and *Hotel* and *Portnoy's Complaint* and *The Love Machine* are all where we've been rather than where we're going.

The Secret Lives of William Kennedy

Scott Christianson / 1974

Published in *The Washington Park Spirit* (Albany, NY) 4–17 September 1974: 10. Reprinted by permission.

"You never worked twenty years to teach yourself everything there was to know about how to do a thing. You never read all the books so that the only thing that surprised you anymore was your own imagination, and, you never learned to value that, use it, wash and polish it until it was the shiniest imagination on the block. And you never put it to work and saw it work out your ears and your eyes and your mouth and your fingers and all your body situations. You never talked to people on doorsteps and deathbeds and in jails got them to spill their guts, and you never learned how to talk to pool-room punks and professor punks and how to figure out how each was a punk and each wasn't. And you never learned how to con bishops and mayors and writers and whores and blacks and whites and spicks and dicks and loonies and goonies and all there was to con and deal and be with, for that's what the con is, to be with a man and have him know you know what he's all about and get him to tell you about his life and his loves and his faults, which is the trick, to get him to tell you where he's weakest."

—William Kennedy, *The Ink Truck* (1969)

Probably, you haven't done all those things, but William Kennedy has. Done them, and then some, for 25 years. First as a roving newspaperman (Glens Falls, Albany, San Juan, Miami), more recently as a literary critic and a serious novelist who is just coming into his own, he has known exhilaration and ecstasy of the most intense kind—the kind which only creation can provide. He also has experienced hideous pain, shock, humiliation, agonizing frustration and unfathomable depression, and labored in obscurity under the most terrible loneliness.

Since graduating from Siena College in 1949, where he worked on the school newspaper, Kennedy has served a long and arduous apprenticeship as a writer, during which he has accumulated piles of publishers' rejection slips and learned what it was like to be without a job. He has toiled for months on projects only to see them flop and sometimes—just when things seemed to be working out—forces have conspired to cheat him of his due. Magazines have bought certain articles, but never published them. Newspapers for which he has worked have gone bankrupt beneath him. Shortly after *Look* made him its book critic, the magazine folded.

Through it all, Kennedy has persevered. Finally, after years of struggle, he seems to be on the verge of something. Though it was not a huge financial success, his first novel has lately enjoyed some modest critical attention, and only last week, a publishing house made him a solid offer on his second. Gradually, his luck has improved. Now the big magazines offer him assignments, whereas not so long ago, they didn't know who William Kennedy was.

In the course of this struggle, Kennedy has learned a lot about himself, his time and his place and others. He has witnessed revolutions, stalked the slums as a chronicler of human misery. Chatted with Nelson Rockefeller in Rockefeller's plush apartment. Interviewed practically every major living American author, probed the slick armor of vacuous men in power.

All of this swells within him, grating and caressing his brain and flickering at times into his typing fingers. "He had all the truth he could stand," he wrote of Baily in *The Ink Truck.* "Any more truth about himself or others would tip the balance, turn him into an ape, a goat, a pig."

As a writer, Kennedy has been forced to constantly psychoanalyze himself and the imaginary characters he has constructed from himself and others. "Sitting up," he once wrote, "he looked through the window of his pajama crotch, saw his pubes growing wild, plucked a few, held one."

Writing has also required constant study of fine craftsmanship. Although he has read them and other great literary works countless times, he still marvels over the ENORMITY of *Finnegan's Wake* and the lyricism of *Ulysses.* James Joyce, he says, somehow knew it all. "And the rest of us sit here like puny little piss ants and *worship!*"

For a recent article in *The Atlantic Monthly,* Kennedy made the pilgrimage to Dublin to attend the Fourth International James Joyce Symposium, "a week-long revel in Joyce's real and imaginary worlds." He visited number 7 Eccles Street, where the Blooms (*Ulysses* characters) had lived, and he talked privately with Joyce's niece, Mrs. Bozena Dellmata.

For another *Atlantic* piece, he flew to Barcelona to interview Gabriel García Márquez, the celebrated Mexican novelist and short story writer who has captivated the literary world with his masterpiece, *One Hundred Years of Solitude.*

Márquez was an especially meaningful writer for him because like Faulkner, creator of Yoknapatawpha County, Márquez had invented—in the mythical South American town of Macondo—another world. He also had explored the vast reaches of absurdity, a quality that Kennedy appreciates and seeks to convey in his own fiction. "It is this sense of a second part to life, which rationality has no grasp on, that I feel I know," he told me recently. "It exists! I know it exists and that is why I use surrealism in my work."

Having only a few weeks ago completed his second novel, he is now struggling to put the five-year project behind him and get his teeth into another. The book centers around Legs Diamond, the flamboyant gangster of the 20s and 30s who was murdered in Albany.

"I feel like I'm coming out of a big BUBBLE and the world is out there for me to reunderstand," he confesses. "Cause I've been immersing myself in Helen Morgan, Al Jolson, Texas Guinan and Dutch Schultz. People, don't even know who Owney Madden was, but I know, because I have *lived* in that era for five years now. The thing has taken me totally out of the contemporary age and involved me in the same sense that civil rights reporting did when I worked for the *Times-Union*."

He wanted the Legs book to be authentic, yet imaginative, and he sought to penetrate the secret, private life of a gangster in a way that would have relevance today. In a playful jab at Truman Capote, who a few years ago proclaimed his book, *In Cold Blood,* to be "the first non-fiction novel," Kennedy refers to *Legs* as "the first fictional non-fiction novel." "Because I was really fictionalizing the character, who had existed. And in a sense, the narrator is presumably telling the truth about that character as he knows it. But of course, I have invented the narrator also."

Why does he write?

"The desire to be immortal is at the heart of anyone who wants to produce anything in this world," he says. "It's certainly at the heart of Nelson Rockefeller, or writers, or artists. If that South Mall isn't a major thrust for immortality, what the hell is it? It'll goddamn outlive the Sphinxes. It has a deeper foundation than the Great Pyramid and the Great Pyramid stands forever."

Why did he leave the relative security of newspaper journalism for the insane world of fiction writing?

"In Journalism, you can destroy anybody if you want to. That's one of the reasons I left the business. I found it was a very cruel profession the way I was practicing it at a certain point. I found it very easy to make fun of anybody. You could just go out and quote them to death.

"Very few people were deserving of that. Some people are, but the vulnerable people, the people that I was having fun with, were probably somewhat embarrassed by it. It took me awhile to sense that there is a medium of honesty and integrity to other human beings.

"I started to write a book about the Albany slums, for instance. I knew *so much* about the private lives of those people! So much that if I really portrayed them in their private lives the way they really were, it would have destroyed them in their environment. Maybe not truly destroyed them, but *I felt* that it would. As a result, I never finished that book.

"The secret things that we don't understand—these are what is truly fascinating. That's why fiction is important to me. I *read* it for that, I *write* it for that."

To him, secrets are what writing is all about. Secret lives and the unveiling of inner absurdities. "Every writer is trying to tell you what he thinks, how you should live. 'You should listen to me, pal. I'll tell you what the story is, I'll tell you how to live. All you gotta do is follow my book, follow my theory and we'll be all right.' Ah, that's such shit! Such egocentric nonsense."

"Except, you know, every once and awhile, it works."

Jack "Legs" Diamond: Alive in Legend

Barbara Fischkin / 1975

Published in (Saratoga Springs, NY) *The Saratogian* 25 May 1975: 1D. Reprinted by permission.

During the Prohibition years, Saratoga Springs spun like the wheel of fortune at the old Chicago Club on Woodlawn Avenue. There and at the lavish gaming houses by the lake, places like Riley's, Newman's and Piping Rock, Helen Morgan and Sophie Tucker sang to the tune of shooting craps while an internationally known gangster named Jack "Legs" Diamond cavorted in highest Runyonesque fashion, building upon his reputation as "the most active brain in the underworld."

The Chicago Club is long gone. So is Piping Rock. Newman's became the College Inn and then collapsed during a snow storm a few years ago. Riley's still stands—surrounded by the Interlaken Trailer Camp. A man keeps curious visitors away from its boarded doors and windows.

The memory dissolvers have done a good job. But not with Legs Diamond. Legend has preserved the gambler, bootlegger and lover extraordinaire and now a novel has brought that legend back to life.

The man responsible for the reincarnation is William Kennedy, former Albany journalist turned novelist and author of *Legs* published this past week by Coward, McCann and Geoghegan.

It is a novel not only of Diamond's life, but also of the times of his life. They are times which mean a lot to Kennedy. "I've always felt I should have been born in that era; been a contemporary of Damon Runyon. I love the music of the era. I love the journalism. I loved Helen Morgan . . . even the Yankees. And Jolson, I've been Jolson freak all my life. It turns out so was Diamond."

But bringing Legs back to life was not quite as easy as remembering old names and faces; and was nearly as difficult as killing the gangster, who escaped at least five murder attempts before he finally succumbed.

For more than five years Kennedy studied, interviewed and researched, doing everything from reading old copies of *The Daily News* to driving four hours to talk to a Diamond contemporary just out of jail.

He explains, "What I've done, in a sense, is to piece together legend and make it seem as real as I could. You know, I researched him for a long, long time. I stultified myself. I must have read 200 to 300 books about the age, about 'Murder Incorporated,' the sociology of gangs. . . . I don't remember them all. I had so much of them in my head it became a problem to me."

In the process of turning this problem into what Kennedy calls a writer's "imaginative rage" there were eight drafts and two stints at isolated country cottages. Out of them came an intimacy with the Legs of different minds and different places: the Legs out of Philly making a name for himself in New York; the Legs whose gang was thrown out of the Catskills; and the Legs who came to the Capital District to start anew his "beer and booze" empire. It was during this time that Diamond mixed with Vincent Coll and Arnold Rothstein, gangsters known in the Saratoga Springs area.

According to Kennedy, "Diamond became a constant presence in Saratoga. He was an habitue of the track. Gambling was wide open in those days. . . . You must think of Saratoga in this age as one of the great vacation spots for underworld people. They came and took the baths and gambled at night. There was a kind of raffish elegance that the town had."

It was an elegance easily worth the price of bullets. Kennedy tells of a shootout in an isolated outskirt region of Saratoga called "Bloody Pond" during which, Diamond in conjunction with Vincent Coll was meeting the resistance of local bootleggers and Lucky Luciano and Dutch Schulz. The State Police at the time said that it was Diamond. There was another confirmation from another state trooper."

The stories are never ending. They are about Diamond's involvement in everything from a still in Mechanicville, to a card game outside Poughkeepsie. They follow Kennedy wherever he goes and especially when he comes near the places Diamond used to frequent.

The author tells of a man who in Caffe Lena in Saratoga Springs, "told me he was sure Diamond owned the Chicago Club. It's not true, but that's the kind of rumor associated with him. Diamond stories are like 'George Washington—slept here.' After you write this I'll probably get letters from people with more stories."

Still, Kennedy listens. Both to the truths and the lies, as if to echo Diamond's fictional lawyer, Marcus Gorman, the Kennedy-created narrator of

Legs who, in talking about perpetrators of Diamond stories says, "I like all their lies best for I think they are the brightest part of anybody's history."

Kennedy knows the process of finding, pulling, conjuring and imagining stories about this man and understands the obsession it creates. He explains, "We're gangster freaks in this country and we have been for 45 years. It's our morality play that we keep staging over and over again. I've rebelled against that. It is a super simplification. If you committed a crime you had to get killed."

Through the listening he is excited. And hopeful that the book will be received as more than another gangster story. Kennedy has recreated this man Diamond, whom he both admires and condemns; writes about, dreams about and whose ghost he imagines himself one day picking up on the highway. He has portrayed Diamond as more than just a common criminal; "as a man who was not a psychopath, but who found his calling and followed it." And he has written the book also to "depict how we look at criminals in America."

There is, too, the wish that the novel will be recognized as good literature. Kennedy has filled it with the same art found in his journalism and his first novel, "*The Ink Truck,* a surrealistic rendering" of a newspaper strike.

The wishes have not been in vain. Enthusiastic reactions from the literary world have included high praise from authors such as Mario Puzo, Seymour Krim and Hunter Thompson. *Legs* has been selected as an alternate Book-of-the-Month Club Selection and a few filmmakers have expressed interest in the story.

But more important, the essence of the novel has come alive in Kennedy. Comparing authors to their characters is a tired thing to do. Kennedy himself says "I would never make the mistake of thinking that a man only lives what he writes."

Yet, the temptation here is strong. It would be most rational to compare the author to Marcus Gorman, the lawyer who in the novel defends Diamond and relates his story.

But it wasn't the rational in Diamond that interested Kennedy. It probably wasn't the rational in Kennedy, either, that sent him on his five-year rampage. And that is perhaps why, when the author walks into a room and someone calls out, "Hey Legs, How are ya?" it somehow sounds just right.

Legs Diamond, Gangster, as Cultural Hero in a Book of the 20s as Written by a Historical, Non-fiction Novelist of the 70s, William Kennedy

Robert Friedman / 1976

Published in Sunday *San Juan Star Magazine* 11 January 1976: 4–5.
Reprinted by permission.

There's no denying it: one of the most noticeable, if not notable, "contributions" of the United States to the modern world has been crime organized, like so much in America, on the grandest of scales.

And the gangster as superstar seems to be predominantly an American phenomenon, even though it does crop up from time to time in other lands. Like, for instance, in Puerto Rico, 1974, when one Tono Bicileta captured the minds of men by capturing the bodies of women. Still, crime as a major growth industry and the criminal as a cultural hero is as American as the absence of gun control laws.

The scrolls of the American Gangster Hall of Fame are riddled with the names of such greats as "Dutch" Schultz, Frank Costello, Louis Lepke, Bonnie Parker, Clyde Barrow, "Scarface" Capone, "Mad Dog" Coll, "Machine Gun" Kelly, "Pretty Boy" Floyd, "Baby Face" Nelson, "Lucky" Luciano and "Legs" Diamond, to mention a mere couple of handfuls. They were all, as they say, legends in their time. Take, for instance, John Thomas "Legs" Diamond.

Which is what was done by William "Bill" Kennedy, former *San Juan STAR* managing editor and *Look* magazine book reviewer and current journalism instructor at State University of New York (SUNY) at Albany and "historical fictional non-fiction" novelist. Kennedy took the life and times of Diamond and turned them into *Legs,* a book that has been praised by, among others, Joseph *Catch-22* Heller, selected as a Book-of-the-Month Club choice and sold to Warner Brothers for a movie with such big guns as Warren Beatty and Jack Nicholson being mentioned for the title role. *Legs* is Kennedy's second book. *The Ink Truck,* a less successful novel, was published in 1969.

The author, who is married to Dana Sosa, well-known San Juan dancer

and former Broadway star, was on the island last week to celebrate the holiday season with his Puerto Rican inlaws. He said he had given the "historical
fictional, etc." tag to his book jokingly during a recent lecture at SUNY.
What *Legs* is is "basically an historical novel done in a modern way."
Whereas historical novels, as most readers know them, are set in swashbuckling days of yore or down on the ol' miscegenatin' plantation, *Legs* deals
historically with a man of relatively modern times: the prohibition era of the
1920's and early 30's.

Kennedy spent two years researching the book. He had little trouble finding
newspaper and magazine stories on Diamond, who, the author said, "got
almost as much publicity in his time as Lindbergh. His exploits were always
on the front pages—including the *New York Times*. There were series on his
life in the major newspapers. The *New York Mirror* ran a series of 25 articles
on him."

Diamond, said Kennedy, was a "pioneer" in his field. Besides being a
topflight bootlegger, he was one of the first of the major gangsters to go into
dope smuggling in a big way. He was also one of the earliest organizers of
marauding gangs. Up until that time, most gangs had been content to shake
down their own neighborhoods. In New York, the Jewish gangs ran the Lower
East Side, the Irish hoods hovered over Hell's Kitchen (the west 40's.) But
Diamond, an Irishman, decided to spread havoc all around the town through
the use of automobiles.

Diamond may have been one of the most notorious criminals of his time,
but he appears in Kennedy's book as a far from unsympathetic character. In
his last years—he was gunned down in 1931 at the ripe old age of 34—
Kennedy imparts a Jay Gatsbyish quality to him. Kennedy feels Diamond
could be portrayed "sometimes as a sympathetic guy, but capable of incredible cruelties. He wasn't a psychopath, but he was very impulsive and you
never knew what he would do next. You might like him, but at the same time
have a feeling of fear and apprehension just being in his company.

"Yet he had a white core fantasy that gave him mythical status. He wanted
something not reductible to venality. Such as to have a good time."

To prepare for the writing of the book, which was redone eight times over
five and a half years, Kennedy also read "about 200 or 300 books" about the
era, in particular, and about criminology, in general.

"Crime was much different in the 20's than it is now," he said. "Criminals
during that time were much less involved with legitimate businesses than

they are now. Diamond was clearly and purely a criminal. That was his profession. He was, among other things, a crazy gunman."

But today, Kennedy said, your most important gangsters are "relatively
respectable. In Diamond's day, the big gangsters went out and killed their
enemies. Today, more often than not, they buy them out of existence."

"In fact, organized crime has reached such respectability in America
today," Kennedy said, "that the CIA hires professional killers to try to assas-
sinate Castro and the FBI finds it more important to hunt Communists than
to break up crime syndicates."

He added: "I think what this says about America is that we're very ambivalent about crime. We've built a mystique around the criminal and think of
him very fondly. Look at the success of a movie like *The Godfather*. The
whole mythology of cops and robbers has replaced cowboys and indians. On
TV, all you see nowadays is cops and robbers series. And most of the time
the criminals are as likeable and as clever and no more venally motivated
than the cops. And that's the key thing about my book: the ambivalence of
people, myself included, about Legs Diamond."

This ambivalence, Kennedy feels, has its roots in both the social structure
of America and the nature of man. The gangster was admired as a hero in the
20's and especially the Depression-era 30's, because he stood for defiance of
a law-and-order establishment that was repressive to a good many people. In
the 20's that establishment was withholding booze; in the 30's, more seriously, it was taking away people's homes and pushing them out on the road.
Nowadays, ambivalence is rife because more and more you can't tell the
gangsters from the alleged good guys without the help of a congressional
investigating committee.

"Watergate is the code word," Kennedy said, "but it stands for all sorts of
things: CIA assassination attempts, the FBI destroying evidence, coverups,
law enforcers working against the best interests of the society."

And this ambivalence toward the acknowledged criminals among us is
also, according to Kennedy, "a primeval thing. I don't think we're that much
up from the ooze. Civilization hasn't had that much of a refining effect on
the human being. We admire those people for doing something that deep
down we might want to do ourselves."

While Kennedy thinks that "the criminal is always going to be there in
society—there's no way of propagating absolute virtue or eliminating evil,"
only in America has criminality become business. And it all began—the rise
of the criminal blue chip firms, that is—because of prohibition and "the

fantastic infusion of money" that went into the rackets during the era. "In
our effort to be virtuous," he said, "we created the reverse."

The reverse kept growing during the stress and strains brought about by
new waves of immigrants and the extremes of wealth and poverty in the
nation, Kennedy said, until, just recently, the Mafia and the White House
have been connected through a woman friend of a former president.

"Except for Germany under Hitler, who was the supreme gangster, or
Cuban under Batista, I don't think any country has allowed gangsterism to
flourish to such an exhaustive degree as the United States," Kennedy said.

Which, in this Bicentennial year, is nothing to celebrate about.

The "Genius" Writer of Old Albany

Barbara Fischkin / 1983

Published in *Newsday* 31 July 1983: 10, 16–19. Newday, Inc., © 1983.
Reprinted by permission.

William Kennedy had spent 20 years writing novels—and struggling. Now his latest book, *Ironweed,* was getting the kind of attention authors crave. The critics loved it, Saul Bellow loved it. Even politicians loved it. Mario Cuomo stayed up all night to read it. And then he recommended it to Daniel Patrick Moynihan.

Kennedy's friends had always said he was going to make it big. This time they swore it.

But "big" in the literary world can mean many things. Good reviews don't always lead to good money. Bill Kennedy did not write the kind of adventure or romance novels that invariably wind up on best-seller lists. Instead, he wrote about the adventure and romance he found in his city—Albany, N.Y.

This year he was not broke. But the plumbing in his house still needed to be fixed. And his car, a 1975 Chevrolet Monza, was still falling apart.

His call came in the morning. Jan. 14, 1983.

"Hello. Is this William Kennedy, the writer?"

"Yes."

"Congratulations! You've been given a MacArthur Fellowship, which gives you $264,000 tax free over the next five years."

This is America's new fairy tale.

Since 1981, it has come true for 80 people. Among them are writers, composers, historians, scientists. They have all been given a grant that sounds as though they concocted it themselves. There are no requirements, no instructions on how to spend the money. The recipients, who include poet Robert Penn Warren, child psychiatrist Robert Coles and Barbara McClintock, a Long Island geneticist, are told they can do whatever they like with it, even throw it away.

Their benefactor, Charles MacArthur, was one of the richest men in the United States. A Chicago insurance mogul, he died in 1978, after setting up a foundation worth $840 million. "I figured out how to make the money," he is reported to have told the foundation's directors. "You fellows figure out how to spend it."

They decided to use some of this great midwestern fortune to relieve the financial pressures on "exceptionally talented individuals"—the kind of people who would probably keep working regardless of how much money they have. So far, $15 million has been pledged to them, and there will probably be more.

In academic circles, the MacArthur Fellowships have been dubbed "the genius awards." And although some conventional geniuses are represented, the recipients also include a Boston community activist, an English professor who wants to write a book that will be sold in supermarkets and the creator of a film about New Jersey teenagers.

And William Kennedy.

This is his fairy tale.

Albany has its problems. There is the snow and the freeze. Downtown on Sunday mornings, there is also an emptiness that reminds downstaters Manhattan is always awake.

But William Kennedy, 55, bristles at any suggestion that there is nothing interesting here. Kennedy's Albany has a rich history of bootleggers, gamblers and political bosses, a background of music from jazz sessions and lunchtime dances at the once-glorious Kenmore Hotel. It also has a future. He sees it in the gleaming modernistic mall across from the State Capitol and the new, chic restaurants. Kennedy, a lanky Irishman with wavy, dark-red hair, lives in the countryside near Albany. But outdoor activities seem to interest him less than even just taking a walk through this city. He was born here. He has lived here for years. But he still finds new details to jot down in the small memo pad he always carries. This is his home. And the material of his literature.

Legs, the first of three books in Kennedy's "Albany cycle," was published in 1975. It is a fictional account of the 1920s' gangster Legs Diamond and his times in Albany, the city where he was murdered. *Billy Phelan's Greatest Game,* published three years later, is a novel based on the 1933 kidnaping of the nephew of one of Albany's most famous political leaders, Dan O'Connell. *Ironweed* is a sometimes surreal look at Billy Phelan's father, Francis, a Depression-era hobo who comes home.

A nonfiction book called *O Albany! Improbable City of Political Wizards,*

Fearless Ethnics, Spectacular Aristocrats, Splendid Nobodies and Under-rated Scoundrels is expected to be published later this year.

"I can't imagine that I would leave Albany out of anything," Kennedy says. "But I can't say. I don't know. There's no rule, and I have no dogma that I must write about Albany. But it seems that the characters that are most engaging to me have a connection to Albany. . . . I feel that there's a kinship between almost everything that happens in the city and what makes me tick. I can talk with a 92-year-old baseball player about what was happening in North Albany in 1902 when he was a kid. I suddenly understand the world more clearly because he has given me two or three facts."

Kennedy was the only child of a working-class couple from North Albany. His father sold pies, cut hair, worked in a foundry, wrote illegal numbers and then became a deputy sheriff. The younger Kennedy, an Army veteran and Siena College graduate, began working at the Albany *Times-Union* when he was about 25.

Three years later, bored and itching to get out of his hometown, he took a job with *The Puerto Rico World Journal,* an English-language daily in San Juan.

It was in San Juan that same year, at a party given for the eligible bachelors of the city, that Kennedy first spotted a petite young woman with long black hair and the graceful body of a dancer. Three weeks later he married her.

Dana Sosa, Puerto Rico-born, New York-raised, had left the Joffrey Ballet to perform on Broadway. And she had just made her mark. The show was "New Faces of 1956." For the sake of comedy, she sang and gargled at the same time. Brooks Atkinson gave her a rave review.

When the show closed, she went home for visit. Bill Kennedy, the newspaperman who loved Ernest Hemingway, came over to her at the party. His first words, Dana remembers, were simple and honed, like those of his favorite writer. "He said, 'You have good hair.' He was in his Hemingway stage then."

After their wedding, the Kennedys moved to Florida, where Bill wrote about Cuban revolutionaries for the *Miami Herald.* A year later they returned to Puerto Rico and by 1959 Kennedy had become managing editor of the *San Juan Star,* another English-language daily. Dana modeled and performed on television.

They had lots of friends and enough money for socializing. But Kennedy, encouraged by a special creative writing class taught by Saul Bellow, who was a visiting professor at the University of Puerto Rico at Rio Piedras,

wanted to continue the fiction writing he had begun in college. He would
come home at 11 PM, eat dinner and try to write. Only there were too many
nights when he fell asleep at 2 AM in the middle of a sentence. In 1961, he
quit his job and worked only as a part-time editor. But that did not solve the
next, more pressing problem. He did not know enough about the city where
his fiction took place—Albany, his home.

So, in 1963, Kennedy moved back there, taking his wife and two young
daughters. They did not have a lot of money. But there was a charm in just
coming home. The Kennedys found a white farmhouse in Averill Park, in the
countryside just east of Albany. It was not only graceful, it was furnished
and cheap.

"It was the bargain of the century," Kennedy remembers. "I did everything I could. I went to all my friends . . . And I got a 98 per cent mortgage.
Then I had to borrow $400 from one of my buddies to buy a car. I borrowed
the $400, and we bought a station wagon, and I had another $600 left over,
so we bought a house. So, for $1,000 I got a house on five acres and a car
. . . I didn't figure this was going to last forever. I'd write a book, and I'd
make some money. Sure, we always thought it was around the corner."

Instead, there were some years when he worked for little money, doing
articles for the local newspaper and magazines and book reviews to support
the time spent writing four novels. And he taught journalism part-time at the
State University of New York in Albany. Meanwhile, the Kennedy house,
even with its faulty plumbing, hid most of the signs of financial insecurity. It
was on its way to becoming what it is today—a social center for writers,
newspaper reporters, students, professors and other friends. They joined Kennedy in two of his passions: watching old movies borrowed from the public
library and holding off-key Irish songfests. Dana knew how to cook elegant
food without spending a fortune. And she kept money coming in. She opened
two clothing stores that doubled as dance studios. At one time, Kennedy's
writing was subsidized by her disco lessons. "I could never stand the idea of
knowing how much money you were going to make in a year," Dana says,
when asked how she coped with a life grounded in financial uncertainty. Her
attitude—and work—did not go unappreciated. "You can't separate me from
Dana," Kennedy says. "As soon as you talk about me, you talk about Dana."

There were good years. But their friends knew there were also monetary
valleys. Sometimes they'd supplement the Kennedy party fare with covered
dishes. Dana kept the family books and attempted to keep financial worries

from her husband for as long as she could, especially when he was deeply into one of his novels. But some things were obvious. Kennedy spent three years researching Legs Diamond's life. But when he wanted to go to Philadelphia, where the gangster grew up, he couldn't afford it. So his vision of a Philadelphia freight yard filled with "liens of empty boxcars, stacks of crossties, piles of telegraph poles covered with creosote" came from his imagination. "It meant a whole trip and staying over in a motel," Kennedy says. "I didn't have the money to do that. I was broke. I was always broke."

But by January of this year, things had turned. *Ironweed* was published by Viking Press, which also agreed to reprint in paperback *Legs* and *Billy Phelan*. That was Kennedy's most lucrative breakthrough, but he was hardly set for life. The advance, his largest ever, was $20,000.

And then, the morning phone call from Kenneth Hope, acting director of the MacArthur Prize Fellows Program.

Kennedy acted as a "skeptical reporter," taking down Hope's name and checking the veracity of the call with his book editor. "He didn't sound like he was joking. But then again, a lot of practical jokers do not. It was something I could believe nor disbelieve because about two years earlier I had a hint that the MacArthur was investigating me. I had heard through the State University of New York that somebody had asked for a vita [autobiographical sketch], and the word got around that they wanted a vita for the MacArthur. . . . I found out after the award was given and announced that almost everybody I knew had been contacted by the MacArthur people."

That is the way the MacArthur program works. Individuals cannot apply. Instead they are "discovered" by any one of 100 anonymous scouts. The scouts talk to people who know the prospective fellows or their work and then recommend them to the foundation, which makes the final decision. Among those contacted about Kennedy were Tom Smith, an English professor at Albany State, one of those to whom *Ironweed* is dedicated; critic and novelist Doris Grumbach, and two other writers who are also friends of Kennedy's, Alison Lurie and Hunter Thompson, the creator of "gonzo journalism." Thompson, who was the inspiration for the Doonesbury comic-strip character, Duke, met Kennedy in 1960 after writing what the novelist says was "an insufferably arrogant letter," asking for a job on the *San Juan Star*. Thompson never actually worked at the paper but he did stay in San Juan for a while and the two became friends.

"Nobody said a word," says Kennedy about the MacArthur investigation. "They were told not to, and they all honored that. That's one of the striking

things, that even people like Thompson, who honors very little, in that respect. I mean, he's an honorable man in his own way. But I think he has very
little use for rules and regulations. I asked him, 'Well, what was it made you
keep a secret?' He said it was all those zeros after the numbers they were
talking about." Later, in a letter of congratulations, Thompson wrote: "If I
had to pick one writer in this country who really should have been chosen
for this kind of insane windfall, I'd have coughed up your name anyway."

The MacArthur Foundation is like a circumspect grandfather who ex-
presses himself with lavish presents rather than generous explanations, an
intellectual prognosticator who believes he is making a good investment.
Kenneth Hope, when asked why Kennedy received his award, says: "Beyond
saying that the selection committee admired the work, I can't be specific. The
committee does not issue a statement with each fellowship. And, it is not
made for past work. It is made for future achievement."

Kennedy says: "I feel that MacArthur must have been a gambler somewhere. They even use gambler's language in the press release. Like 'taking a
chance,' or 'the risk factor.' The idea of playing the long shot, believing in a
particular person, believing that this guy, who we've chosen out of—how
many writers are there in this country?—this guy's going to do something in
his work. I think the only way they can really do that is by circumstantial
evidence. Nobody really knows what a writer is like this afternoon when he
gets the telegram or the phone call."

Kennedy got his first monthly check for $4,040 two weeks later and fought
off the temptation to buy a Mercedes. instead, he traded his Monza for a
brown Chrysler Le Baron with plush seats, "the velvet tunnel," he calls it.
But beyond that, he has not changed much. He needed a belt, but the only
one he liked cost $40. Too much, he decided. And he says he sits down at
the typewriter as the same person—just less anxious.

"What you get is the freedom to do whatever it is you choose to do. Now
I can go to Europe. I want to write a book about Germany, about my time in
Germany during the war, and I mean to do that. I hope to go at the end of
this year and visit Frankfurt again, where I was. Just to look at it to try to
reconstitute some memories. . . . Even just listening to the language and
remembering what the taxicabs and the trolley cars used to sound like will
be important to me. Not that I have to have it accurate. It's just that memories
will coalesce. It's like self-hypnosis, I suppose, or going under hypnosis to
remember something you had forgotten. That's what an act of the imagination is. In certain ways, it's rekindling things that you'd forgotten and putting

them into a modern perspective or else creating what you never knew. I think it's a fusion of both things. That's the luxury of what the money can do. Or you can hire somebody to do some research which you might spend a year doing. Or you might be able to buy a word processor with it and save six months of typing and retyping and retyping."

The MacArthur money will do much for Kennedy. But there are some who feel that he has gotten a head start with the publication of *Ironweed*. Kennedy's other books received good reviews, but not so many. *Ironweed* was a Book-of-the-Month-Club alternate selection. It is one of three main summer selections of Quality Paperbacks, an arm of the book club. Since the Viking deal was struck, about 35,000 copies of the "Albany cycle" books have been sold.

Movies based on *Ironweed* and *Billy Phelan* are being discussed. Publishers in Finland and Sweden have agreed to translate it, and a Yugoslavian novelist is translating it into Serbo-Croatian. Sen. Pat Moynihan, who took the governor's advice, liked it so much that he invited the Kennedys to dinner.

But in the beginning, there were those who believed it, too, was a gamble. Prof. Tom Smith is an effusive man who enjoys an Irish song as much as his friend Kennedy. And, along with being the writer's musical compatriot, he is often his literary sounding board. That was the role Smith was playing on a cold night in 1979, when he sat down in his own country house on Crooked Lake, three miles from the Kennedys. He began to read these first lines of the manuscript that was to become *Ironweed*:

"Riding up the winding road of Saint Agnes Cemetery in the back of a rattling old truck, Francis Phelan became aware that the dead, even more than the living, settled down in neighborhoods. The truck was suddenly surrounded by fields of monuments and cenotaphs of kindred design and striking size, all guarding the privileged dead. But the truck moved on and the limits of mere privilege became visible, for here now came the acres of truly prestigious death: illustrious men and women, captains of life without their diamonds, furs, carriages, and limousines, but buried in pomp and glory, vaulted in great tombs built like heavenly safe deposit boxes, or parts of the Acropolis. And ah yes, here too, inevitably, came the flowing masses, row upon row of them under simple headstones and simpler crosses. Here was the neighborhood of the Phelans."

"I started to read it by my fireplace at the lake house," says Smith, "and I looked at the first couple of pages and I said this goddamn crazy Irishman is not going to get away with this. Who is ever going to read a book that begins with a bunch of bums in a graveyard in Menands, New York? And, of course, before I finished the chapter, I knew that Bill Kennedy was writing one of the masterpieces of American literature."

The first chapter ends with Phelan, the hobo, speaking to his dead infant son, Gerald, whom he accidentally dropped and killed years earlier. It was that act that drove him finally away from his family and roots among the Albany Irish. Now he is back.

Grumbach, who views *Ironweed* as a part of Kennedy's whole Albany cycle, says: "I think for some reason that isn't quite clear to me—and I think it may have something to do with marketing it together with the two other books—that *Ironweed* was the one that caught on. Perhaps it is the most skillful of the Albany cycle, but it seems to me *Billy Phelan* is an equally good book. I don't think it's *Ironweed* that puts him among the good writers of our time. I think it's the whole cycle. He has created a parish the way Faulkner did for Yoknapatawpha County. And Albany is his parish, old Albany. He's just finished a book on the history of Albany, and really, the novels are histories of Albany, too.

"My feeling is that he's done what I guess any good writer does. He's taken an unlikely place and dug down far enough to realize it isn't unlikely. . . . Bill isn't what you'd call a popular writer. He doesn't make either wild jokes about the Phelans, nor does he go deep down the way Faulkner might into their psyches." The first chapter, she says, is "a leap of the imagination. It takes a certain kind of reader to see what Bill is doing."

In part, what Kennedy says he is doing, and has done ever since his first novel, about a newspaper strike, *The Ink Truck,* is to view the extreme. In a staunchly political city such as Albany, there is nothing worse than having something happen to a political figure as it does in *Billy Phelan.* Phelan, the gambler son Francis left behind, has been asked to report on the activities of a particular character who might be involved in the kidnaping. Only Billy calls it "finking on Morrie." And he doesn't like it.

"I've always been intrigued by extremism," Kennedy says. "Not political extremism so much, but extremism in behavior. . . . Legs was an extreme character. Billy Phelan carried himself into the realms of being an outlaw. Bailey in *The Ink Truck* is an extreme outlaw. He's the last striker. And, of course, Francis. Francis is an outlaw all his life. He's always on the run. And those extremes seem to me to be where you're coming in touch with the deepest elements of your being. When you're strung out, then you find out who you are and who you are not, what you will do and what you will not do."

Legs, in talking about morality in the underworld, Kennedy adds, "sums it up by saying, 'There's always somebody who will do what you won't do.' "

Martin Daugherty, a character in *Billy Phelan,* often plays the mollifying force, the balancer of extreme behavior. He is a newspaper columnist who tries to calm Billy, who talks his editor into holding off on the kidnaping story. Kennedy lets Daugherty express self-doubts but treats him kindly. Kennedy writes that Daugherty's "column was frequently reprinted nationally, but he chose not to syndicate it, fearing he would lose his strength, which was his Albany constituency, if his subject matter went national."

With Kennedy, it is not so much fear as conviction. He spent the past school year as a writer-in-residence at Cornell University. He, Dana, and the youngest of their three children, Brendan, 12, rented a professor's dream house overlooking a waterfall and gorge. When the MacArthur awards were announced, Cornell offered Kennedy a permanent job. But he decided, once again, to come home, accepting a similar offer from Albany State.

It will be especially sweet for the author to be back home when his *O Albany!* book is published. It is, in many respects, his personal history of the city and the characters he has known there. Included in this group are Nelson Rockefeller and Mayor Erastus Corning II, who was the country's longest-serving mayor when he died in May after 41 years in office.

This story, about both those men and the mall—formally called the Nelson A. Rockefeller Empire State Plaza—will be in the Albany book:

"They were going to present the whole mall project to the press, and Rockefeller wanted to know how he should characterize Erastus' role in the financing," Kennedy says. "What he really was saying was that he wanted to take credit for himself. So Erastus said to Rockefeller, he said, 'Nelson, I've always made it a practice to tell the truth—whenever I can.' That's one of the greatest lines any politician has ever uttered. And he told me this very candidly. He really was a wonderful character."

During the late 1970s, one place where Kennedy's love for the city came to life was at his table at the Marketplace. It is a bar and restaurant built on the spot, downtown near the mall, where contemporaries of the author's characters used to buy fruits and vegetables. Every Thursday afternoon for years—until "I stopped going because I couldn't afford it"—Kennedy would gather many of the same people who came to Averill Park. They were joined by local characters, such as Andy Bakarian, who was responsible or looking after the ruins of the Kenmore Hotel and often took friends on tours. Almost every week, Kennedy and Tom Smith sang their rendition of "Dear Old Donegal," which begins with: "There came Brannigan, Flanagan, Milligan, Gilligan, Duffy, McGuffy, Malarkey, Malone." When Isaac Bashevis Singer came to give a talk at Albany State, Kennedy took him to the Marketplace, where he gave his appraisal of Rockefeller's "egg," the large, oval-shaped arts center at the mall. "It could be an egg," said Singer, over a plate of fried eggs. "It could be a blintz."

That line is also in Kennedy's *O Albany!* book. Many times at the Marketplace, the author's memo book would come out to take down details. Some of them may find their way into the novel he is now writing, tentatively called *Quinn's Book*. It is the story of Francis Phelan's grandson, Danny Quinn, and the family of Danny's father. Some of it will go back to the 1800s.

"I've felt I wanted to understand where everything was in 1880, in 1884," Kennedy says. "I had a dream one night that I went back to 1884 or 1886 with a tape recorder. The tape recorder was about as big as this table, here. And it was in the back of a wagon, a horse and wagon. There was no electricity. I don't know how I was going to make it turn, and there I was driving up to this mansion, and I was with this woman, and this woman said to me, 'You're really stupid. . . . You're going to get everyone on tape, and you're going to bring it back to the 20th Century and nobody's going to believe you."

William Kennedy doesn't have money problems any more. Now, he can worry about important things, like tape-recording the 19th Century. "I'm absolutely liberated from all financial anxieties," he says. "Now, as far as writing is concerned, I can totally indulge in my emotional anxieties."

An Interview with William Kennedy

Larry McCaffery and Sinda Gregory / 1983

Published in *Fiction International* 15.1 (1984): 158–179.
Reprinted by permission.

We arrived at William Kennedy's home in Averril Park, New York (just outside Albany) late in the afternoon of August 23, 1983, only three hours after Kennedy and his family had returned from New York City. For the past six weeks Kennedy had been keeping a grueling pace working (sometimes around the clock) with Francis Ford Coppola on the script for *The Cotton Club*, Coppola's latest movie project. It had been a high-powered, high-pressured project, full of impossible deadlines and Coppola's usual theatrics, and we expected to find Kennedy exhausted and drained from the experience, with little energy to entertain questions from strangers. Instead, Kennedy was animated, lively, anxious to talk about books and writing. It was a long interview which began at 5 p.m. and continued through and after dinner; when Kennedy's wife Dana excused herself at midnight, we assumed the session was over. But Kennedy danced Dana off to bed (literally: to the strains of Duke Ellington's "Mood Indigo") and came back for more—more talk, more music, more Irish Whiskey, more living. We listened to Bix Beiderbecke and Louis Armstrong (an autographed photo of Armstrong is prominently displayed in Kennedy's study), we chatted about Damon Runyon and Francis Coppola, and when Kennedy played his favorite Sinatra song, "New York, New York," he got up and put it back on when it was over ("I played that song twenty-one times a while back at a party," he explained). When we finally said good night at six in the morning, Kennedy was still going strong—flipping through records ("Listen to this one!"), talking about his favorite films, about the wide-open city that Albany used to be, bobbing to the best of the early Miles Davis. Upstairs, as we lay exhausted in one of the many guest rooms the Kennedys keep ready for friends, we could hear "New York, New York." When the last rich note played out, there was a moment of silence—and then Kennedy and Sinatra rocked on.

William Kennedy was born, raised, and has spent most of his adult life in Albany, New York, the locale which has become the inexhaustible context for the fictional universe he inhabits in his imagination. Albany is the place where Kennedy's magic works, and it was here that Kennedy began his writing career as a journalist for the Albany *Times-Union* in the late forties. His first published novel, *The Ink Truck* (1968), is a highly experimental, surreal work loosely based on an actual newspaper strike Kennedy had witnessed as a young man. His next three novels—*Legs* (1976), *Billy Phelan's Greatest Game* (1978) and *Ironweed* (1983)—form a trilogy set in Albany during the 1930s. His latest book, *O Albany!* (1983), is a highly personalized, anecdotal history of the city. It is in this dog-eared American city that Kennedy has found his subject, and the result is a fusion of a real landscape—of loud, swinging speakeasies, all-night diners, and hobo jungles—with the landscape of Kennedy's imagination, where the dead walk side-by-side with the living and a bowling alley becomes a mythic battleground.

Larry McCaffery: The brief biographical end notes in your books state simply that you're a lifelong resident of Albany—implying that this is the most relevant feature to your background. Could you talk a bit about what there is about Albany that has kept you physically rooted to this area and has sustained your literary imagination throughout all your fiction?

William Kennedy: To begin with the physical element—being rooted here—I find that Albany is a most civilized place to live. It's small enough to let people feel they're in control of their lives, and yet it's close to major cities—New York, Montreal, Boston—if you need big-city action. Most of my life I've never needed that action. The day-to-day life was what was really important: a circle of close friends, a private life in a crazy household where you never know what's going to happen in the next ten minutes. That has satisfied me enormously. Living here in this house, close to Albany, provided me with all the things anybody could need to nourish life—except money. Until this year I never made any money to speak of. My condition might have been described as pleasant impecunity. But I was never writing for money anyway. I was writing to say what I wanted to say, to write the kind of books I wanted to write, to do the kind of journalism I wanted to do. What difference did it make if I did it in a Greenwich Village apartment or this Averill Park farmhouse? The end product is all that really matters, and I realized that very early on in my life, long before I aspired to write fiction. I knew I probably wasn't going to become a New York City journalist because I never wanted to live there. There were also a lot of reasons, at one point in my life, *not* to live in Albany, either. When I was a young man, just out of the Army,

I felt like a displaced person. I had gotten enough taste of cosmopolitan life in Europe to believe that Albany was a backwater and would stifle me forever.

McCaffery: That sounds like the kind of classic response that a lot of American writers have gone through—they go to Europe, like Hemingway, and then say, "I'm not going back and spend the rest of my life in Oak Park." But you came back . . .

Kennedy: I came back after the Army for three and a half years, but then I took off to Puerto Rico for an extended period. While I was gone I found out some of the answers to the second part of your question, about how Albany sustains my imagination. Before going into the Army (this was the Korean War), I had been a sports writer for three years. Then instead of being sent to Korea, where we thought we were heading, we went to Europe. We were the first division (the Fourth Infantry Division, which was Hemingway's, by the way) to be sent back to Europe after World War Two. When I came out of the Army I knew I'd had enough sports writing, even though I'd had a great time with it, and I went to work for the Albany *Times-Union* as a general assignment reporter. That meant I could write about anything, interview anybody—writers, entertainers, politicians, whatever. I covered the police beat early on and I loved it. The fact that so many dimensions of the world were opening up for me kept me here a while. But then I began to feel I was wasting my time in Albany, because I was working under some very limited editors. All young writers and reporters think their editors are limited, or stupid, but in my case it was true. This was confirmed when I took a job in Puerto Rico and had an editor down there who was *not* stupid. It was like night and day. His name is Bill Dorvillier and he and I became great friends and I wound up being assistant managing editor in a matter of a few months. This was a very small, brand-new newspaper, the *Puerto Rico World-Journal,* an adjunct to a big newspaper, *El Mundo.* That work was fun and it was good journalism, but the paper went under because of problems with distribution and advertising. Eventually I met my wife, Dana, married her within a month, went to Miami for about a year, and then moved back to Puerto Rico where we lived very happily for another six years. In 1959 I wound up being a founder with Dorvillier of another newspaper, the *San Juan Star.* It evolved into significant journalism, vastly different from the kind of thing that had driven me out of Albany. One of my buddies, Andy Viglucci, another of the founders, is still running the paper down there.

Sinda Gregory: This whole experience sounds very positive—so what was it that you discovered about Albany while you were down there that made you eventually return?

Kennedy: While I was in Puerto Rico I started to write about this expatriate life I had chosen for myself. Puerto Rico was certainly exotic enough as a setting. It was a Spanish-language community, full of both hostility and reverence for the United States, with all sorts of politics and beach bums to write about. But while I loved Puerto Rico, I found that I really didn't give a damn about it as a basis for my fiction because I wasn't Puerto Rican. I couldn't identify with the Puerto Rican mind because I couldn't read the language well enough. I felt I'd always be a second-class citizen in Puerto Rico because of the language barrier, that I could never possess the literature, could never possess the intellectual world of the scholars, or the political theorists. I'd written some short stories set in Puerto Rico with the beginnings of political contexts, but they were shallow, and I realized it was because I didn't know very much about the place. Finally I just said to hell with it and started to write about Albany. And the transition was extraordinary. I found myself ranging through sixty years of the history of a family, the Phelan family—Billy and Francis Phelan were part of the characters in that first novel I began down there. I found that by focusing on these people and locations something happened to my imagination that freed me to invent very readily. With Puerto Rico I always felt I was a tourist. But I could understand the psychology of a wino in Albany, or a spinster, or a clandestinely married woman. I didn't know *why* I understood them, but I did. It became magical.

Gregory: Was this "understanding" a product of your own experience in a direct way?

Kennedy: Certainly the Phelans were not my own family. There may have been paradigms from my family for some of those people but there was no real transposition of biography into fiction. They were all invented characters and yet I felt very much at home with them. Two or three chapters into the novel I realized that the people were substantial to me. There was some "sand" I could deal with. I was no longer a Yankee trying to use Puerto Rico as an exotic locale, the way so many writers tried to capitalize on Paris after Hemingway—all those people going to the Left Bank in all those boring, boring imitations.

McCaffery: So what became of that book?

Kennedy: I wrote the book, which I called *The Angels and the Sparrows,* three or four times. It went around to maybe twenty publishers and nobody took it on, but nevertheless that was when I decided I was a real writer. Oh, I wasn't a *real* writer—you're never a real writer until you publish something, right? "Writer" is a sacred word. You can't use it until somebody consecrates you by putting you in print. But I was aspiring to something serious, and there were enough people taking me seriously that I felt confirmed that I had written something pretty good. Because Albany fired my imagination, I also felt I should know more about it. Even before we moved back to Albany in 1963 I started taping conversations with my family. Just before he died in 1975 I even taped my father talking about his life, his random, senile craziness—wonderful conversations. He didn't really know what he was talking about, but every once in a while he would be absolutely lucid. Much earlier I had quizzed my mother and my aunts and uncles about their lives and I began to see patterns and structures among families and political relationships and the social dimensions in the gambling world and nighttown and the world of music. I was also coming to know the newspaper world, hanging out with reporters and editors who knew the old days of Albany and understood what it was like to cover all those gangsters in the Prohibition era when Albany was a wide-open city—and Albany *was* wide open for years. This all fertilized my imagination to the point where there were no dimensions of Albany I didn't want to understand.

Gregory: Could you talk about this "fertilization process" more specifically? How exactly does this kind of research help your imagination?

Kennedy: These random flashings in and out of history create atmospheres. I need the sense of a specific world that is definable, like the Jazz Age, or the Depression, so that if I want to set a book in that time I know the thrust a character will have. I want to understand how an era affects the life of Albany, not in a sociological way—I couldn't give a damn less about that for fiction—but what was happening to people's emotional lives.

Gregory: So it's the "feel" of the era that gives your fiction its impetus.

Kennedy: That's exactly what I'm talking about. Once I have that, I have everything I need. Then I can begin to shape and cut away things that are not important. By knowing what would be possible in this age, or outlandish in this age, I can make the intuitive leaps you need to make in terms of character psychology—the arbitrary graftings, the sculpting. If you don't have a sense of where somebody comes from, you don't know who they are, imaginatively speaking. If you don't know their roots, or have a feeling for their origins, or their family, then they become characters in a tourist novel, the Left Bank story, or whatever. When I went down to New York City to write the screenplay for *The Cotton Club* with Francis Coppola, I didn't have anything except my sense of the Depression era, I didn't know what I was going to find. All I knew was that the script was going to be about the Cotton Club, and I didn't know much about the place. But I did have the sense of the era and so it was a matter of finding out what was useable from it. So Coppola and I began to create this Dixie Dwyer character, who took shape slowly. By having certain elements of the era to work with we were able to piece together a life on the fringes of music, movies, and the underworld; and by forging that experience into an Irish family situation, we had the basis for something that seemed original.

McCaffery: Could you talk about your family background? I'm especially interested in what your father was like, what your relationship with him was like—some of the most powerful situations in your books revolve around the father-son relationship, and in particular the primal fear of the son being abandoned or betrayed by the father (that's especially important in *Billy Phelan* but also central to *Ironweed*). That fear is presented so forcefully and in so many variations, that we sensed it might have deep-seated roots for you, if not in autobiography then perhaps in some dark corner of your psyche.

Kennedy: As to the fear of being abandoned, I believe it's basic to the unconscious life of a child. We outgrow it, usually, unless there is some trauma, but we don't really forget it. There was certainly never any abandonment of me by my father; in fact there was always a very strong feeling of family as I was growing up. My family was a Catholic working-class family, Irish on all sides. We weren't poor but we never had much money. My mother and father both worked. I had a wonderful relationship with my father; he was one of the main reasons I came back to Albany.

McCaffery: In reading your reminiscences about your Uncle Pete McDonald in *O Albany!* I got the sense that he might have been a model of Billy Phelan.

Kennedy: He was the prototype for Billy. Actually when I was writing *Billy Phelan* what I did was use the circumstances surrounding an actual kidnapping that took place in Albany (Dan O'Connell's nephew) as background music for Billy's story. I knew I wanted to write a novel about politics and in particular about Dan O'Connell, who ran this city for sixty-two years. And I was interested in the dramatic possibilities inherent in the intersection of Albany's nightlife and politics. This fusion of the kidnapping and politics truly did take place during the O'Connell kidnapping. Dan's nephew was kidnapped because the kidnappers assumed the Albany politicians had access to a vast amount of money. They asked O'Connell for a quarter of a million dollars ransom, which he could have paid, but they kept talking until they finally agreed on forty thousand, which *was* paid and then they got the nephew back. But the mechanics of that, the dynamics of it that were unleashed, always fascinated me. I knew there was a great story there but when I started to do it I couldn't place it—I was originally going to use the Jazz Age and examine the beginnings of the O'Connell political machine on up into the present. But then I discovered Legs Diamond and he took over and pushed the politicians aside—there was too much going on in his life for me to deal with them both. When I went back to the material the holdover element was the era in which Diamond functioned and then disappeared. Eventually I found the focus in 1938 that let me tell a political story centered in Albany's nighttown.

Gregory: So far all your books except *The Ink Truck* are set in the 1930's. What is there about that period that makes it especially interesting to you?

Kennedy: The kind of life that was being lived then. By the time I was in high school and college in the 1940s Albany was in decline as a hot city. But I had lived through enough of what it had been, still knew the stories, was still listening to people who had really lived through it all. Even as a child I knew it was a unique situation to have this absolutely wide-open city where gambling was condoned by the powers who ran the town. I knew there had been gangsters around but not "around" the way they were in other cities— they could not have stayed here if the boss had decided that should not. That's one of the points I make in *O Albany!*: I think the Machine killed Legs Diamond because he was beginning to get uppity and overstep his boundaries. So what we had in Albany during that period is a unique city, a unique social situation in which power came from the top right down to the gutter, which is what I wanted to show in *Billy Phelan*.

McCaffery: A few reviewers of *Billy Phelan* complained that your involvement with the people and places of Albany and its history got you sidetracked from what they took to be the "main plot" of the book.

Kennedy: The context of the city in that age was one of the points of the novel: the fact that the political machine touched everybody's life; and if it didn't touch you, you knew it could. If you merely voted Republican they could up your taxes by reassessing your house and then you'd have to hire a Democratic lawyer to get it reduced. They could put the word out and somebody like Billy Phelan could be suddenly "marked lousy" to the point that he couldn't even get a drink in his own territory. *That* is real power, and in the kind of controlled environment that Albany was, the individual became a totally subordinate figure whose freedom was very much in question. Everyone cowtowed, everyone had fear, because Dan O'Connell (or Patsy McCall in *Billy Phelan*) owned the city. Everyone used the same taxicabs and the same cigarette machines because the Ryan boys (associates of Dan) had an interest in them. These things were made manifest to the public and the public responded. But Billy didn't understand the way the world worked, even though he thought he did. *Billy Phelan* is about this curious misreading of his own extraordinary moral code that Billy has to deal with, come to grips with. Contrary to what those reviewers apparently thought, I had to reconstruct the-city-that-was in order to show how Billy was enlightened by its singular power.

Gregory: You create an equally vivid sense of place in *Ironweed*—but for different purposes, I gather.

Kennedy: Creating this sense of place now seems to be an important part of my function as a writer. I'm bored most of the time with these abstract stories where psychology is everything—and too often nothing. If people don't interact with the place where they live and with the artifacts of their lives, then they are voices in empty rooms. Even in Kafka's *Metamorphosis* there is a fully, furnished society—it's about *those* mores in *that* room, with *that* family, *that* food they feed him, and so on. I've heard that people are now taking *Billy Phelan* to downtown Albany to find the places that exist in the story. With *Ironweed* people can go over the same turf and see what the city was through another and older character's eyes.

McCaffery: One thing that links many great writers of Irish descent—Beckett, Joyce, Fitzgerald, and so on—is an ear for the music and sensuousness of language itself. Certainly your own language has these qualities. Do you see yourself working out of a specifically Irish literary tradition?

Kennedy: I really don't. Certainly I love some of the Irish writers. I revere Beckett and I live constantly with Joyce and Yeats. But I don't aspire to be in their tradition any more than I aspire to be in Faulkner's tradition or the tradition of Kafka. As an American writer the useful influences are so varied. The Irish have been an important influence on me, but I don't consider myself an Irish writer. I'm an Irish-*American* writer, which is very different. I value Ireland enormously and I am enthralled by its history, but I could no more live there than I could in Puerto Rico. I don't even consider myself wholly Irish-American, but that's how people are perceiving my work. I believe I write out of a set of influences that extend well beyond Ireland—Grass and Camus and Ellison and Greene and Bellow and Nathanael West, and many more. Critics keep citing the Irish dimension of my work, but I suggest to them that if they look elsewhere they will find a very odd assortment of benefactors.

Gregory: The first part of your writing career you were a journalist. When had you settled on that direction?

Kennedy: As soon as I was old enough to fool with one of those tiny toy printing presses. Sixth grade, maybe. I went on to think of a newspaper career without much knowledge of what it would involve—it was a kind of fantasy future that kids grow up with. My high school experiences were minimal, but they confirmed the direction I was taking because I was thinking about writing; I was valuing things like Poe's stories and *Our Town* as a sophomore, and also reading Dashiell Hammett and Raymond Chandler and Damon Runyon, understanding that Runyon was an incomparably comic writer. I was also finding the journalists in the daily paper to be generally valuable citizens. That's where I decided I wanted to go, and I did go into journalism as a serious sideline as soon as I entered Siena College, a small school outside Albany, run by Franciscans. I didn't think much about literature then because it seemed beyond possibility, though enormously desirable (in grammar school I used to collect literary classics in comic book form) but somebody else's province.

Gregory: When did you decide to be serious about fiction?

Kennedy: I was doing it from my last two years in college, and I continued to write it badly in the Army, and later when I went to work for the *Times-Union.* I'd work on short stories on my days off, give all afternoon to it, and likewise in the late hours in the city room, when no news was breaking. I produced maybe thirty stories, none of which were ever taken for publication, but which all contributed to both my commitment and my apprenticeship in the use of language. The journalistic experience was a marvelous matrix, but a confusing one.

Gregory: Was it difficult to make the transition from journalism to fiction? They seem to require different skills, a different use of language and imagination.

Kennedy: I went for maybe six or seven years writing fiction the way a journalist would write it, transcending that now and again but still believing my fiction would be more or less a transcription of life. Philip Rahv has written about the cult of experience in American writing and singles out Hemingway's "bedazzlement by sheer experience." That experience has loomed excessively large for writers of my generation, so much so that if you lacked it, your fiction seemed watery. But that's the journalistic trap of this age; for the writer needs to know that essential as it may be, experience is only where fiction begins. What sets a good fiction writer apart from the journalistic guppies is that he, or she, understands that the truth comes up from below, that it develops from the perception of the significance of experience, and not from the experience itself.

McCaffery: I've never bought the notion that writers like Hemingway or Crane were great fiction writers because they had "a reporter's eye" or a journalistic background. Crane wrote *The Red Badge of Courage* before he had seen a war; and Hemingway's world is not *really* realistic—it's highly stylized, a world of language. I mean, listen to that dialogue he wrote . . .

Kennedy: You're absolutely right. Hemingway was a reporter and he conveyed ideas of what it's like to be alive and functioning in the real world, but he's telling you in a way that gives you access to a *private* conversation that was not the real world. His dialogue is certainly not that of a reporter; it's novelistic dialogue that gives the illusion of speech the way a Van Gogh painting gives the illusion of life—his private vision of life.

McCaffery: Or the way Damon Runyon gives that same illusion.

Kennedy: That's a very good leap. Runyon was also creating a very private world, and maybe that's why I liked both him and Hemingway so well. Both valued language and the internal dialogue. As soon as you put Hemingway's dialogue into the movies it becomes instant caricature, the same way Runyon's does. You can't put in the conversation of Regret, the horse player, or the Lemon Drop Kid, or Nicely-Nicely Johnson, because they were meant to be private eavesdroppings on fantasy worlds. Runyon's dialogue is wonderful, but it's not far from dreams. Faulkner is often the same way with his dialogue. Nobody in his right mind would mistake the dialogue in *Requiem for a Nun* for real people talking. It's absurd, it's so stilted and formalized, so "Faulknerian." It's also fascinating.

McCaffery: And it's that "Faulknerian" quality—or the Kennedy quality of language—that we respond to. It's that highly personalized, distinct *style* that I look for in a writer, more than for what he's writing about.

Kennedy: The great writers I value all create their own language. It's the measure of their supreme originality. Runyon is not very interesting as a writer of substance. He really had very little to say about the world. It wasn't what he said but the way he said it that makes me still able to read him today. That presence of language was there, so he survives even though he wasn't able to do what almost any serious writer is able to do, which is to synthesize experience and make it significant for us. Runyon was working at a silly, gossipy, journalistic level, underworld fairy tales, really. But nobody else used words quite like he did, or gave us the comic, quirky sense of what it meant to be alive through language that way, listening to the world and re-creating it through words alone. Of course, he didn't have access to his own soul. It's a matter of gift, I suppose—not everybody can be Melville or Joyce. But a writer can still be interesting when he or she gets to the point where language alone becomes so important, the way it does with Runyon.

Gregory: Your first novel, *The Ink Truck,* is so absolutely opposed to any kind of journalistic style that I was wondering if its style grew out of a self-conscious desire to break with "reportage" of any kind.

Kennedy: *The Ink Truck* was a willful leap into surrealism. It grew out of expressionism, out of dream, out of Kafka, Beckett, and Rabelais. I can't remember whom I was valuing when I wrote *The Ink Truck*—certainly all those people and dozens more, including the surrealist painters themselves, whom I love, especially Magritte. I've always wanted to be able to do with language what they do with painting.

Gregory: Even though *Legs* is probably your most realistic novel, you conclude it with a very dreamlike scene in which Jack awakens momentarily after his death and is then pulled into the void. Larry and I have puzzled over that scene endlessly—it seems to suggest that Jack has, in some sense, failed to make that final leap into transcendence, that he's doomed to be reborn into other incarnations, maybe like the book we're reading. The whole scene seemed very mystical . . .

Kennedy: The whole thrust of that last scene has to do with Legs being reborn into this life as a legend, then a mythic figure, a figure in American history who will be with us a long time to come because of his inability to purge himself into being one with the "whiteness," however you want to look at that image. You're right about the mystical element. At one point in its trajectory through many, many forms, the novel was going to be structured as a totally surreal work, based in part on the *Tibetan Book of the Dead,* from which that last chapter derives. There is very little left of that original conception except that last chapter. What I wanted to suggest was something very aligned to the sense of transmutation that is one of the most striking things in the *Tibetan Book of the Dead*—the notion that people are born again into this life or they transcend it, cease to exist, enter Nirvana. The principle I was working with—it's an utter metaphor—is that Jack Diamond is still alive. He could not have gone into the great white beyond, Nirvana, having lived the life he had. He was destined to be reborn, maybe in the gutters of Calcutta, or somewhere other than in that whiteness, perpetuated in this society by people like Marcus, and me, who have retold the legends that grew up around him; and not just legends about Diamond alone, but all gangsters, I mean, here I am *still* writing about Dutch Schultz in *The Cotton Club.* Of all the people in the world, I think Schultz is one of the most useless, yet I've spent the last five weeks of my life writing about him. And why? Because men like him have galvanized the imagination of the American people and of people all over the world. People are fascinated by their extremism. That's one of the important things I was driving at in *Legs,* that sense of the gangster as myth, that idea that Legs was moving into mythic status after his life here on earth.

McCaffery: The notion that life is utterly capricious, and the view that life indeed has some sense of plan or design, compete with each other in your fiction, and they coexist there in part because you present an almost mystical view that life is more fluid and interconnected than most people suspect. This view seems to owe more to Oriental philosophy than to Catholicism. Is this a view that evolved out of your own experiences, or does it owe something to your reading in theology or philosophy?

Kennedy: I'm absolutely not interested in either Oriental philosophy or the formalities of the Catholic Church. I find I can watch the institution of a bishop and marvel at it or be entertained by it the way I can be by watching the New York City ballet. But I'm only seriously interested in religions, or anti-religions, to the extent that they suggest something of the mysticism that is at the heart of everyone's lives. I believe in the mystical relationship that exists among things. It has surfaced so many times in my life as to confirm my belief that it's worth writing about, thinking about, trying to figure it out. I don't believe in practicing mysticism as a religion but I do know there are certain affinities and transferences of ideas and confluences of thoughts and interactions that are inexplicable in the ways we usually think or function. In *Ironweed* I'm interested in religion only insofar as I want to present anything you can imagine, including atheism and Catholicism, that would be on a man's mind in extreme situations where he's confronting the deepest part of his own life. And that seems to me to be the *only* thing worth writing about. All the rest is so much gratuitous sociology or out-of-date philosophy or theology.

McCaffery: Your books are about violent times—the Depression era—but you also seem to be suggesting something very much about America itself: our love affair with violence and with the people who perpetuate violence. Do you think that American society has a different relationship to violence from what is found in other countries?

Kennedy: Maybe we're more interested in a certain *kind* of violence—the gangsters and outlaws. But are we really more violent than Latin America, or Turkey, or Germany, or the Soviet Union? Think of the kind of death that García Márquez or Juan Rulfo would write about. Or Grass in *The Tin Drum.* I don't particularly want to write about violence as such, but sometimes it gets in the way of life. That's what's happened with Francis Phelan—he commits these very violent acts almost by accident, due to the situation he finds himself in. There is a time, when you're involved in a strike, for instance, when violence is on the table because your life is in jeopardy. It's a form of war. Francis Phelan throws a rock at somebody and happens to kill him. Later somebody tries to cut his feet off and he retaliates and kills his assailant, because he's the stronger man.

McCaffery: The opening image in *Ironweed,* of the dead relatives speaking to each other, is very striking and immediately demonstrates that *Iron-*

weed is going to be more magical, more non-realistic, than the two preceding novels. We were both struck with the similarities to the way Márquez uses ghosts in his fiction as a literalization of the way the past affects the present. Was Márquez a specific influence on *Ironweed?*

Kennedy: Those ghosts probably come more from *Our Town* and Dickens than from Márquez. I was already fixed in a matrix of influences before I encountered Márquez's fiction. But he's one of the great writers alive and we can all learn from the world of his fiction. I'm sure Márquez has affected me in the same way that any of my contemporaries who depart from the norm have—the way Beckett has, for example. We've all learned from Beckett. Márquez is my age and he comes out of Faulkner and Hemingway and Kafka, it turns out, in much the same way that I did, independently of him. And we both came out of a journalism background, so there are some parallels. But my sense of what my fiction was all about was cast fairly early on, certainly by the time of *The Angels and the Sparrows,* of which all my books, from *The Ink Truck* to *Ironweed* are extensions. From the beginning I had this desire for the surreal, the desire for extending the reality of the fiction, the feeling that many writers of my age had that naturalism is dead, that ordinary realism is dead, that the writer can't seriously engage us any longer with that alone. It also seemed to me that if I was going to try to really talk about the deepest problems that everybody has, and the deepest worlds that we inhabit, then I had to move into that world of mysticism I was talking about earlier. In that regard, *The Tibetan Book of the Dead* was obviously a direction for me in *Legs,* as was Martin's foresight in *Billy Phelan,* and going back in time to a mystical Albany in *The Ink Truck,* and the use of the ghosts in *Ironweed* as the reconstitution of Francis' past, which is hardly a new thing—it exists in Joyce, and in films like Fellini's *8½* and Bergman's *Wild Strawberries.* If there was ever an influence on my work it was *8½,* which I think is the greatest movie ever made. And I revere Buñuel even more than Fellini because he did more quality work than Fellini, went deeper into people, wasn't obsessed by imagery alone as Fellini eventually was.

McCaffery: Despite your use of these unconventional devices, every one of your novels (except possibly *The Ink Truck*) seems to re-create the people and places of the era so meticulously, that fact and fiction often seem to blur. Certainly this is true of *Legs,* which seems at once utterly mythical and yet utterly faithful to Diamond's real life. Did you set out from the beginning with the intent of trying to present the "real" Legs Diamond, or was that not really central to your conception of the book?

Kennedy: When I first started *Legs* I didn't give a damn about the real Jack Diamond because I was inventing everything. The first start was a free-floating, ahistorical version in which Legs Diamond was going to be a mythical, generalized gangster whose name was just a designation that people would recognize. In the early version everything was being done as a movie, with a director following Legs everywhere in life to use him as the hero of his film. The only thing left of that version in the book is at the end, where the cameraman is at the courthouse when Legs brushes up against the pillar and dust falls, and the cameraman asks Legs if he'll do that again. But the camera became, as you can imagine, a gimmick that began to interfere with the story. Every time Legs turned around, I had to invent where the hell another cameraman was going to be. This had nothing to do with what I was really interested in—it was just a way of focusing on Legs as mythic hero, who was to be made into a movie hero. But that notion of myth remained with me and became central to the final version of the book: the idea of how myth is created: an act which becomes a public fascination, and then is blown out of all proportion, so that the doer is given legendary status; then the legend is passed on, and becomes one of the defining myths of the age. That notion of myth is what I began with, and because of that I didn't give a damn about facts when I started the book. But the more I went into the book, the more respect I had for facts.

McCaffery: Sounds like a bit of your background as a journalist coming through.

Kennedy: Yes, I suppose I always had the sense of myself as a journalist looking over my shoulder at myself as a novelist, telling myself that you can't *do* this to a historical character. You don't abuse his history for the sake of myth, no matter how good your intentions are. I began to feel that it was very important not to be cavalier about his words and his life, so I wasn't. I then began to accumulate information so I could write that same mythic story, only this time using his particular facts as accurately as possible to build the myth. Once caught up in that desire, I began a period of intensive biographical research, and the farther I went, the more distance there was to go—new information presenting itself to me every day: more books, more magazines and newspapers, more people who knew Legs, or thought they did. And it became an endless process. It also became obsessive and then counterproductive, because I was a novelist; I wasn't supposed to be interested in writing history. But I became so fascinated with the history of the man and the age that I couldn't stop. I became a history junkie, compulsively reading still another set of fakey, wrong-headed articles about Diamond, poring through pages, 2, 3, 4, 5, 6 and 7 of the *Daily Mirror* and then switching over to the *Daily News* to read 2, 3, 4, 5, 6 and 7 of the same day. I exhausted the files of *The Times, The Post, The News.* I was having such a great time in the library that I was turning into a mole. I hoarded my notes, was happy only under a microfilm machine . . .

McCaffery: That sounds a lot like the experience that Bob Coover went through in compiling his research for *The Public Burning*—he couldn't stop, even though he sensed that his research was becoming counter-productive after a while.

Kennedy: The reason my research finally stopped was that I knew it could go on forever. History had become very important to me because I had seen so many renderings of gangsters in so many different contexts—theater, magazines, movies, books, newspapers—that I felt were all wrong. I was convinced that my mission in *Legs* was to write a meticulously accurate, historical gangster novel. Then I found out that the mission was not possible. There is no such animal. It could never be done because of the conflicting stories of who did what to whom, who paid for it, and who got killed because of it. I became aware that all this information was actually *preventing* me from writing the novel I wanted to write. This goes back to what I said before about the novel coming up from below—your imagination still has to grapple with all this information at gut-level. It's never the case that you ingest the information and then create a story *because of* the information. It's got to begin somewhere in your center—which is where Jack Diamond originally began in that fist mythic version I wanted to write.

McCaffery: Was there any specific reason you settled on Jack Diamond as your central character, rather than any of the other historical figures associated with Albany?

Kennedy: The Albany connection was the basic thing. He was killed here, he was hanging out here. I grew up reading about him and I knew people who knew him. I even knew his two favorite songs, one of which I've still never heard: "My Extraordinary Gal."

McCaffery: My relatives in Duncanville, Texas, talk about Bonnie and Clyde like that.

Kennedy: You see, *that's* what people talk about—these things and people that are so far afield from their own lives. Talking about them helps them define their own lives in ways they could never arrive at through even-handed reasoning. Through this extreme development of the argument you begin to see things more clearly, see the patterns of what's possible when you take something to its ultimate possibility; and this is what my fiction has been doing, I've discovered. I perceived somewhere along the way that my books had this element in common. In seeing how far the individual will or won't go, we discover things about hierarchies of values.

McCaffery: What was behind your decision to have Diamond's lawyer, Marcus Gorman, narrate the novel? Had you discovered something about the real lawyer that intrigued you, or was it more of a technical matter? Why not have Legs himself narrate, for example?

Kennedy: I didn't want Marcus associated directly with any specific individual, but there was a famous lawyer in Albany who represented Diamond, and who could have been close to him in the way I projected Marcus as being close; I know that Diamond was, in fact, present socially at the lawyer's house, knew his kids. But I created a private life for Marcus which would in no way invade the private life of any lawyer I knew, actually or historically. As far as using Diamond to narrate his own story, I couldn't make that work. I couldn't make him see himself without artificializing him. He was not as interesting a character when he was narrating his own story as he was when others were looking at him.

Gregory: The parallels with *Gatsby* are obvious, and you even have Marcus refer to Gatsby at one point, but I was wondering how conscious you were of using *Gatsby* as a model?

Kennedy: There's no doubt that *Gatsby* was a conscious model. That's one reason I used that reference. But Nick was different from what I wanted Marcus to be—Nick was a smart but boring presence, as far as I'm concerned. A lot of people have made cases for Nick as an interesting character, but he's not deeply interesting to me, mainly because he rarely *does* anything. His relationship with that golfer, Jordan Baker, is boring, boring. The only time he's interesting is when he gets drunk at that hotel scene and suddenly he's outside himself, almost as if he's no longer the narrator. It's what Percy Lubbock says about James pulling back from the center of consciousness to fall silent except for the description of action; and when the action does take place you discover that the character has become visible in a different way. That's what I sought to do with Marcus—have him act and react, be the person who's subtly and slowly corrupted, into the fallen figure he becomes in addition to being the contemplative narrator who can put Diamond into a social and moral perspective.

Gregory: At what point did you realize you were going to write a series of books that would be interrelated? *Billy Phelan* and *Ironweed,* for instance, seem much more closely intertwined than *Legs* is with *Billy Phelan.*

Kennedy: Even when I was working on that first book, *The Angels and the Sparrows,* I realized how compelling it was to write books like *The Sound and the Fury,* with the Compson family's saga, and *Portrait of the Artist* and *Ulysses,* with Stephen, and Salinger's Glass family stories—works that carried people, not in any sequential way, through great leaps in time, maturity, and psychological transformation. When you see these people in a later time, having known them at an earlier age, there is this cumulative knowledge that rivets the mind; it makes you believe they did exist in the same way you believe in that uncle or grandfather who, you find, was really visually there—in that old family photograph that just turned up—long after you've heard his legends. And they *are* just as real, you've made them that way. That struck me early on as a thing that was very desirable to do, but I didn't set out consciously to weave a web of novels. You can see that if you compare *The Ink Truck* with *Legs,* for they have little in common except they are both set in Albany. It's interesting that *The Ink Truck* dips into the 1840s, which is where I am *now,* in 1983, in a new novel. And I'm there probably because I was there then, only now it's vastly different. Even though Albany is never mentioned in *The Ink Truck,* I feel I have the same streets, and the same newspaper as I have in the work-in-progress, with the same characters running saloons, the same traditional figures existing in the history of this mythic city I'm inhabiting in my imagination. My worlds are interconnected because that's the way life is, and if you can only track the interconnections of any particular family, then the web of coincidences, influences, and prefiguring is extraordinary. That's what I want to represent.

Gregory: That image of the ink pouring out on the snow is a vivid, constant one throughout *The Ink Truck.* One of the ways it could be interpreted is to see it as the writer pulling out the plug, of letting all those inked words go all over the page, a kind of personal liberation. This was the first book you had published—*was* it like pulling the plug?

Kennedy: It was that, and I had that sense of all my previous fiction being dammed up inside me. But more fundamentally, that image is a metaphor of anything that's obstructed. It was ink because it specifically had to do with a newspaper, but it also represents any letting of blood or bile. But remember, actually only a few drops of ink come out. That struck me as being the nature of what happens; if you get into a fight as a kid and give the guy a bloody nose, that can be traumatic, even if he only bleeds a little bit. And when you try to enter into any world and you achieve something, you usually get at it for only a few seconds where it really matters. But when you turn that pet-cock and get a drop, that's absolute ecstasy, an orgasm of a kind. It's any achievement, any arrival, the ink being your first story in a newspaper, your first novel, your first entrance into manhood as a macho figure who wins at pool, or love.

McCaffery: *The Ink Truck* deals with union issues, worker oppression by management, strikes, and other highly political issues, and yet its odd, surreal form is certainly not the traditional, social-realist presentation we expect from a work which deals with these issues. What's your feeling about the view that many "committed writers" have expressed, that stylistic oddities are a luxury political writers cannot indulge in, that to deal with these issues the writer needs to present things as directly and realistically as possible?

Kennedy: The thirties' communists, led by Granville Hicks as editor of *The New Masses,* probably would not have approved of *The Ink Truck* because it would not have been sufficiently on the realistic mark for them. But that was the thirties. When *I* was writing I was in the middle of the civil rights movement, and it was energy from that movement that informs *The Ink Truck.* There are no significant blacks in the book, but Bailey is really, for all intents and purposes, an isolated nigger. Now I don't believe that Bailey is a black man in the sense that he has had to face the same things that black men have faced, because Bailey is white and has had it better than the blacks. But the civil rights movement definitely contributed to the energy that moves that book, and so did my residual affection for the Wobblies and the other labor organizations of the thirties and forties. I became disaffected from that, as others did in the age of Hoffa and Fitzsimmons and so on, but

I've never entirely lost that sense that the man on the street is still a man who needs to fight for everything he gets because there will be no gifts from on high. As soon as the chance presents itself, the people in power will take it away from you. What I'm describing has never been any clearer than it is right now under the Reagan administration; the retrogression of humanism we see now is beyond belief, and so is the retrogression on racial and environmental issues. Reagan is far more a criminal than Jack Diamond ever thought about being because he is affecting the whole society. It's beyond my comprehension that any man in this day and age could allow things like the chemical waste situation not only to prevail but to proliferate. And for what reason? Money and power, pure and simple. He doesn't give a damn about racial or human values; he has this vision of a reign of oligarchs. And this reign must be fought every time you turn around, in every age. *The Ink Truck* is a statement about that, and so is *Ironweed*.

McCaffery: But of course the *form* of those statements is very different from that used by writers of earlier generations, the same way that Godard presents politics from a different aesthetic standpoint than earlier filmmakers.

Kennedy: Absolutely, and that opens up another interesting point: Godard certainly *is* different from Odets or Abraham Polansky and all those writers from the Hollywood Ten, and those figures out of the thirties like Dos Passos when he was a leftist. But what those earlier people were involved in seems simultaneously noble and futile today. There was a wonderful commitment, but what did it prevent? What did it change? It galvanized the right wing and led to McCarthy, when so many of those guys had their balls cut off. When I was writing for *Look* magazine Albert Maltz put out a book called *Afternoon in the Jungle,* a collection of stories he'd written back in the thirties and then revised. The title story was about a kid who finds a 50-cent piece down a sewer and then a bum comes along, sees what he's doing, and pushes him aside saying in effect, "I want it." Then the story tells about the fight between the kid and the bum. It's a great realistic story, a classic statement that synthesizes something about the time in the same way that the song, "Brother, Can You Spare a Dime?" did. Those pieces are wonderful, but you can't keep doing them over and over. Should we go on making the same statements about social issues in the same old way? If you do that you become boring and tired. The stories fundamentally won't *mean* anything anymore, they won't *affect* people. We've *been* there already, everyone has heard and absorbed their lessons. If one's politics can be effectively dismissed by

William Buckley, what good are they? Fuck Buckley. The writer has to find a way to leap over such people, make one's own political message transcend both the left and the right. You know that pair on *60 Minutes* that does the "Point-Counterpoint"? They're cartoons. You know exactly what position each will take on every issue. Set up the issue and you already know the opposing elements. They could switch sides and nobody would notice. Or care. Who is convinced? What good is that? That's the kind of approach many so-called political writers take. It's like most newspaper editorials—so many of them are dumb and obvious. If you're a Republican you're going to deplore the Welfare State and if you're a Democrat you'll worry about cuts in welfare. That kind of art isn't going to move people.

McCaffery: It's interesting that so many of the best recent political novels—like Márquez's books and Coover's *The Public Burning* and Coetzee's *Waiting for the Barbarians* and Barth's *Letters*—seem to demonstrate exactly what you're talking about. They're trying to create new ways of talking about these things, of forcing people to examine the issues from a different perspective . . .

Kennedy: That's true, even though a lot of people still haven't realized that we're living in a different world today, a world that requires different ways of talking about it. There was criticism of *The Ink Truck* by certain people on the same grounds that Hicks would have criticized writers in the mid '30s (Hicks became a neighbor and good friend of mine in the '60s and went out of his way to praise *The Ink Truck*). The old criticism was that writers who aspired to be more than entertainers weren't meeting their obligations if they didn't toe the leftist line, or if they weren't sufficiently realistic so that people could get an easy handle on what was being said. This is the urge for propaganda, Boy-Meets-Tractor-Yet-Again. Now Odets and Dos Passos were enormously important; strong voices during a period when things were really happening politically. But I was writing during a period when a new kind of politics was also happening. *The Ink Truck* is a book that grows out of the late 1960s and it absorbs a lot of the radical atmosphere of the time: the hippie movement, the drug movement, the sexual revolution, the crazy politics, all the death and assassination that was going on with Jack, and Bobby, and Martin Luther King, and so on. My book doesn't reflect these things directly, but they all helped make the book what it is. I think its rebellion is not only in the wild style of writing and storytelling, but in the resistance to the social determinism that the naturalistic writers of the 1930s found so valuable. It seems to me vastly less important to castigate a society, which is easy, than it does to demonstrate how the individual can survive its evils and perils, which is not easy.

Gregory: Really, all four of your novels can be seen as "political" novels of one type or another; this is very obvious with *The Ink Truck* and *Billy Phelan,* but it's also true in *Ironweed,* which deals with the disenfranchised in a different way. But it's very striking how really *different* all four of your novels are from one another. Could you talk a bit about the evolution of your style, where it's been taking you?

Kennedy: So far I've gone through three stages in my writing. At my first level, *The Ink Truck,* I was trying to talk about the world the way that book does—through surrealism, through expressionism, all those things we talked about earlier. I was trying to leap out of realism because I felt the whole world of Dos Passos and O'Hara, a world I had once revered, was now dead for me. I knew I couldn't do that any longer, couldn't write another realistic line. I was trying to make sense of a new age in which, for me, Kafka was far more of a prophet than anybody with realistic politics.

McCaffery: Even Kafka can be seen as a highly political writer—

Kennedy: Exactly. *The Trial* is an extraordinary piece of political thinking, and so is "In the Penal Colony." When you read these books they react on your soul forever. Anyway, when I finished *The Ink Truck* there were several reasons why I wanted to move into a new kind of statement, a new form, for my next book. In *The Ink Truck* I had been able to say what I wanted to say in a non-taditional way, and yet still be true to the impetus for personal achievement in the world, and for political resistance. But I felt I couldn't go on writing this hyperbolic comedy which is always six inches off the ground. I needed to be grounded in reality, yet I didn't want to write a realistic novel. *Legs* is a consequence of that, although, as I've told you, I started off trying to write myth from the beginning. It was a different style from *The Ink Truck* but it wasn't working, it was still too far off the ground. So the next stage for me was to say something at the level of realism, which I'd come to value, but in a different way. I felt that if I didn't have a realistic foundation in *Legs,* I wouldn't have anything. It would have been like William Burroughs' *The Last Words of Dutch Schultz,* which has nothing to do with reality but is a most original reconstruction and invention of society to suit Burroughs' private purposes. That book uses Dutch Schultz and Legs

Diamond as names, as mythic signifiers, the same way my original version of *Legs* did. When I first read it I could see that it had nothing to do with what I was trying to do. It reaffirmed my belief that when you're dealing with historical figures like Schultz or Diamond, realism must be there at the first level; then you can build. So I could not be satisfied with designating my book as mythic. The myth had to grow out of the real, otherwise I wasn't writing from substance but was inventing lifeless metaphors that didn't say anything interesting about gangsters or anything else either. *The Ink Truck* had substantial elements to it: it was about a strike that really did happen, it was about the civil rights movement, and about being a writer and an individual. But to talk about gangsters and deal with them *only* as a myth seemed absurd to me. So what I did was to go back down to the documentary level in order to understand the history, and to work from some concrete basis on which that reality—which I was about to reinvent and pass on—would have some historical significance. Remember, I was not inventing a gangster. If a writer reinvents Jesse James without knowing what a six-shooter is, he runs a certain risk of inauthenticity. A genius like Kafka can invent an entire cosmos from scratch and we accept it all. But without an historical context for their work, what most writers produce is isolated psychology, poetic music. So I was working for authenticity of a kind in *Legs,* and *Billy Phelan* is an obvious extension of that.

Gregory: You're leading up to *Ironweed,* which, I agree, has a totally different feel from your other books. It seems both grounded in reality, and operating on other levels, too.

Kennedy: That sense of multiple planes is something I was aiming for. By the time I'd gotten to *Ironweed* my realism was still there, but something else was going on. I'd realized that I didn't want to loosen that hold on reality, didn't want to let the fiction hover six inches off the ground. I still wanted the craziness of *The Ink Truck* but I wanted the craziness to emerge at the level of a more grounded significance. What I wanted to do in *Ironweed* was to take *the reality* of a man and try to move into his *soul.* You might think of Francis Phelan as always being aware of where he is, and yet also always aware of all his history. Deeper inside he's aware of the obligations and evasions that go with his existence, and the kinds of conflicts that conscience generates. Then deeper still is his center, and there isn't any way he can *ever* articulate what is in there, and he knows this. That's the center of his soul, the ineffable element of his being. That's what I was trying to suggest—that we're enormously complex beings who can never know everything about ourselves. I know that's true about me. The center of Francis is the place I'd like to go to forever. It seems to me the only thing really worth writing about: the absolute center of somebody. Of course it's very hard to get there; also to find somebody who has a center worth reaching.

McCaffery: Did you do any sort of research on bums, or model Francis on a real-life prototype?

Kennedy: *Ironweed* wasn't researched exactly. I hung out with a few winos, and I've been in saloons and watched them. Bums seem to me to have more interesting lives than most businessmen. I did a series of articles on them in Albany during the early sixties and there was one articulate bum whom I got to like. But that bit of journalism was really just an extension of my imagination, since I had already created Francis and the whole Phelan family in that first book I wrote that was never published, *The Angels and the Sparrows*. Francis of *Ironweed* was not the same character who was in that early book. The first man wasn't a ballplayer, for example—but he was the basis of Francis.

Gregory: Despite the vividly drawn, depressing nature of life that Francis and Helen lead, there's a sense that Francis has won at the end, beaten them all. He's alive and has come to terms with certain contradictions about life, and himself, that most people never arrive at.

Kennedy: Well, some people do learn how to save their souls. Not everybody, but it does happen to some people. I decided that Francis probably could. When I began to explore his nature he seemed to be a man of wit and reason, and a pawn of fortune in the sense that he didn't create his own fate. Oh, in a way he did, but he didn't really mean to kill that scab, and certainly not his son. Those deaths, those fated circumstances and events, marked him for life in ways that he grows to understand.

Gregory: That kind of acceptance you're talking about is not granted to some of the other characters in your fiction that you also feel obvious affection towards, like Francis' son, Billy. What's the essential difference between these two that allows one to develop this wisdom and the other not?

Kennedy: Billy hasn't had the experience Francis had: nothing of the sort. Experience is usually the basic ingredient of a complex character. When I teach writing my students are always writing poetry about their love affair and its breakup yesterday, and they fill their writing with allusions to *Tristan and Isolde,* or they try to find metaphysical meanings in their valentines. What Faulkner once said is that the problems of children aren't worth writing about. I believe he said that not to disparage children, who can have problems beyond belief, but because in fiction the complexity of life is arrived at through consciousness; and children are not fully conscious of what is going on. Billy Phelan does not have anywhere near the conscious awareness his father has. Billy hasn't gone through the valley, has not slept in the weeds, hasn't had to kill people to stay alive, has not been a fugitive unable to come home. Billy has had it relatively easy; he's interesting, I think, and a nice guy, but even his moral complexity, which is the basis of the book, he only intuits, doesn't fully understand.

McCaffery: The sense of play and games is central to the development of *Billy Phelan* and, perhaps more abstractly, it seems relevant to all your writing in various ways. Was Huizinga important in helping you formalize your notions about this?

Kennedy: The sense of play being basic to us all—to even the animal species, that was important; and you're certainly right that *Billy Phelan* is all about games. Just about every form of game you can imagine is being played out in that book. But that notion of play, the way people live life as a game, has always been valuable to me. I feel now I am constantly at play. I've been trying all my life to do nothing except play, and now I'm finally doing it.

McCaffery: Is that what writing is—play?

Kennedy: Absolutely. It's the supreme game. There's nothing I'd rather do tomorrow than go upstairs and play at my typewriter. Writing is the most satisfying game of all for me—you're matching your imagination against everybody else's. Is that a game or isn't it? I've always loved games, always considered myself a gambler—a rotten gambler—at most things. I could never win at craps. I was a pretty good poker player, and a fair pool player. I played bogie golf and got a hole-in-one one day. I was a good bowler—I bowled 299 once, just like Billy. I was a pretty good first baseman. I wasn't bad at any of the games I played. But the real game for me is writing. It's the pleasure principle at work at every imaginable level. What else is as great as creating a world out of nothing? You project yourself out into the beyond, to where you want to go, but you don't know how to get there. And everything after that is a quest for lucidity, a game of light and shadow.

PW Interviews William Kennedy

Joseph Barbato / 1983

Published in *Publishers Weekly* 224 (9 December 1983): 52–53. Reprinted by permission.

"There was a time, in the 1960s, when I knew I was working blind and might never get published," says William Kennedy, whose three-novel Albany cycle—*Legs, Billy Phelan's Greatest Game* and *Ironweed*—earlier this year won the author and his native city a literary prominence neither had ever experienced. "People would tell me, 'Don't worry. You're going to get published and taken seriously.' But I never really believed it. Then it happened, and it was very lovely."

Indeed, after two decades of quiet, little-noticed fiction writing, Kennedy, now 55, finds things simply *keep* happening in his writing career. "A good friend in Albany called me *homo mirabilis* [wondrous man]," he says. "Everything happened this year—and things still seem to be happening."

His new book, *O Albany! An Urban Tapestry,* just published by Viking (*PW* Forecasts, Oct. 7), is a nonfiction account, part history and part memoir, of New York's state capital, a city much-maligned for its dreariness, but which Kennedy celebrates unabashedly.

"It's a nonesuch book with no particular reason for being except my rather peculiar attitudes toward the city," says Kennedy. *PW* called it "an unusual, deeply affectionate history" that "blends research, old-timers' recollections and personal observations into an engaging, unpredictable narrative of life, both high and low, in the city he once loathed but now claims as his own."

In fact, the book is a nonfiction delineation of Kennedy's imaginative source—an upstate city of politicians and hoodlums, of gambling dens and ethnic neighborhoods, which for all its isolation remains, he insists, "as various as the American psyche" and rich in stories and characters. Based in part on an article series he wrote in the 1960s for the Albany *Times-Union,* the book "doesn't take away from what I want to say imaginatively about the city," Kennedy explains. "I can still go over some of the same territory in fiction and find new things to do with it."

Kennedy's breakthrough year began last January, with the publication of *Ironweed,* the last novel in his trilogy. "For a while, I thought nobody was going to buy it," says the author, who has the mild, pleasant manner of an ex-newspaperman caught sitting on the wrong end of an interview. "Editors were saying it was too downbeat, and who wants to read about a bum, and other silly things." Cork Smith, his editor at Viking, not only took the book but simultaneously reissued the earlier Albany novel, *Legs,* first published in 1975, and based on the life of gangster Jack "Legs" Diamond; and *Billy Phelan* (1978), about the Depression-era kidnapping of the nephew of Albany political boss Dan O'Connell.

"What a coup that turned out to be," says Kennedy. "I couldn't imagine the kind of response the whole thing got when it was looked at as a body of work. Almost everybody reviewed all three books. It was amazing."

That same week, while his novels were receiving major treatment in leading review media, the John D. and Catherine T. MacArthur Foundation of Chicago named Kennedy a winner of one of its no-strings-attached fellowships for "exceptionally talented individuals." The award—"an absolute surprise"—consists of $264,000 over five years.

"Then came the film option for *Billy Phelan*—I'm writing the script now. *Legs* had already been optioned, for about a year, but they had never thought of me as the writer. I'll be writing that script next. Gene Kirkwood is producing, and Michael Rourke is committed to star in it."

Next, in June, came a call from a reader of *Legs:* filmmaker Francis Coppola. Would Kennedy—a self-described "film freak" who tried unsuccessfully for years to get screenwriting assignments—be interested in serving as dialogue consultant for Coppola's latest movie, *The Cotton Club,* about the gangster-run Harlem nightclub of the 1920s and '30s?

That was the beginning of a summer-long collaboration at New York's Astoria Film Studios, where novelist and filmmaker sometimes worked 17- and 20-hour days. After three weeks off for a European trip, during which he attended a writers' conference in Yugoslavia, Kennedy had just returned to New York when he met with *PW* in his publisher's offices. He would rejoin Coppola that afternoon to do new rewrites on the movie. "Working with Coppola has been an exotic episode in my life," he says. "Great fun—that's the main thing. I've learned how to write a movie, I'll tell you that."

On the day before, Kennedy had sent a letter of acceptance to the State University of New York at Albany. He has taught there part-time for about 10 years. "Now they've given me a professorship in the English department. I'll be teaching writing up there eventually."

For many years, Kennedy was a newspaperman ("I loved the business and still do") who left journalism reluctantly to pursue his ambitions as a novelist. He grew up in North Albany, an Irish-American enclave shaped by religion and politics (his father and many relatives were on public payrolls), attended Christian Brothers Academy and went on to Siena College, a Franciscan school, where he edited the campus paper and earned a bachelor's degree in English in 1949.

"I came out prepared to be a newspaperman," he says. After a year of sportswriting at the Glens Falls *Post Star,* he served in the army, then spent three years as a general assignment reporter at the Albany *Times-Union* and finally went to Puerto Rico. In San Juan, in the late 1950s, he met two important figures in his life—his wife, Dana, a dancer, and the novelist Saul Bellow.

By 1957 Kennedy was free-lancing for *Time* and other magazines while beginning to write fiction seriously. He wrote what he calls "one bad novel"—and threw it away. Then during two years as managing editor of the San Juan *Star,* he began an Albany novel (*The Angels and the Sparrows,* still unpublished) and enrolled in a course taught by Bellow, then a visiting professor at the University of Puerto Rico at Rio Piedras. "He confirmed my belief that I had something to say," notes Kennedy. "He was very, very encouraging, and helped me get an agent."

In 1963, having left full-time journalism and convinced that he should write novels (and that they should be about Albany), Kennedy returned to his hometown. "My mother had died, and my father was gravely ill. Nobody was taking care of him. He was a stubborn old Irishman who wouldn't listen to anybody. I got him straight, and then realized I probably ought to come back for good. And I did. It was time."

It was then, while working several days a week for the Albany *Times-Union,* that he spent four months writing a 26-part series about the city's neighborhoods. In the same period, a strike at the newspaper inspired a short story that became Kennedy's first published novel, *The Ink Truck* (Dial), in 1969. The book will be reissued by Viking next year.

Several years ago, a friend who runs the Washington Park Press Ltd., a small Albany publisher, asked Kennedy if he was interested in republishing his Albany articles in book form. Pleased by the idea, Kennedy reread the series and found "the prose was dead. Also, I realized the neighborhoods had changed drastically in 17 years—some weren't even there any more. So I had to do a lot of new reporting." The press ultimately became co-publisher with Viking.

Besides expanding sections on such figures as Legs Diamond (who died in Albany), boss Dan O'Connell and long-time Albany mayor Erastus Corning, Kennedy wrote new material on his childhood. Among those portrayed is his uncle, Pete McDonald, a gambler, bowler and hanger-on, now dead, who delighted in recalling Albany's "sin city" years of the 1920s and '30s—the period for each of Kennedy's Albany novels to date.

"Pete was very important to me," says Kennedy. "He had a special quality in his attitude toward life, which was one of great vivacity. He had a great sense of humor and absolutely original attitudes. He was a magical character. He personified that age. He's one of the prototypes of Billy Phelan."

Despite his screenwriting commitments, Kennedy has made progress on a new Albany novel, begun some years ago. Set in the mid-19th century, it will focus on ancestors of his cycle's characters. His wife Dana has been entering the draft on a word processor.

"I absolutely believe in them," he says. "I can't turn one on, but I'm going to learn. Coppola works with one. Once, we had four drafts over a weekend. We tore it apart, wrote new scenes, and every time we'd come out with a full, clear set of pages.

"I really know that's an important change in the writing world. Especially the way I write—I make so many changes. I rewrite so heavily. I scratch to the point where I can't read it myself anymore. So this will be a great new sense of control. It's a very satisfying thing to have a clean page."

William Kennedy: An Interview

Kay Bonetti / 1984

This is a print version of a recorded interview by Kay Bonetti in 1984 for the American Audio Prose Library (PO Box 842, Columbia MO 65205. Phone 1-800-447-2275). First published in *Missouri Review* 8.2 (1985): 71–86. Reprinted by permission of Kay Bonetti and *Missouri Review.*

KB: This has been a spectacular year for you, hasn't it?

WK: Yes. This week I became grandfather. My grandson, Casey Michael Rafferty, was born the same day that the Pulitzer Prize for Fiction arrived. It was a day of double glory. But it got to be so impossible to live in the house here that we went to New York to get away from it. It's been like that—the phone ringing off the hook—since January of 1983, when *Ironweed* was published and *Billy Phelan* and *Legs* were both republished. On top of that came the MacArthur Fellowship, on my birthday, January 16, 1983. That whole thing was my birthday week, and the MacArthur was totally unexpected. It liberated me for five years from any kind of need to have income from anywhere else. And then came the movie options, on *Billy Phelan* first, then an offer to go to work for Francis Coppola writing "Cotton Club," and on top of that contracts to write screenplays for *Legs* and *Ironweed.* Later in the year I published *O Albany!* which was a nonfiction history of the city, so I published four books in one year, plus contracting for four movies, and getting the MacArthur on top of it.

KB: And you won the National Book Critics Circle Award.

WK: In January of this year, and now has come the Pulitzer and being a finalist for the P.E.N. Faulkner award. It's staggering for this to happen at all, but for it to happen in such a short span of time is bewildering, a very strange thing to live through.

KB: Do you feel there's anything *behind* all of this?

WK: The secret? Some cabal? Some conspiracy? God likes me. (chuckle) I think that it is the sudden concentration of books about a single place with interconnected characters, and people recognizing now that there is a cycle here, which is how I see it and what I've been calling it for about 10 years. I knew that the books were going to be overlapping on certain characters, interconnected. It was something that I came to early on because I knew I could write about Albany at great length and not exhaust the subject matter.

KB: But why *Ironweed?* Why did this one capture people's hearts and attention, over a book like *Billy Phelan's Greatest Game* that some readers liked best of the three?

WK: I don't know. I think the presentation of three at once was important. Reviewers like to discover something new. Most of them reviewed all three at once. They were distributed that way deliberately by Viking and Penguin, and attention was called to the cycle. But *Ironweed* was the new one and so it had that going for it. I always thought it was my best book. I feel that I've come through an apprenticeship, that I'm a journeyman now, whatever, and I felt that I really knew what I was doing in structuring that book. That was the best language I could bring to bear on the story, and I also felt I was able to penetrate more deeply into Francis Phelan's soul than in any other work. The other books were experimental in other ways. The city of Albany of the 1930s and 40s was as much a character in Billy's life as Billy himself was in that book. And *Legs* of course was written from various points of view.

KB: I read someplace that you wrote that book eight times.

WK: That's correct. I wrote it over a period of about six years and it never worked until the final version. It worked up to a point, but I never was very satisfied. It started out as a kind of novel being written about a movie being made about this mythological hero, or anti-hero, and I found that to be contrived. It was a bad gimmick. The cameraman kept getting in the way of the story. Then I tried to tell it as a surrealistic work to the point that it was mystical, and that didn't work. I tried to tell it chronologically from the very earliest days, an accumulation of voices connected into a narrative and that didn't work. I tried to tell it totally through the last day of his life, the trial and his farewell party, and that didn't work, and so on. Finally, I focused on a way of telling it.

KB: Marcus Gorman?

WK: Marcus Gorman became the narrator and that was necessary. I found out that I could not have all the multiple voices and make it work. I had to have somebody collating all this. Maybe Henry James turned me around. I was reading his marvelous prefaces and notes on the novel and he was talking about the importance of an intelligent narrator and I realized that was what I needed. So I began. It just fell into place then and I also found a dramatic focus to build to a climax of his life which was the torturing of the trucker, Clem Streeter.

KB: That "mistake" he made?

WK: The mistake he made by torturing that man and then not being the villainous character he might have been and killing him. And that brought down his empire and was the end of his life.

KB: Several reviewers picked up on the *Gatsby* connection. Just as *The Great Gatsby* is really Nick Carraway's book, in a larger sense isn't *Legs* really Marcus Gorman's book?

WK: A lot of people feel that way. Marcus is a much more complicated human being than Jack is, although Jack is a singular character.

KB: In a way Marcus Gorman sort of becomes all of us.

WK: There's something in our makeup that is fascinated by the lawbreakers who carry things to extremes, by "extremity" in our attitudes toward life, and that's what my books have come to represent, to me anyway: the treatment of characters in extreme conditions. Marcus is a man who speaks for our fascination with abomination—with Bonnie and Clyde, the Godfather, Cagney and Bogart. And I go back to Diamond as the phenomenon of the age. Diamond fascinated the public in the way a movie star might be today. He had this enormous popularity. He sold newspapers like crazy. He embodies a kind of pleasurable self-destructiveness that we all have—an inability to accept anything that contravened that maverick element deep in him. Francis Phelan had it also, and Bailey. These are people who have a very clearly defined sense of themselves—what they want and what they don't want—and will pursue that to exotic degrees by other people's standards.

KB: And it has to do with individualism?

WK: Absolutely. I mean it comes to the fore in the first book, *The Ink Truck,* where Bailey becomes the solitary striker in a year-old newspaper strike. The point is that even when the strike is taken away from him, *he* continues to strike on behalf of this cause that he is still defending even though it has ceased to have for any other people any logic. It has become an utterly absurd pursuit by any standard except his own. You have to know that that kind of madness is certainly going to define the individual as an eccentric, maybe a madman. You know, these extreme attitudes really create the possibilities for our existence. And if you can carry them through politically, or literarily, or sexually, or criminally, you'll come up with new answers, or new questions maybe, about what it's all about.

KB: *The Ink Truck* is a very different book from the books you've done since then, it seems to me, in that the region in *The Ink Truck* is the region of the mind. It works in a different plane—the landscape of the psyche.

WK: It was willful on my part to write *The Ink Truck* the way it was. I used to talk about it being six inches off the ground at all times. But the sense of place also impinged on me when I came back in 1963. I began to discover Albany. It's a monstrously old city and a sprawling city in its own way, even though it's small by American big city standards. But it was a cosmopolitan place, because of the various ethnic groups, because of the high level politics, because of the money that was here, because of the commerce, the capitalism. It was a crucible for capitalism. It was a crucible for presidential politics. And so, suddenly, that became as interesting—far more interesting—than my own psyche and my own problems as translated into Bailey's psyche. I began to think of other dimensions of fiction, and I began to think that I should write a political novel. I started to write a novel about Dan O'Connell, the old Irish patriarch here, the boss of bosses, who died in 1977. Then I discovered Legs Diamond, and I decided I should use Legs Diamond in that novel because he was in Albany and the relationship was obvious . . . that he was tolerated by the political machine. But then I got to know more about Diamond's life and he became so fascinating. Shot five times, this fabulous celebrity. I looked him up in the New York Times Index and it took me two years to research him, to figure out what he meant in this society, what gangsterism meant, and what prohibition was all about. I knew it from the movies and all that stuff, but there was an element I didn't know, and the small details of those days were very important to me. So I spent two years fooling around with microfilm machines and old newspapers.

KB: Did *O Albany!* grow out of that same research?

WK: Well, I was researching in general at some point, just trying to discover Albany. I did a series of twenty-six articles on the neighborhoods and the various ethnic groups in 1963 and 64, and they, very much transformed, became the basis for *O Albany!* I couldn't just reprint them because I didn't like the prose anymore, and I knew a lot more about the city's history than I knew then, so I sat down and wrote a new book which was *O Albany!* In those days I was spending a lot of time in the library just looking up general history, trying to discover what it looked like here in 1880 and 1870 and so on. That's translating even now, because my new book, which is called *Quinn's Book,* is set in Albany beginning in 1849 and going on until maybe the Civil War era somewhere, the 1860s, 1880 maybe, I don't know, I'm not sure yet. But there's a wealth of great history, and as a source of background and matrix crucible for fiction it's marvelous.

KB: You gave yourself a "historical memory," as Mary Lee Settle calls it.
WK: That's true, that's a very good way of putting it.

KB: At what point did you realize what you were going to be doing with that historical memory that you were giving yourself?
WK: When you start to work on a book, you begin to eliminate and winnow and something comes out, like Diamond emerged from that throng of historical personages that existed in the teens, 20s and 30s here. I do have the first book still in mind, and I'll probably get to it some day. I hope I will. It will be a book that will have my father in it, I think, and Dan O'Connell, but Diamond just took over. He demanded the attention of my imagination and so I stayed with him.

KB: You started researching a political novel, giving yourself this historical memory, and the first kind of "aboutness" that came out of it was *Legs.* Then he took over for a while . . .
WK: Yeah, right. Knowing about *Legs* helped me to understand the period in which the kidnapping of Dan O'Connell's nephew took place, which was 1933. That was the basis for *Billy Phelan.* Basically *Billy Phelan* is a political novel. It's all about the power of a few politicians to control everybody's life, right down to the lowly hustler on the street—who only wants to play pool and cards, and they can lock him out of every bar in town just by putting the word out. That absolutism, that despotism if you will, that kind of life existed here and it doesn't exist anymore. It's gone. It existed until last year, in a certain way, when Erastus Corning died. He was mayor for 42 years. He represented a continuity of the machine. Corning's own father, Edwin, had founded the machine back in 1921. They ran the county and the city uninterruptedly, without interference of any significance—including a five million dollar investigation by Governor Dewey in the early 1940s—until Dan died in 1977 and Erastus died in 1983. That was the whole era of my life. I never knew anything except the power of Dan O'Connell, and it's a great story.

KB: Why the 1930s? You were born in 1928, right?
WK: That's right. I was a child of the depression without knowing it.

KB: And now you're going back even further in time.

WK: To a time when I wasn't alive. I mean 1849 obviously is a century before my time. But I feel I know something about that city. I don't want to know everything. I want to explore it. I want to be able to hang out in the library again, and look in those old newspapers and have fun just reconstituting a city a century and a half earlier. I feel that there's value in that. I'm not tired of the 30s at all, but there are so many other things that intrigue me. I'd like to play with the Erie Canal for instance. I love the concept of the building of the canal, the way it functioned, and the river, life on the river. And the lumber district in North Albany where I was born and raised, though I never knew it. It had been torn down and disappeared by the time I really was old enough to even look where it had been. I think if I can look at those things maybe I'll have some nice stories to tell about those people who lived in that period.

KB: You came on, somewhat early, to the father and son relationship.

WK: Yeah, it was very important to tell that relationship, that notion that we are all in conspiracy against the next man, against the next generation. Something wrote that line in my brain one day, and I just saw it. I didn't know what it meant, didn't know what I was talking about at that time, but it became one of the motivating principles of building that father/son complexity throughout the whole thing, in various ways, the conspiracy against the children. The thing is that I didn't feel it personally. I had a very fine relationship with my father. We used to fight when I was little and he'd yell at me. But he never hit me. He never denied me anything. I had everything I ever wanted that he could possibly provide, and it went on right to the end of his life. So it doesn't come out of personal denial or neglect or anything like that. It just comes out of a feeling of familial relationships that I see in all directions, and that was one of them.

KB: There are not too many happy relationships, either, with mothers in these books.

WK: The maternal problem is, again, ah . . . I had a great mother, she was terrific. Not my problem, again. I can see how these things destroy certain people in other families, and in my family in other generations there was this maternal problem. My great-grandmother was very much like Francis' mother, but I never knew her. I just knew the consequences of how she controlled the family. I wrote a novel about that. She was a far more sinister character in that book and that may have been one of the problems. It was too much of a negative vision of her but she was the figure who really kept the family from becoming what it should have become. And this Catholic puritanism, this kind of matriarchal possessiveness wouldn't let the children out, wouldn't let them become what they were capable of becoming. That principle certainly was at work in that first novel, which was called *The Angels and the Sparrows,* and it's obviously at work, in other dimensions, in *Billy Phelan* and *Ironweed.* But in different ways, different ways entirely. I mean *Ironweed* is not about that kind of control, it's about the absence of control. It's about flight and refusal to take responsibility.

KB: "The fugitive thrust."
WK: Right.

KB: But one of the things that thrust Francis Phelan out was his relationship with his mother.
WK: Yes, and a few critics accused me of not treating women seriously enough in *Billy Phelan.* That's a ridiculous criticism because that was a book about men, about a society of males. You didn't *see* women in that society . . . tables for ladies, back entrance, that's the way it was.

KB: Well it was a sexist society and these are sexist men. It's institutional. It's cultural. It wouldn't have been an accurate book otherwise.
WK: That's the point, exactly. When Billy Phelan goes home in *Ironweed* you find out that he has this sister, he has this mother, and they're quite different from his life on the town. You can't satisfy partisan critics, advocacy critics, in every book and I think generally it's unfair to attack a writer on those grounds until you look at the body of the work and see if he's truly what you say he is.

KB: A lot of people have criticized contemporary fiction for being sterile because of lacking a sense of place. Do you think this is possibly true?
WK: That's the way I feel. I don't single out any individual and I don't want to tell anybody how to write, what to write, what not to write, but I just find myself pretty bored these days with the endless concern with style, with writing about writing, with writing about the pure psyche, with writing about yet another Beckettian landscape, or Kafkaesque dream, though Kafka's dreams were really interesting, and they were rooted in place and event. A little piece like "The Fratricide" is just like a film, it's so visual and so set with detail. I think that if you leave out place, you leave out one of the principal ingredients of fiction. We are what we are because of the place to

some degree. We interact with it. We interact with its mores. This place is not like the next place. New York City is not like Albany. There's a more provincial feeling in this city. There's a more familial feeling in your relationships to politicians and local people and you behave differently, therefore, than you would in the hostility of a big city slum or in an indifferent depersonalized culture of some urban glass cube. "Place" is so significant.

KB: So I take it that you believe that American literature, by definition, is regional literature.

WK: I don't say that. I think that, well, if you think of a writer like Melville, his region was the sea. If you think of Hemingway, he had place wherever he went and he was this cosmopolitan character. But he really was writing about the provinces of his own existence. There's always an exception. Kafka is one and Beckett is another. I can read those men forever but they do something else, and that's fine. Just think of John Cheever—where would we be without his place? The culture that he knew so well. His were not sociological stories, they were stories about people who lived that suburban/ exurban upper middle class lifestyle, and out of that he created mythological characters. He's a marvelous writer! God I love Cheever, I'm so sorry he died. I wish he'd written about ten more books.

KB: Language is very important to you, obviously.

WK: The people I value are people like Cheever and Faulkner and Joyce for whom language was the principal element. You can exist without a place, as Kafka and Beckett will prove. You can just create the life of the mind and be extraordinary, but they too had language—great language. It's the thing that makes me want to read anybody. Suddenly a man like Milan Kundera comes along and you want to read everything he wrote because he's so witty. He plays with the words. And so does Cheever. His sentences—you can read them aloud, they're works of art. His paragraphs . . .

KB: But there is a point of view, among some writers, that language is all there is, that characters are purely "linguistic constructs."

WK: I would agree more than you think with that. Language is the *sine qua non,* if you don't have that language on the page, I won't read it. I mean I just can't. I might read it dutifully if I have to review a book or something, but the chances are I'll hate it, and I'll drive myself through it. Or if it's a bad translation it's painful to read and I hate it. It's the element without which I won't get through the book. I'm not talking about florid language.

I'm not talking about Joycean convolutions or portmanteau words or anything that's not necessary, but the language as style, language as elegance, language as life itself. That's what I care about, more than anything else, and if it doesn't have that, forget it.

KB: Does the magical, the supernatural element in your books relate to "the life of the soul?" Is that the thing, beyond language, that concerns you the most?

WK: I don't think you can talk about the life of the soul if you don't talk about surrealistic, metaphysical elements. We live and think, and we also dream. And dreams are very illogical and surrealistic, that's why I'm a great lover of Luis Buñuel for instance. Or Fellini. They transcend realism. Realism goes just so far, and no farther. You're stuck with James T. Farrell and Dreiser, and however great both of those men are, and they are in their best work, they stop at a certain point. I want my people to go on. I want to have that mystical element that I know exists in everybody's life.

KB: Did you feel like a writer you had to work up to that to be able to do it in *Ironweed?*

WK: No, because I think that it exists in *The Ink Truck.*

KB: It's there, that's true.

WK: That's a crazy book. It's motivated by a desire to not write a realistic novel. I think I went in that direction as a resistance to the journalistic realism that had so pervaded the novel through so many years. When you have great language, as you have in a book like *Gatsby,* which is realistic, the language transcends. The language carries you into that vision that Fitzgerald had. He could rhetoricize you into a dream. I was trying to find it and I went in search of it by, I suppose, courting a wild surrealism. People think that I was up on acid or something when I wrote that book and that's utterly untrue. You could never write anything that made any sense on any drug. But the feeling of looking into somebody's mind and soul by these wild abstractions appealed to me far more than did any kind of conventional reporting. That was why I quit to write fiction. From then on it was a matter of deciding how to discover what was really going on inside my mind, and I wasn't able to ever go back to that mundane world of realism. But when I began to do *Legs* I was still looking for a *whole* surrealistic novel. I was structuring it on *The Tibetan Book of the Dead,* and all sorts of wild and crazy things, stylistically departing because I didn't want a conventional narrative anymore. Yet I had this feeling of being meticulous about history. I was trying desperately to tell the real story of Legs Diamond and not just another wild and imagined gangster story. And when I began to write, I realized I had to come down to the real Diamond. I moved back into realism and I found it very valuable again. Yet I think there's still an element of the surreal that moves in and out of that book. It's not entirely there. Kiki's confrontation with the penman on the street, or the birdman that Legs meets on the boat, and the final chapter. Those elements are meant to convey what is valuable beyond realism, to me, in trying to define that character.

KB: If you look at the physical world intensely enough and long enough, if you look at a place hard enough, it starts to "bend" on you?

WK: It's that sort of thing. But the danger in treating this stuff is that you might move into mysticism yourself. I never feel myself really mystically involved.

KB: You're not a Martin Daugherty, who was clairvoyant?

WK: No, but I've had experiences like Martin Daugherty. An element of that is essential in order to convey in literature the complexity of human beings. If you don't get close to the unconscious, then you're only dealing with part of any individual. That's why I really have this kind of split in Francis Phelan. When he begins to think, he thinks in far more complicated and more abstract ways than he could ever speak, but don't we all?

KB: I have read that you are a real film buff. Do you think that film has had an influence on your choice of narrative style?

WK: I don't see how I could not be influenced by film. I've lived my whole life in this generation where we spend half our time watching films in one way or the other. When I was a kid, I always wanted to see every movie that came along. Later, I became a movie critic so I could go to New York and hang out at the New York Film Festival and see all those foreign films that you'd never get to see in Albany. I worked as a movie critic for a couple years in Albany and learned a lot about movies. I started a film club up here and I brought all of these terrific movies in that nobody could get to, and then wound up writing movies. It's not an illogical direction to go in. Obviously, I have translated this into visualized fiction at certain times. When there is a scene it ought to be visual. When there is language it ought to be as powerful in its own way, as remote from the visual as it needs to be. So I don't have any overwhelming influence where everything is cinematic. I learned as much from Hemingway as I learned from the movies. He too was influenced by the movies; he grew up in the age of film. His scenes are very visual.

KB: So I guess what you're saying is you think that film is part of the vocabulary of all writers in some way or another.

WK: Unless they are writers who just militantly have never seen movies.

KB: What about reading in your life?

WK: (Laughs) Well, I've collected a few books as you can see.

KB: What kind of a reader are you?

WK: I don't know how to answer that question. I read all the time, and I read everything, but I tend to read about writing and about fiction and about writers whenever I can. I just bought Kundera's new book. I'm going to review Mario Cuomo's diaries—he's a brand new writer on the scene. I read a lot about the movies, now that I'm in the movie business. I go back to Cheever every once in a while. I need to have a little Cheever input, and a little Faulknerian fun. I love Nabokov's essays. He's such a scandalously irreverent man. I read a lot of Latin American writers. When you think about men like Juan Rulfo in Mexico and Mario Vargas-Llosa in Peru, and of course García Márquez in Colombia, and so many of the Cuban writers . . . oh, and a Puerto Rican writer, Luis Rafael Sanchez who wrote *Macho Camacho's Beat,* a wonderful crazy book.

KB: And those writers all use magical elements, don't they?

WK: Right, they all do. That's a basic ingredient in Latin American fiction. Jose Donoso and *The Obscene Bird of Night,* you think of the wildness of that book . . .

KB: Combined with the strong political thrust. I guess that's what fascinates me about writers like yourself. The combination of the intense realism, the political and social vision, but also a lot of the elements of mythology and romance . . .

WK: Well, why not? Why shouldn't you use it all? That's what it is all about. When you leave something out it's at your peril. If you leave out language, if you leave out mythology, if you leave out love, or money, or power—it all has to be there, somewhere along the line. You can't get it all in one book, or maybe you can, sometimes, but it takes a lot of books to get to the point of what it is that you see.

KB: Can we talk about the ending of *Ironweed?*

WK: I don't want to explicate it, if that's what you're moving toward, but . . . okay.

KB: Did you make a conscious decision to shift the voice at the beginning of the final section of *Ironweed?*

WK: Oh yeah, I can talk about that. The conscious change that people have remarked on—going into the conditional . . . I did that not in order to make it hypothetical, that was not the intention. As far as I'm concerned that's real, everything that happens there is real. The change in language, in syntax, is meant as a kind of overview that here we are, looking at the last moments of this book, the last moments of this man's story, and I saw him walking down Pearl Street and I began with that sentence and it seemed right.

KB: The "It would be . . ."

WK: "It would be . . ." such and such an hour by the clock on the first church by the time he. . . . It was taking into consideration a great deal of his psychological and temporal motion, and yet doing it in a very short space, and I felt that was the way to tell it. I can't tell you why. It was just a stylistic leap I felt that changed the mood.

KB: It gives you narrative distance so that you're able to handle some emotionally loaded subject matter and avoid melodrama, among other things.

WK: If that was the achievement there, it was instinctive. I avoid melodrama at all costs.

KB: At what point did you know you were going to both begin and end the book with Strawberry Bill's visit to Francis Phelan?

WK: That was evolutionary. I knew he had to confront somebody at the end and Strawberry Bill was a likely character. He had to have a dialogue with somebody who was friendly, who had a way of looking at his life that he couldn't look at himself, and he had to be one of the dead. So here came Strawberry Bill, into the boxcar.

KB: You say you don't want to explicate the ending, but the total and complete intent of the ending, whether he's physically dead or not, either way he is in fact home under the eaves, am I right? I mean, he does come home.

WK: Well, I would rather not go on record as saying what precisely that means. I think it speaks for itself. I can't say it better than I said it there. I can't say it more clearly. It's a very complicated situation in which he exists at that moment, and I think I'm representing the complexities, variously. It's not simple realism, nor is it simple mysticism, if mysticism can ever be simple. But it exists, and describes where he is. I don't want to make a puzzle out of it. However the ending can be interpreted, it still has an integrity of conclusion. I'm not leaving you up in the air. What those last two or three pages say is what Francis Phelan's condition is when we take leave of him.

KB: As I've been reading the Albany books, I couldn't help but think about the Thomas Wolfe—*You Can't Go Home Again*—syndrome. But you appear to have been received very well here in your home territory, in Albany.

WK: People want me to run for governor, mayor, for congress, anything (laughs). I don't know. That's a joke.

KB: They've had a William Kennedy Day here.

WK: They had a William Kennedy Month, and then there's going to be a week in September. The city celebrating itself is what it really is and it's wonderful. What they're doing, among other things, is using *Albany* as a basis for some discussion of neighborhoods. People who have been written about in Albany, people like Howard Simons who's the managing editor of the *Washington Post,* or people like John McLoughlin who's a TV reporter here and used to be a colleague of mine in the *Times Union.* And they're mentioned in the books and so they're going to be brought out into panel discussions to talk about politics, the neighborhoods, etc. There will be, I guess, use of the various books for some kind of guided tours of the city or something: "This happened here in this book. Here's where Francis Phelan walked." It's a mix of fiction and realism, or fiction and journalism. It's really authentic, but that's the way the books are.

KB: But what about the . . . say the O'Connell family? Are there any of the O'Connells left to . . .

WK: There are, you know, heirs and nieces, and so on, and cousins.

KB: Has there been any criticism?

WK: Oh no, they all seem to accept everything. You occasionally get a disgruntled citizen. A bit here and there, but mostly, everybody has been waiting for that book to be written, somebody to put Dan's story into hardcover.

KB: Then there really was a kidnapping?

WK: Oh yeah, it's a very famous case. It took place in 1933 and I set it in 1938, and it didn't happen in quite the same way, and there was no Billy Phelan involved in it. Not that I know of anyway. But the kidnapping was pretty much the same way it is.

KB: Where do the fictional characters come from? Are they composites?

WK: The people are invented, however much they were inspired at one point by certain living characters, including Jack Diamond. I invented Jack Diamond as he exists in *Legs.* I followed the line of his life, he got shot on such and such a date, he was on the boat going to Europe on such and such a date, he died on such and such a date.

KB: Did he meet Fitzgerald or did you make that all up?

WK: No, I invented it. I really thought that he was an extension of Gatsby, but way beyond what Gatsby is. Fitzgerald treated Gatsby with kid gloves and Diamond was a gangster. Those gangsters were cruel and vicious people.

KB: What about the private people in the books? They're purely invented . . . how do they come to you?

WK: Well I don't know . . . that's a question that would take about six years to answer. But there are certain paradigms. I had an uncle who lived in that world of Billy Phelan. I talked with him a lot. I moved in that world myself when I was a kid. I played pool in some of those places, and had turkey sandwiches in some of those saloons, and things like that.

KB: But did you set out to catch a type, in the way Henry James talks about catching a type?

WK: No, that never appeals to me. I think that's maybe what you *do,* but that's certainly never the motivation. What I try to do is find a character on whom I can build, who really intrigues me, and who is therefore usable and creatable. There has to be some sand there at the beginning and when there is, I go with it—that's all.

KB: But you did build a history. You've spoken about feeling that you have to know how everything came out before you can even begin.

WK: If I said that I must have said it in another context. I don't know where the new book is going—*Quinn's Book*—I have no idea what is going to happen in that book. I've had some idea. I see events out there. I have a time, I have an era, I have a kind of complexity of character. I've got the clay and once you've got that you've got a book, it seems. Then you can go ahead and work. *Quinn's Book* is evolving from a book I started, probably in 1977. I worked all summer and produced a novel's worth of notes. They were all dead in the water. I couldn't make anything come to life, I don't know why. I tried. I created characters, I defined them down to their shoelaces, and I had plots . . . but nothing was happening and so I had to throw it away. And instead of that I wrote *Ironweed* or *O Albany!*, or something.

KB: We've talked about the way you conceived these books . . . you had a heck of a time actually. You must feel vindicated right now, in light of the very devil of a time you had getting *Ironweed* published.

WK: That's a very mild way to put it, vindication. I mean, exaltation! The feeling I had all those years that maybe I wasn't going to be recognized ever, seriously. I had been published and I was having fun along the way. I was not denied any taste of success, but it was just a taste along the way. *The Ink Truck* came out and then I sold *Legs* right away and I had a time working it up, but it was a complicated book. I had a lot to learn. That came out and got wide attention. I got, I don't know, 100, 150 reviews, I don't know how many reviews I got. There was an option for a film, it was made into paperback, it sold in England, and so on and so on. And then came *Billy* and that was okay. I got great reviews on *Billy*. *Billy* didn't make a nickel.

KB: Didn't they just put it out there and let it drop?

WK: That's exactly what happened, and it didn't make a nickel. But it got marvelous reviews, not anywhere near as many as *Legs* had gotten because *Legs* had been reviewed on the basis of the gangster element. It was badly publicized and cheaply publicized too. It was scandalous the way they treated *Legs*. I was an absolute innocent and let it all happen. They treated it like a Mafia book, as if that were the way to go. Then came *Ironweed* and I sold that, but then my editor, Cork Smith, left publishing for a time and the book began to go round and round. Nobody wanted to buy it. They were afraid of Albany, they were afraid of bums. They didn't like the fact that I had not made any money on *Billy Phelan*. They found the kind of dialogue between the conscious and unconscious language of Francis unfathomable, and what you're talking about is a lot of bad editing as far as I'm concerned. The way the book was received by people who were close to me was quite the opposite of this. What it really comes down to, I believe, is that a good many editors are unable to express conviction for fiction which is not automatically translatable into money. If it looks even skittishly negative, forget it. They will find reasons on which to base their rejection. Now this doesn't mean that they are not literate people, or not sensitive people, but it's the nature of what has happened in publishing in our time. I think I'm kind of an odd example now of how that world has made one mistake. Their judgments were based on my track record, the subject matter—and the book had nothing to do with my track record. It's an extraordinary financial success at this stage. And it's been critically received, as you know, which delights me no end. I didn't aspire to best-sellerdom. I didn't aspire to big movie money or anything like that. I hoped for it, but all I wanted to do was have a way of life and be able to write some fiction. And it was very, very difficult. The better I got the more difficult it became. There's an object lesson here and I don't recommend the profession to everybody. I just think that people who are writers will have to go on and be writers no matter what happens to them, and that they'll continue to write whether the climate is friendly or hostile. And maybe it will happen, as everybody seems to be saying it's going to, that fiction will one day go the way of poetry and there will be no money in it. I don't think so. I think we're going to always have a need for storytelling, and that people will always come back to the story.

William Kennedy: An Interview

Peter J. Quinn / 1985

Published in *The Recorder: The Journal of the American Irish Histori-cal Society* New Series 1.1 (Winter 1985): 65–81. Reprinted by per-mission.

It's the writer's dream: the National Book Critics Circle Award for fiction; a MacArthur Foundation "genius" award of a quarter of a million dollars; the Pulitzer Prize for fiction; movie deals, fame, acclaim, wealth, a success story so improbable that even Frank Capra might have turned it down.

But it's true. It's as real as this man sitting on the porch of his house in Averill Park, outside Albany, a novelist whose life reads like a novel, who spent years of struggle and anonymity, writing books that, despite praise and plaudits, never seemed to sell.

"I was broke," Kennedy says. "I didn't have any money. I didn't have any future. I didn't have anything." Nothing, that is, but the writer's craft, nothing but the redemptive satisfaction of his own creativity as he came "to under-stand that the writing itself was the most important element in my life."

Kennedy's literary odyssey began in good Irish fashion when he turned his back on the parochial world of pols and prelates and left Albany for Puerto Rico. But, also in good Irish fashion, he remained a prisoner to the place, with a knowledge of himself now as "a person whose imagination has be-come fused with a single place. And in that place finds all that a man needs for the life of the soul."

Kennedy's "Albany cycle" of novels—*Legs, Billy Phelan's Greatest Game,* and *Ironweed* brought fame to that place, putting Albany on the Amer-ican literary map, where, if the progenitor of the James brothers (William and Henry, not Frank and Jesse) had not left Albany for New York, it might have arrived sooner. Kennedy is currently working on *Quinn's Book,* the fourth revolution of that cycle, and is also writing screenplays for the other three.

Bill Kennedy has it all now. But sitting with him on a soft summer after-noon, warmed by the sun and the smooth assurance of a glass of Irish whis-key, you realize that the work goes on, that while the fame and good fortune are welcomed and even relished, they are still beside the point. For Bill Kennedy the point is what it has always been: the sentence, words strung together into complexity, words transubstantiated into life, words that jump off the page.

"That's what the whole thing is still all about," he says, "what it's always about: the invention of something out of nothing. That's the classic statement of what writing is. And I believe this is the whole satisfaction that comes from writing: that you are able to create something out of nothing that seems new to you."

What follows are some of Bill Kennedy's reflections on life, art and the Irish-American experience, a self-portrait of an artist in progress.

Quinn: John Updike in a recent piece in the *New York Review of Books* mentions a story that he wrote called "The Happiest I've Ever Been". He says that "While composing a single paragraph I had the sensation of breaking through a thin sheet of restraining glass to material previously locked up." Did you ever have a similar kind of experience, a moment—an epiphany—when you knew you were going beyond the material?

Kennedy: Yes, I wrote something once and I showed it to a friend of mine. He asked, *"Who* wrote this?" and I knew I was on to something. But it happened to me seriously when I was in Puerto Rico. I was working on a first novel that has never been published and when I read back the next morning what I'd written the day before I knew I had done *something,* probably just as Updike knew what he had done. It's when you discover that there's something else going on in your head, when you find the right metaphor, or symbol, or whatever it is you're groping for—and suddenly the work begins to blossom in directions that you couldn't possibly conceive for then. That's precisely the way I felt with *Ironweed* which is the most recent example that comes to mind. You create the structure, you create the character and a number of events, and then you find out that what you've done is beyond what you intended to do. Of course, you understand the new developments as soon as you touch them, and in my reading of that paragraph back in Puerto Rico, I realized I knew more than I gave myself credit for knowing. It comes out of your fingertips as you write, the unconscious becoming conscious at the instant that you need it. It first seems a very happy, wonderful accident, but it's not so accidental—it's really everything that you always were and hoped to do that is emerging.

Quinn: What about the "Muse," the sense of something speaking through you? Some writers seem to experience its presence. Have you?

Kennedy: Never had that. I never understood the Muse. I used to wait for it when I was a kid. I'd stay home on Thursday afternoons and expect it to arrive. That was my day off, and also the Muse's day off. It never did show up, but I'd like the stuff anyway. Nobody ever bought any of it, so I felt there was some other element in writing that I didn't understand. That was a question I asked in *The Ink Truck*. "What is it that I don't understand? What is it that I can't figure out?"

With *Legs*, I began to understand writing a little more clearly. I would work for hours sometimes and nothing would happen, but then after ten or maybe eleven hours, suddenly, something *would* happen. I used to go to a friend's lake house and put in time. I knew I wanted to say something, thought I knew what I wanted to say—I had all the material, but nothing would come together. I couldn't figure out what to do or how to do it. But after those long hours, I would begin to write, and feel very good about what I'd achieved by the end of the day. I came to understand in those days that writing itself was what was important. It was enough. I mean I was broke, didn't have any future, didn't have even a prospect. But I would come away from those sessions at the lake house feeling quite happy. It was amazing. I went over to Cape Cod, I went up to the Adirondacks, all by myself, and just hung out and wrote. At the end of the day, I would be ecstatic about the fact that I had produced whatever number of pages it was. I was somehow making something worthwhile out of nothing at all.

Quinn: There's a scene in *Legs* that strikes me as being one of those moments when you felt both a sense of "breaking through" and a sense of achievement. It's the scene where Legs's girlfriend, Kiki, is hiding in a closet. It's a tautly woven, exciting example of what—for lack of a better phrase—is called "stream of consciousness."

Kennedy: That's a true fact of her life. Kiki was actually arrested in a closet in her friend's house. She was hiding when the police came and got her. I guess I got to know Kiki. I felt it one afternoon when I was writing about her. That piece didn't get into the book, but it was a most ecstatic afternoon, another one of those moments when I felt I had done something that I hadn't expected to do. It was a leap beyond the surface of Kiki. I had gotten beyond the journalistic sense of who she was and into what she truly was, the kind of kookiness of her life, the voluptuousness of her life, and it was all in this page and a half that never got into the book. It was giving definition to something that had not been very clear before, and that is what

I really loved. It was a new sense of writing, a breakthrough in saying things
obliquely.

Quinn: John Gardner has described the writing process as getting to the
point where you just look at your characters and let them act, let them live
their lives. They're so real that you're writing down what people are doing,
rather than attempting to invent. Have you ever had that experience?

Kennedy: That's the idea of the characters running away with the writer.
I've never really felt it. I must say that's probably true for some people.
Maybe it was true for Gardner, but it's not been entirely true for me. My way
is to impose myself, my new information, my new interest, my new attitudes
on anything in the book. Whatever I read tends to turn up in the next chapter.
You may not know that I read it yesterday afternoon, it may be something
that happened back in 1846, but quite possibly it can turn up in the writing
as a brand new perception.

Quinn: You spent several years writing *Legs*. How well did you get to
know him? Was he a real person for you?

Kennedy: I believed I knew Jack Diamond, but it took me a long time. I
started to write him in the first person, and I couldn't, because I didn't know
him. I started to write his life as a movie script which would become a novel,
a form that now is a cliché, and I could see it was a cliché even then. I only
got about two chapters done, and then I was asking myself, "Where am I
going to put the camera now? Where is the cameraman going to stand?" All
those artificial aspects of the constructed world, the stylistic world, were intrusive and ridiculous, so what I did was spend about two and a half years
trying to figure out how to tell that story. I wrote it eight different times. I
finally arrived at a narrator who could see Diamond in the round, and when I
did that, I began to see Diamond myself. And then I began to wait for him
on the road. I figured he'd be a nervous hitchhiker and I'd pick him up. Dana,
my wife, had a dream about him being on the front lawn after the book was
finished. She went out on the porch and there was Diamond. He rolled around
in the grass and kicked his legs up in the air, and Dana asked "What's going
on?" Legs said to her, "Bill got it just right." That's Dana's dream, not mine.

Quinn: *The Ink Truck* was your first novel. It's said that there's a special
relationship between authors and their first novels, a parent's pride in their
firstborn. Do you feel that way about *The Ink Truck*?

Kennedy: Yes. I love it. Some people badmouthed it after the fact, and before the fact for that matter. Actually, it sold as soon as I had finished it. It sold the first time out. I had a little problem trying to sell it before it was finished, but when it was done, my agent sent it over to Dial Press where Ed Doctorow was the managing editor, and he bought it. Thereafter, it went out of print fairly quickly, but that's the nature of first novels. Writers who are serious about themselves don't worry about that. If you're going to cut your wrists after your first novel, you're not a writer. After the twenty-eighth novel, and nobody will buy it, well . . . But you think of Farrell. He never quit. It's an admirable thing, because he was getting pleasure out of what he was doing. If there are enough people who understand that, if there are other writers getting some pleasure out of reading your twenty-eighth novel, then maybe that's enough. I don't know.

Quinn: What about the influence of other writers on you? James Joyce must certainly be one of them?

Kennedy: Yes, absolutely. I've been reading him just lately. I've read books about him, by him. There's no end to that man. He's the greatest man of letters in the twentieth century. I don't think there's a close second. If there is, it's Faulkner.

In America, there's *nobody* close to Faulkner, but Joyce has transcendence. Leopold Bloom is someone who is never going to die in the history of literature. Faulkner did great things. He did wonderful, wonderful things. But there's nothing like Leopold and Molly, the Blooms, in all of twentieth century literature. I don't know where the hell you go to find their equal.

Quinn: What about the similarities between you and Joyce?

Kennedy: Similarities? I don't aspire to similarities.

Quinn: People have compared the opening of *Ironweed* to "The Dead" and to the "Circe" chapter in *Ulysses*. Is there any validity to that?

Kennedy: I wish I had heard somebody say that, but I never heard that before. Joyce is Joyce. He's by himself, and I wouldn't make any comparisons. No, it's not an attempt at conscious imitation, if that's the question.

Quinn: Your careful reconstruction of Albany, your fascination with place, certainly evokes Joyce's obsession with Dublin.

Kennedy: That's true enough. Joyce made things easier for all of us. He prompted us to become aware of our entire heritage, including dishpans and the jakes in the backyard.

Quinn: You both are absorbed with the place where you grew up. And you both left it. Did you choose, as Joyce did, "silence, exile and cunning," and set out to chronicle Albany at a distance? Or did you pack up all your cares and woes and only gradually come to understand your relationship to Albany?

Kennedy: Silence was imposed on me by all my editors. My might-have-been editors. Exile came because I couldn't stay in Albany any longer and still function effectively. I had to go elsewhere. I went to Puerto Rico, which is exile under the American flag. It's as far away as you could get, and still be in the U.S.A. But cunning was not in my kit bag. I never felt that that was necessary. I was always above board. I always put out my work for stomping, whatever I did. And I usually got stomped. But I never felt that it was necessary to retreat and stay home and nurse my wounds and never try again until I had a masterpiece. That was never my understanding of how to write, or how to live as a writer. Somewhere along the line I came across a phrase about "renewing your vulnerability." And that seemed to me a most important thing for a writer. You renew your vulnerability. Constantly. You start out feeling so vulnerable that you're afraid the criticism will kill you. But if you're not afraid of being vulnerable, if you say, "Go ahead, hit me again, I can take it," you get a thick skin.

You get that as a journalist. Letters to the editor demanding "Throw this guy in the river." Or, "Why did you hire him to begin with? This man should be destroyed." Or "This is a radical, or this is a liberal,"—or some other dirty word. You get to live with that. I remember I wrote a series of articles on the slums of Albany back in the sixties. The mail attacking me came in like you couldn't believe. I got hate calls and hate mail from grand bigots, wonderful bigots, really *creative* bigots. It didn't faze me, because I realized early on that when you get into the business of putting yourself out on the public chopping block, you have to figure you're going to get chopped at.

Quinn: With *Legs* did you set out to write a trilogy about Albany?

Kennedy: No. As a matter of fact, the new book—*Quinn's Book*—will make it a quartet, or a tetralogy, a double set of twins. I don't know what you call it. The reason why I chose the word "cycle" is that it's an open-ended and related series of novels. I'm writing a book right now that's set in 1849 and it's about Daniel Quinn, the grandfather of the boy Daniel Quinn who appears in *Legs* and *Billy Phelan* and *Ironweed*. It's the same family, and all the Daughertys are going to be there, and the ancestors of Katrina.

Albany is still going to be Albany, but I'm going backward now to discover patterns that anticipate the twentieth century present. It's preconsciousness I'm working on right now.

Quinn: The other three are set in Albany in the Depression, which really seems to have captured your imagination. Why?

Kennedy: *Legs* was 1931, and that was researched to discover that era. And once I discovered the twenties and Prohibition and the gangland world, I began to see that it had tentacles that went forward, that people I was writing about in *Legs* were going to be significant in future books I wanted to write. When I got around to writing *Billy Phelan,* which was the next one, it should have taken place in 1933, which was only two years after Diamond died, but I felt what I needed to do then was to move deeper into the Depression, into the grit of it, into the end of it, and the feeling of coming out of it. I set *Billy Phelan* in 1938, which was just before the war begins and was also a political year. I manipulated history to suit myself. I made the real-life kidnapping of Dan O'Connell's nephew take place five years later than it actually had, and I used the "blackout," for instance, in *Billy Phelan,* but placed it in 1938. Dan O'Connell [Albany's political boss] "blacked out" Governor Dewey in '42 or '43. He had the civil defense behind him when he turned off the electricity so nobody in Albany could hear Dewey's speech attacking the Albany politicians.

Quinn: *Ironweed* is the latest completed part of the cycle. You said in a recent interview that it came "like a bullet." Is that because you had lived in that world for so long, were so familiar with it from all the research you'd done, that you already knew the characters?

Kennedy: No. *Ironweed* was something else, and had a pre-existence in both journalism and early fiction. In that unpublished novel I wrote in Puerto Rico I created Francis Phelan, just one of several characters in a family chronicle. Then, in 1963, I wrote a series of articles on a wino couple for the Albany *Times-Union,* and I fused the fiction and non-fiction when I started to create Francis Phelan again for *Billy Phelan.* The early work was all dead at this point, which is what usually happens when you leave it in the drawer, so I began from scratch, and Francis emerged as a new and more complex character in *Billy,* so much so that I knew he should have his own book. So by the time I got to him in *Ironweed* I knew far more about the history of the city, and I was reflecting a complexity of life that I had not been able to get to in the first novels. I felt I was into higher mathematics, and that I really knew this man. And the book was written in just about seven months.

Quinn: You mentioned Farrell before. Are there any other Irish-American writers who've had an impact on your writing?

Kennedy: Fitzgerald, if you call him an Irish-American. Actually, he was the original Yuppie. The Yuppie Irishman.

Quinn: There are similarities between *Legs* and *Gatsby.* Several critics have mentioned them.

Kennedy: Deliberately so. *Gatsby*'s a great book, I think. And I make that comparison in homage as much as anything else. I wouldn't want anybody to think I was cavalierly using the narration of Marcus Gorman about a gangster without understanding the precedent. But I also feel that the narrator in *Gatsby* was boring as a character, and I don't think Marcus is. Fitzgerald's narrator came to life only when Fitzgerald let him stop talking about himself and allowed us to see him in action. That, very clearly, was when he leaped off the page for me.

Quinn: *Legs* and *The Great Gatsby* are both outsiders trying to force their way into America. Is that right?

Kennedy: Right. But you never see Gatsby doing it seriously. There are some people who have made the analogy that Diamond *is* Gatsby, but I don't think Gatsby was like Diamond. I don't think Gatsby was a gangster. I think he was just a thief. I don't think he was a killer. People said he killed a man *once,* but they said that about everybody in the twenties.

Quinn: That's the American story. The immigrant or the immigrant's son forcing his way in.

Kennedy: The ambition was always to reach fame and fortune. Some people tried to shoot their way into it. Some survived, were acquitted, or just got rich and went straight. Big Bill Dwyer did that. He was one of the great rumrunners, and he wound up in Cafe Society, Palm Beach, racetracks, hobnobbing with the rich, hanging out in tuxedos. A number of Irish-Americans chose that route.

Quinn: Any other Irish-American writers besides Fitzgerald whom you value?

Kennedy: O'Hara, even though he tried to bury his Irishness and come on as a WASP clubman. But his stories still have great vigor and wit. I got lost in his novels, that deluge of information that now seems the trademark of the pulp writers. Eugene O'Neill was a great favorite of mine, especially his *Iceman* and *Long Day's Journey.* Wonderful Celtic gloom and irony in those works. I liked Farrell's *Studs Lonigan* but I never wanted to write like that—the naturalism of the city. I was too interested in the dream element in life, the surreal. Flannery O'Connor is terrific, now and always. I always thought Edwin O'Connor's *The Last Hurrah* was a marvelous book. I fell off the chair reading those great lines about the Curley days and I could see he understood the tension between the Church and politics extremely well. But I also felt he was leaving out things either to be polite to the Church or to Irish society, or perhaps out of squeamishness. I felt at times that he didn't reflect Irish-American life as I knew it. I felt I had to bring in the cat-houses and the gambling and the violence, for if you left those out you had only a part of Albany. The idealized Irish life of the country club and the Catholic colleges was true enough, but that didn't have anything to do with what was going on down on Broadway among all those raffish Irishmen. They were tough sons-of-bitches, dirty-minded and foul-mouthed gamblers and bigots, and also wonderful, generous, funny, curiously honest and very complex people. I felt that way of life had to be penetrated at the level of harsh reality—its wit, anger, sexuality, deviousness. It also needed to have the surreal dimension that goes with any society in which religion plays such a dominant role. Those lives are worth recording, and I'm not done with them by any means.

Quinn: Do you think, in fact, there is such a thing as an "Irish-American literary tradition?"

Kennedy: When we talk about Irish-American writers—or Irish-American anything—we're talking about an evolution. You can't really be negative about Finley Peter Dunne, or Farrell, or Fitzgerald, or O'Hara, or O'Connor. They all lived in a certain time and reflected that time. And for some of them, maybe, there was a sense of marginality about their background. There was an uncertainty. Certainly, in the days of Fitzgerald and O'Hara there was. The Irish were aspiring to rise in the world. You had Finley Peter Dunne satirizing those "donkey" Irishmen in order to make them become something beyond what they could become. Everybody is a climber. Everybody is trying to come up from below. That's the first law of motion in America. Nobody wants to live in the Five Points in New York City forever. Nobody wants to live with the stereotypes that were associated with Irish thugs—the derbys and the cock-eyed look, the readiness to break your ankle for a nickel or your wrist for a dime.

God knows where I am in all of this, in this evolution, but I *know* all that has come before. I know that those who come before helped to show me how to try to turn experience into literature. I know all that came before in the same way I know that the Irish ascended politically to become Jack Kennedy. After Jack Kennedy, anything was possible. Goddammit, *we've* been President, and you can't hold us back anymore.

Quinn: Is there a certain defensiveness about the Irish? We know all about the lecherousness and the sinfulness but we prefer to present outsiders with the other face, the saintly side.

Kennedy: I just got a letter from the son of the owner of a bar in Albany. You know what he told me? He said, "Dan O'Connell told my father that he closed all the poolrooms in Albany, so how come you've got a poolroom in *Billy Phelan*?" O'Connell didn't want any poolrooms in Albany, he said, because they were corrupting influences on kids.

Quinn: As opposed to cock fights?

Kennedy: Or as opposed to saloons? And whorehouses? I don't see how you can leave all that out if you're going to talk about life in the twentieth century. Irish-American life or any kind of life.

Quinn: But haven't the Irish been blessed by a wonderful sense of guilt? Isn't that part of their Catholicism?

Kennedy: I don't think Catholics feel that much guilt anymore. They're more and more like other Americans.

Quinn: Isn't the loss of guilt the loss of a wonderful strength? Isn't it one of the essential ingredients in the Irish-American mind, as it is in the Jewish-American mind? It's the one thing you can be sure of never losing.

Kennedy: Well, there's always a sense of sin. I don't think we're ever going to lose that. Norman Mailer was unnecessarily worried about the loss of sin, in terms of sex, back in the sixties. He was suggesting that the only thing that makes sense is to have sex when you're sinning. Otherwise, it's no fun.

Quinn: But isn't Catholicism one of the things that makes those earthy Irishmen you write about unique? The tension created in their lives by the Church?

Kennedy: That's only part of it. You only go to church on Sundays, and maybe you talk about it the rest of the week. But politics is far more impor-

tant than church, because politics is survival. You would postpone your concern about the salvation of your soul. You could always say, "I'll get to that
when I get old," and if you got a heart attack, God forbit, and died in the
blossom of your youth, the chances are you would go to Purgatory.

Quinn: What about the Catholic element in your novels? One reviewer
has seen in *Ironweed* a parallel between the liturgy of the Catholic Church
and the events of the three days the book encompasses. Is he right?

Kennedy: Absolutely, but not for reasons of celebration and liturgy. In
Ironweed, it was all accidental because I had already created the time frame
in *Billy Phelan.*

I created it because I had to have it all happen during the pre-election
period. That was the whole purpose in *Billy Phelan.* So I made the kidnapping
take place in an election year, and also at election time. Then it moves forward into the campaign. Once I had that, I went back, and if you notice, *Billy
Phelan* and *Ironweed* end on the same day. And they do that only because
having created the dynamics of Billy meeting his father, the logical thing
when I dealt with Francis was to see him in those post-confrontational days
with Billy—to discover what it was that made him go home.

Francis Phelan wouldn't go home until he knew that Annie had never
condemned or blamed him. So first come these two things: the invitation
from Billy and the knowledge about Annie. They stay in his mind. He dries
up. And he wants to go home. All of *Ironweed* is this tap dancing into reality,
trying to figure out, "How am I going to do it?" Talking to Helen, getting rid
of Helen, walking back, putting her in the car with Finny, walking up to
where he used to live, confronting that reality, going back and making some
money so he could buy a turkey, and so on.

Quinn: Editors kept turning down *Ironweed* because they said it was too
depressing. Nobody would want to read a novel about bums. But it's actually
a very hopeful novel, isn't it? a novel about redemption? and forgiveness?

Kennedy: Redemption is the key word. That's what it's all about. It parallels the *Purgatorio.* When you talk about the liturgy or Catholic thought, you
think of Dante, and eventually you think of the *Inferno,* and the *Purgatorio,*
and the *Paradiso.* From the epigraph, you enter my book with Dante, and it's
a journey through planes of escalation into a moment of redemption out of
sin. Francis cleanses himself. It reflects something I think is profound about
human behavior. I don't look at it in the way that I used to when I was a kid,
when I believed in everything, believed it was the only way to look at the

world. Today I believe Catholic theology has great humanistic dimensions, great wisdom about how to achieve peace of mind in relationship to the unknown, the infinite. Maybe it's a palliative. Maybe it's one of the great lollipops of history. At the same time, it's beautiful. It's as good as I could see on the horizon. I don't need Buddhism, or Zoroastrianism—I've got the Sacred Heart Church in North Albany.

Quinn: All Saints Day is taken from Irish mythology. It's based on the Celtic feast of Samhain, when the barriers between the living and the dead disappeared. Was Irish mythology a conscious part of *Ironweed?*

Kennedy: No, it was not. I didn't know that about All Saints Day. I just grew up with it as a holy day. But I'm finding out all kinds of things about myself, things that are pushing me, nudging me into places I'm not yet fully aware of.

Much of its seems parallel to what I know about contemporary Irish life. Maybe, if there's such a thing as collective unconsciousness, then this was part of it: a kind of grip that still holds. It's really remarkable that the Irish, like the Jews, have held on so to their identity, that there was this triumphant resistance to death and genocide and their obliteration as a people. But in this case, the Kirsh link wasn't conscious. My consciousness as a Catholic was sufficient.

Quinn: The Irish poet Patrick Kavanagh has written that he lived in a place where literature wasn't supposed to happen. It was too conventional, supposedly. Did you ever face that stumbling block? The thought that literature happened in places grander and more exotic than Albany?

Kennedy: Oh yes, from the very outset. I understood that Melville went to school here. I understood that Henry James touched down here, in one of his less cosmic moments. Bret Harte was born here, and left immediately. Elizabeth Taylor passed through once, stayed at the DeWitt Clinton Hotel. Those kinds of moments, that's about as much as you used to expect out of Albany. But then I began to figure that it couldn't be all that bad, I found out that Albany was, and is, a great place. There are not all that many people who lived and died in Albany creating a literature that would endure through the ages. But there was a sense of the place being valuable, and this was *tremendously* important. As soon as I began to understand this, I realized that the town was unexplored.

Quinn: Was it out of the newspaper articles you wrote about Albany that you began to sink yourself into its history? To sense its depths?

Kennedy: No, I was writing in Puerto Rico about myself and my wife and my ancestors trying to understand it all, and then I realized I didn't understand, and that was it. That ignorance was the main drive: to come back at some point in my life, settle in and do some research in the library, and try to understand. I never expected that I would stay forever.

How can you write about a place if you don't understand what the street names mean, or who the mayor is, or what the machine was all about? I was writing from Puerto Rico at a point when I didn't really understand the political bossism in Albany. I hadn't paid sufficient attention when I was working at an Albany newspaper. I just said, "I'm *mildly* opposed to it." I was very self-righteous.

Quinn: One of the main components of Albany is its powerful, Democratic machine, an Irish-American machine. For the Albany Irish, you've written, "Politics was justice itself; politics was sufficient unto itself." What did you mean by that?

Kennedy: When I grew up, there was no sense of morality in regard to politics. If you were Irish, you were obviously a Democrat. If you were a Democrat, you were obviously a Catholic. If you were a Catholic, you obviously gave allegiance to the church on the corner, and to Dan O'Connell who was a pillar of the church, inseparable from the Bishop and the priests, and who was revered and prayed for. But Dan was also running the whorehouses, the gambling joints, the all-night saloons, and the blackout card games. He was in collusion with the grafters and the bankers, getting rich with the paving contractors.

No matter what it was in town, wherever you could make an illegal dollar, that's where the Irish were, that's where the politics were, that's where the Church was, that's where the morality was. And it was all fused. You couldn't separate it because the families were so interlocked, and the goodness walked hand-in-hand with the evil. But it wasn't *viewed* as evil. It was viewed as a way to get on in the world. But objective morality didn't interest Albany. The Irish didn't care about it. They understood that *they* had been deprived and now they were not. Now they were able to get jobs. In the previous era, when the Irish were not in power, they had *not* been able to get jobs. Their families were starving and starvation for them was immorality. So once they took power, O'Connell became kind of a saint. He became the man who would save your soul by putting you to work.

Quinn: Was he a Robin Hood?

Kennedy: Of course he was a Robin Hood. Of course he was also a rascal.

I don't know what the original Robin Hood was like. Maybe he has been romanticized out of existence, but there's no question that Dan O'Connell as we know him was a Robin Hood. He certainly gave away a lot of money.

Nobody really knows how much he died with. What came out in the papers was ridiculous. A quarter of a million or so. But they would spend $200,000. in five dollar bills every election day. He was raking it in from all quarters. All the beer drinkers in the county were adding to the Party's profit, and Dan O'Connell controlled the beer. Thousands and thousands of fortunes were made in this town through politics.

Quinn: Politics was the Irish stock market?

Kennedy: Yes, the Irish stock market. I never thought of that. That's a great phrase. You've invented something.

Quinn: Politics, then, is one of the common threads among the American-Irish? If anything united them, it was that. In Kansas City, Boston, Albany, New York, always the same story.

Kennedy: What else could they do? They could have done other things if they had the education, but they didn't. They were the people of numbers. That was the important thing about them. They were not the people of knowledge, the people with connections to power, the people of Harvard and Wall Street. What they knew was politics. What they knew was the Church. What they knew was their Irishness. What they knew was clanishness. The network was a great strength. It let Dan O'Connell hold onto the allegiance of the masses. In the face of the most vile declarations by enemies, in the face of the obvious stealing that was going on, and despite the slimy meat and the whorehouses, Dan went on and on and on.

Quinn: Albany is more than a setting for your novels. It becomes kind of a character. But do you think of yourself as a *regional* writer in the way that Flannery O'Connor thought of herself as a Southern writer?

Kennedy: Yes and no. All regional writers are trying to capture the uniqueness of their region, obviously. And most writers who use regions are trying for universality, to speak to life outside the region. It depends, I suspect, on how well you are able to make your cosmos, however small— Milledgeville, Georgia, or Albany, New York, or Dublin, or the Pequod— become a center of vitality, a center of ubiquity, a center of spiritual life that will transcend any kind of limitation that geography imposes. If you never find that center, all you're doing is floating free. Until you have a Midgeville, or unless you've a genius like Beckett, you can't coalesce your meaning. Creating life in an abstrace place—that's very hard to do. you have to really have genius.

Quinn: Do you think you could move to a place, let's say to Scarsdale, stay there for two years, study the place, become familiar with its characters, and then create the same sort of magic that you've done with Albany?

Kennedy: I don't think so. I would probably begin to impose my knowledge of Albany on Scarsdale. I tried to do that in Puerto Rico, and I couldn't do it. I didn't understand Puerto Rico that well. In those days, I could write about Puerto Rico as a reporter, but I didn't really understand the dynamics of the place, what was going on in the *soul* of Puerto Rico, in the *soul* of San Juan. When you don't have that, you don't have anything, as far as I'm concerned. You can do all the navel-gazing you want and until it's centered on a place, it seems to me that it's a vagrant pursuit, a Sunday afternoon in the park, or with the soap operas, it's an absence of significance. If you don't have the place, you don't have the dynamics of the society which exists in that place, and they're very different in Scarsdale from Albany, or San Juan, or Dublin. Georgia is not in any way equivalent to North Albany, where I grew up. No matter how Catholic Flannery O'Connor was, she's writing about a society where you have peacocks on the front porch, you have blacks and whites with great hostility toward one another, and that's not where I grew up.

Quinn: What about Ireland? Does it ever tug on your imagination? Any chance of the Albany cycle spinning its way back there?

Kennedy: I've been to Ireland several times. I'll go again in quest of my ancestors, like so many other Irishmen in this country, to comprehend origin and consequences. But it's very unlikely that I will ever set a novel in Ireland because I don't know enough about the places. It's a foreign country to me. I've thought about writing about Ireland, I've been to the North, I've lived in Dublin, but I feel I don't know enough about any particular place to give me what I'd need for a novel.

Quinn: You're latest novel is *Quinn's Book,* which is set in the 1840s with the "Famine Irish." Haven't you had to go into a great deal of Irish history for this book?

Kennedy: I'm thinking seriously about the Irish-American experience, but that's not the *Irish* experience. I feel that I'd be a fraud if I went to Ireland

and tried to write significantly about somebody there, when I'm not from there. I'm from Albany.

I believe that I can't be anything other than Irish American. I know there's a division here, and a good many Irish Americans believe they are merely American. They've lost touch with anything that smacks of Irishness as we used to know it. That's all right.

But I think if they set out to discover themselves, to wonder about why they are what they are, then they'll run into a psychological inheritance that's even more than psychological. That may also be genetic, or biopsycho-genetic, who the hell knows what you call it? But there's just something in us that survives and that's the result of being Irish, whether from North or South, whether Catholic or Protestant, some element of life, of conscious-ness, that is different from being Hispanic, or Oriental, or WASP. These traits endure. I'm just exploring what's surviving in my time and place.

I don't presume that I could go back in time and find out what was going on in Belfast or Dublin before my own day, to go back as a fiction writer and reconstitute it. For me, it's a question of imagination. I don't feel I own those Irish places, but I do own Albany. It's mine. Nineteenth-century Albany is mine as well. It's a different time and in many ways a different place from what it is now, but I feel confident I can reach it.

Quinn: Do you know your fascination with place is particularly Irish?

Kennedy: The sense of the natural world is always very important to writ-ers. You use it wherever necessary. But it's not peculiarly Irish to have a sense of a place. For me, fiction exists, finally, in order to describe neither social conditions nor landscapes but human consciousness. Essay, documen-tary films, editorials in newspapers can persuade you to a political position. But nothing except great fiction can tell you what it means to be alive. Great fiction, great films, great plays, they all center in on consciousness, which always has a uniqueness about it, and the uniqueness is what a writer can give you that nobody else in the world can give you: a sense of having lived in a certain world and understood a certain place, a certain consciousness, a certain destiny, a grand unknown, all the squalor and all the glory of being alive.

And if you reduce fiction to political or social argument, or to a kind of sociological construct, you lose its real strength. When you think of Chaucer or Boccaccio, you remember the individualistic elements of their characters in the same way you remember the people in, for example, Sherwood Ander-son's *Winesburg, Ohio.* They don't go bad. Great fiction doesn't go bad.

Quinn: Do you write with a certain audience in mind? Do you have an ideal reader?

Kennedy: You know who I write for? I write for people like me who used to appreciate Damon Runyon sentences. I write for people who appreciate writing first, who understand the difference between an ordinary sentence and a real sentence that jumps off the page at you when you read it.

I'm working on a preface from a new book about the state Capitol. As always when I do research, I read an incredible amount of horseshit that's been published on the subject. Tons of it. The same old stuff rewritten and rehashed every which way. But every once in a while a historian gets hold of something and creates a real sentence, maybe one in a whole book of essays, but it stops you. You look at it and say, "Terrific sentence." That's the reaction I'm looking for.

Quinn: Does writing—the creation of a "terrific sentence"—ever get easier?

Kennedy: Some things get easier. Journalism gets easier. I'm not sure it gets better. Fiction, at least for me, seems to get more complicated. Not that it's hard to write a sentence or a paragraph, but it's hard to believe that the current sentence or paragraph is new and that I'm not just saying something that's been said a hundred times before. Making it new, that's what's hard. I don't expect it will ever get any easier. I'm not counting on it.

Quinn: Do you ever look back at what you've written, and say, "I've learned so much since then. I know so much more now"?

Kennedy: Yes, absolutely. But it doesn't mean the writing gets easier just because you know more now. . . . Because what you have to do now is not repeat yourself, at least try not to repeat yourself. You feel that maybe you're in better command of the language, of your ability to write a sentence, of your ability to conceptualize, of your ability to create a new character. But the total is problematical. It's still a great game. That's what the whole thing is still all about, as far as I'm concerned, what it's always about: the invention of something out of nothing. That's the classic definition of what writing is. And I believe this is the whole satisfaction that comes from writing: That you're able to create something out of nothing that seems new to you.

Maybe you don't have the same response to it that you had as a kid, when you were discovering these wondrous elements of your unconscious, or your talent, or even the nature of your existence. But at the same time, what I feel about my life is that there are still so many unknowns. When I begin to write,

I begin to confront things that I never confronted before. I begin to invent
things, willfully going into the unknown. As I face the challenge of an empty
page tomorrow morning—and that's what I live for—what I need to do is
discover something that will surprise me, something that I've never done
before, written before, seen before, heard before.

It's not as if you want to write science fiction, or go to another genre or
invent another bizarre character. But you must penetrate into something beyond an ordinary story. You start with an ordinary story. You have a man or
a woman moving quietly through life. A man and woman in trouble, both of
them. And there's a classical way to create the clichéd situations about how
they meet and get back together, or how they stay together for forty years.
But you can't do any of those things. You must do something that *you* have
never done before. And how do we do that? Mostly, it seems to me, through
language. It can happen through dialogue—sometimes through language
alone. When your language is leading you in, it's like watching the sea, and
the sea is never the same. And it's never the same sentence. And as long as
it isn't, you're in good shape. As soon as it becomes the same sentence again,
you're all washed up.

Quinn: Your next project, besides the new novel, is to write screenplays
for *Legs, Billy Phelan* and *Ironweed.* Any trepidations? Any fear that Hollywood might hurt your writing?

Kennedy: No, I don't have that kind of conflict. I believe it's a very rare
writer in the twentieth century who can separate himself from films. They're
such an enormous and important part of our imaginative lives. Only hermits
haven't been influenced by them. And I love the movies. I'm glad to be a
part of the movies. I don't confuse them with novels. I don't see them as
competition. I think the novel is far superior to the film because of its complexity. But I think the film can also do many things that engage you in ways
that no novel can. You can't get quite such an exciting vision of womanhood
from a book as you can with Garbo or Monroe or Ava Gardner on the screen.
When you see these people idealized up there, there's nothing quite equivalent to it in literature. Literature is an extension of your imagination, but
here's an incomparable illusion of visual reality.

Quinn: How different is screenwriting from writing a novel?

Kennedy: Very different. I'm glad to write the screenplays for the films
that are going to be made out of my books since I've got *some* control on
each of them. I respect films very much. I think film can be a tremendously

exciting medium. It's been that for me all my life, from the time I was a kid on up to the time I began discovering Ingmar Bergman. The whole idea of the translation of any kind of life into cinema is important, because it's a medium that reaches so many people. And if you can reach those people with something that's valuable to you, it's the same as reaching them with your novel in a certain way.

Quinn: What do you most want to preserve from your novels when they're made into films?

Kennedy: I don't know. That's always a challenge. I'd like to preserve the whole novel, but you can't. You can't preserve the language. You can't preserve the unconscious center of Francis Phelan's soul as it's articulated in *Ironweed.* You're not going to be able to depict it, except maybe in a fleeting scene or phrase. You're not going to be able to put that into the movie. One medium is language, the other is the visual. Movies can only do so much. The novel is the supreme form of explaining how it is that any human being exists on this planet, complexly, with a history, with a soul, with a future, with a present, in an environment. You can get some of the environment, you can get a bit of the language, you can get the look of things in the movies. But you only get a small bit of the soul. You can't get the density of the unconscious, you can't get the ineffably complex element of what it means to be alive. It's all but *impossible* in the movies.

At their best, movies can only suggest great complexity. John Huston, Orson Welles, Bergman, they've done it. They've required us to be alert to complexity. But maybe only two percent of the movies ever made have required this of the audience.

Quinn: A final question. We've talked about the "Irish-American experience," literary and otherwise. I don't know if we've come to any conclusions but, in your opinion, what is it that unites us?

Kennedy: What unites us? It's song, drink, wit, and guilt.

Quinn: No politics?
Kennedy: That's included in all four.

The Man Has Legs: William Kennedy Interviewed

David Thomson / 1985

Published in *Film Comment* 21 (March/April 1985): 54–59.
Reprinted by permission.

If anyone anywhere has got more fun or juice out of *The Cotton Club* than William Kennedy, then Orion should find them and put them to training audiences. But Kennedy's having a good time altogether, and sharing the pleasure. It's entertainment in itself watching him on top of the world, grinning like a shy rascal as the prizes come in, or grumbling conscientiously at all the people who want his time. "Hey, I forgot," he said as this interview came to a close, "we've got wine." So we opened the bottle and disposed of its contents in his suite at New York's Mayflower Hotel, hours before the second premiere of *The Cotton Club*. The first had been a week before, in Albany, largely organized by Bill and his wife, Dana, and very likely one of the biggest nights in the history of a city that now sees Bill as a power and an attraction not much less than the Mall. His book, *O Albany* is going to be a PBS documentary. For all I know, there are stars now in the sidewalk where he strolled and chatted with Diane Sawyer.

So long as it doesn't keep him too long from more novels, it couldn't happen to a nicer or a more deserving man. It is already folklore that Kennedy labored in his provincial city for 25 years—some novels published but largely overlooked, *Ironweed* turned down so many times on its zigzag to a Pulitzer Prize. Kennedy is dealing with the fame and the glory with wry zest and insouciance, loving every minute and trusting it about as much as a woman had reason to rely on Legs Diamond.

This is a movie magazine, not a literary review. You can and should read Kennedy's books for yourself. If you do, you'll find not just Albany standing for every self-centered city of politics, religion, booze, guilt, and gossip. You'll find a command of dialogue, action, and rapid character exposition that might have alerted Hollywood, years ago, to the likelihood of Kennedy as a screenwriter. He was a film critic, too, once upon a time; and he's still a movie character. Trim, smart, dry but romantic, he's like the classic Forties buddies to the hero. If you can picture the best of Regis Toomey, Roscoe Karns, and Thomas Mitchell in one person—with a Cagney grin—that's Bill Kennedy. He could play any or all of the reporters in *His Girl Friday*. It's no wonder his three best novels are on the verge of becoming movies, for their author has seen a lot of films and absorbed the rhythm of cross-talk and sudden violence as well as the dark flourish of attractive villains.

That would be wealth enough, but *Legs* is also a book that sees the gangster as an early version of the American celebrity, acting it out for the press and the newsreels. If only, one's bound to ask, *The Cotton Club* had a little more of this (from *Legs*) in its view of Richard Gere going to Hollywood to play a gangster more famous and glamorous than Dutch Schultz could ever be:

"So the newsmen, installing Jack in the same hierarchy where they placed royalty, heroes, and movie stars, created him anew as they enshrined him. They invented a version of him with each story they wrote, added to his evil luster by imagining crimes for him to commit, embellishing his history, humanizing him, defining him through their own fantasies and projections. This voyage had the effect of taking Jack Diamond away from himself, of making him a product of the collective imagination. Jack had imagined his fame all his life and now it was imagining him. A year hence he would be saying that 'publicity helps the punk' to another set of newsmen, aware how pernicious a commodity it could be. But now he was an addict, a grotesquely needy man, parched for glory, famished for public love, dying for the chance at last to be everybody's wicked pet."

If you were to ask Kennedy why he ever gave up quiet, time, and daily writing to do movies, he would list the answers: the fun, the challenge, the money. But there's another, unspoken answer: It's the dangerous appeal of the limelight and the danger, the molls and the talk, that makes lawyer Marcus Gorman chuck a dull career in Albany politics and walk with Legs.

My feeling is that The Cotton Club *will do quite well, but it's not going to make the money it needs to. I think the two central players hurt it.*

You mean Gere and Diane? I disagree. I like them both. Gere is very lively and very vulnerable in the role. And Diane is snappy, self-centered, tough, and lovely.

I don't find Gere charismatic enough. The people around him are wonderful, the supporting characters. I kept hearing things I thought were you, like the watch scene with Owney and Frenchy.

My chief contribution to that was keeping it in the film. That scene came from Fred Gwynne and Hoskins—actually written by Gwynne. People around Francis kept wanting to cut it on the grounds that it was too wacko. I loved it and lobbied for months to keep it.

Would there have been a lot more if you'd been brought in earlier?
I don't know as that's entirely true. There was a lot written that found its way on to the writing-room floor. It was a different movie all the way through. It kept changing drastically. You know, we did between 40 and 50 drafts of that thing. And Francis was constantly trying to reduce the cost, and bring everything to the Cotton Club. We had to accommodate Richard, who wanted to play the cornet. That was his principal contribution to the forming of the character in the beginning. So obviously he had to be a musician. When Francis first wrote the script he was a gangster. I didn't see how it was feasible to have a gangster be also a cornet player, except as a hobby in his apartment or something. So we had to change him. Then there was a problem: Once he was a musician, what do you do then? So we did what we did. [*Chuckles.*] I don't want to give anybody else the rap. Francis and I worked on it. It was that ensemble of a movie from the beginning. If you go in expected a Richard Gere starring movie, you come away disappointed.

Could it have worked better if Gere had been the club owner? As it is, the Bob Hoskins character is almost the center of the film. And since it is so much about the club, maybe the owner would have been an ideal central figure, a man trying to balance lots of different things.
Well, I love the film. I've seen it now so many times, and I don't have any real objectivity about it. I've seen a lot that's not there anymore. But, by and large, I think it's beautiful to look at. The talent is just extraordinary: those dancers and singers, and the beauty of the costumes, and the way the people move. Lonette [McKee] and Gregory [Hines] are just dynamite. The leads *were* problems—trying to create an effective role in the gangster milieu for a man who's not a gangster, not hateful, and has to have some kind of quality.

I think somewhere in Hemingway he tells the story of when he was young talking to a woman in a club and being warned off her because she was a gangster's property.
I think what you're talking about is in Lillian Hellman. Is it in a memoir about Dashiell Hammett? It's at the Stork Club, I think, and Hemingway and Hammett get drunk and Hemingway makes a pass at Kiki Roberts, who was

Legs Diamond's girlfriend. There's a million of those gangland stories; that just happens to be one. I didn't have that in mind when we were doing it.

I remember it being more frightening than the film ever is. There's some-thing about the film that you never quite feel either that they're in love, or that they're in great danger by being in love. I felt more love between Owney and Frenchy.

Those two guys, they could take that act on the road. No question about it. They're marvelous.

Are there particular things that didn't end up in the film that you miss?

I'm not going to second-guess Francis' editing. There was more in almost every direction you can imagine, including Dutch Schultz' mother, an old Jewish woman who goes shopping and has diner with Schultz and Vera; Gregory's relationship to the black numbers barons; Diane's relationship in more detail, to Dutch; Gere's family; the Williams family: Winnie and Bumpy—all these were developed in a lot of directions. Great musical num-bers were cut out. What happened was that Francis decided a long time ago that we were going to have a two-hour movie. And I think the first cut was two hours and 15, 17 minutes, the first cut I saw. It was a draggy performance. He cut out 17 minutes and the next time we saw it, it wasn't there—there were a lot of things out. The watch scene wasn't there. Francis made constant trades with himself, listening to responses from everybody. And finally he came up with this version after a lot of consideration. I remember being part of one editing process, here in New York, after that two-hour screening which didn't work, and we put back about eleven minutes, and that made all the difference. And that week he had very good reactions. Now that wasn't, by any means, the final version. He kept changing and adding and going back, even after the print was in processing. He's a man who just doesn't give up until he gets exactly what he thinks works.

You evoked Hemingway, and that's one thing I've been looking at. This film is a version of a kind of modern short story where what's suggested is important and what's delineated is very little. A Raymond Carver story, or the early Hemingway stuff. Even *The Old Man and the Sea,* where he articu-lated the iceberg principle; one-eighth above water and the other seven-eighths suggested. Whether that works here is a measure of our success. I think the Lonette story, for instance, is very obliquely done. The relationship with Gregory hints at whole realms of her life.

We always knew we were working on something like the *Grand Hotel* principle, and we didn't even bother to see that movie. Francis was always for the short scenes. I thought I was a concise writer, but then his decisions on what could still work in a scene were very instructive. There's a few lines I regret losing, here and there, a little fragment of a scene that I'd remember fondly. But it's not a problem with me anymore. I stand on the film. I like it. I love it. I've seen it, like, 40 times, and I don't get sick of it. It gets better when you see it again and again.

When Raymond Chandler worked on the script of Double Indemnity, *he and Billy Wilder argued over transposing James M. Cain's dialogue to the screen. Everyone agreed that Cain wrote great dialogue—as they would about William Kennedy—but Chandler said that it was written for the eye, not the ear, and he brought in two actors to read it aloud. Sure enough, it didn't work, so Chandler went about evoking the spirit of Cain, but in different words. Have you found something like that in doing dialogue for film?*

I'm writing *Billy Phelan* now, the script, and the same thing is happening to me. I see my own work there and I'm juggling it. I'm taking essences out of it and reducing five, six pages in the book to three pages of dialogue. It's an enormous cut-back, but still you can find the nugget. I don't know how successful you think my dialogue is in *Cotton Club*. I'm not responsible for all the dialogue by any means. It went through my typewriter once, but sometimes it was spontaneous stuff on the set—which the watch scene was to a great degree. What I'd wind up doing is orchestrating. It's a matter of choice what you save and finding that precise word. Take the conversation with Dutch Schultz and Dixie when he says, "Do you want a job? Well, you've got a job. You'd be dead if I didn't like you." And Dixie says, "It's nice to be liked." That to me is a very effective line and it's what? Two lines. You get the boom-boom-boom. Well, I was always looking for that.

And I guess maybe I know how to do that in writing screenplays—find the word that moves the story forward. And Coppola discovered this along the way, too, because he was editing and treating my writing the way he was treating his own. You know, chop and change, and find the way he wanted a scene to look and sound. But then, after a while, he stopped. And he said to me one day—we were on the phone, we were talking about some of the scenes I was writing, I was up in Albany, I occasionally did that, sent them in or called them in—he said that working on the set he usually gave the actors great leeway to improvise. When they're in rehearsal they make up scenes entirely. After a while he stopped doing that, he told me, and told them to follow my dialogue because he found that it was working dramatically. And he seemed happy with it. So from then on we'd talk about a scene and I'd write it and he'd shoot it. There was very little change done on these scenes after a while, unless they got cut and disappeared entirely.

Were there moments when he and you together, maybe, or you individually said, "I wish I could go back and start this again because we're caught up in . . ."

Oh, yeah! We *did* that. We did that again and again. How to recapitulate it exactly, it'd be tough. I'd have to go back and find a lot of those early drafts. I have 15 of my own, or 20. But it was like this. We would be going forward with Richard, and we would be trying to create some activity in which he would be (a) a musician, (b) under Schultz' thumb, (c) moving forward in time toward a new career, either an actor, which is what we evolved to, or another form of musician, or an ancillary figure to Schultz in that he accepts gangland and then somehow prospers and goes down the tube morally, and so on. Well, we'd go in that direction, and it wouldn't work. It'd be creating an unsympathetic character. And yet you'd have the action that would be necessary, and he'd start to carry a gun or be driving trucks or cars for hijacking or something that didn't really work. So we'd have to throw it out and go back and find new ways of doing it.

Also, Francis is an incredible editor who just lifts and moves great chunks of story. He does it by reels. He had it pinned up on the wall, from the beginning of the movie to the end. It looked like paper towels, only he could write on it. And he would roll it out and roll it up at the other end, and finally he had the whole movie. It was a fascinating process, but it was a very difficult way to work. It's not the way I work.

This was while you were shooting?
Most of it, I would say, was before the shooting began.

But you were tied into sets that were built?
Oh, absolutely—the Cotton Club, the apartments, and so on. But Dick Sylbert had also scouted a lot of locations that were eventually just abandoned. In one scene, Richard and Diane sneaked off to a 1930's auto court, and Sylbert found one we could use. But that proved to be so expensive, it was abandoned. But that changed a lot! When you move it from an auto court into his own bedroom and his family is there, you have to redo everything. And once that changes you get new relationships all the way around.

What's the first film you remember seeing?
I think it was Tim McCoy . . . Tom Mix. Maybe it was Tom Mix. I think it
was at the Leland Theatre. It's the first area of memory I associate it with,
because it's really so far back. I always wanted to go to cowboy movies.

You would have been how old?
Five or six. I'm talking about 1932, '33, or '34. Something like that.

So you were taken by your parents?
Yes, my mother, my grandmother, my aunts. My father would occasionally
take me, but he wasn't a moviegoer. He did take me one night; I remember
Imitation of Life. I remember the skyline with this Aunt Jemima billboard lit
up. I went a lot. I loved it. I had a projector of my own when I was a kid, and
I've still got it, 16mm. But it doesn't run. All the gears are rusted, or something. I tried to fix it one time, but I couldn't make it work. I had three films:
a Popeye cartoon; Pluto and Donald Duck; and a rodeo movie that my parents
got me one Christmas. I used to play those things over and over in the kitchen
on a sheet.

When I grew up, the thing to do was to go to the movies on the weekends.
Saturday maybe, and then again on Sunday. And sometimes on Friday night.
I remember a friend of mine said he used to go once a week; that was what
his allowance allowed. But he remembered me going three times a week.
That was a very luxurious thing, but they'd always give me money to go to
the movies. And we used to walk down when we were in grammar school
and see the serials.

What did you like to see?
I saw everything, I'd see the double features. I can remember an Orson
Welles film, *Journey into Fear,* Eric Ambler. I've never been able to see it
since. I would see everything at the Grand Theatre for 15 weeks because the
Shadow serial was one I used to read the pulps: Doc Savage and the Spider
and the Shadow. There was another stretch when I went through everything
at the Ritz because the Green Arrow was on. And I missed the last episode
because they said "Children Under 16 Not Admitted"! There were so many
films to see in those days. My city—Christ! The Palace, which we lit up for
the premiere last week, it was such a magnificent theater. It was new in '31,
and when I was a kid it was awesome with all the marble.

Was your recollection of the theater always being packed?
Oh, you'd have to stand in line. And then sometimes you couldn't get in.

You have to wait for the next show or go to another theater. The Road movies, not a seat would be empty. And sometimes kids would double up in seats. I stood through some of those. They used to have four or five deep, standing room. Two or three deep, anyway.

Was there a time when you began to be more critical?

I preferred this kind of story and that, and B movies too—Mike Shane and the Saint. We were stunned by *Gone With the Wind,* and I remember *Gunga Din. Bride of Frankenstein* and *Dracula* scared the hell out of me. *The Long Voyage Home:* I began to see there was some power and drama that wasn't available in most movies. But the comedies were great. The Preston Sturges stuff, *Sullivan's Travels.*

Was there a time when you said, "What I really want to be is a novelist"? And "Movies are fluff"?

I never thought of writing for the movies, although I loved to see them. It was the Sixties before I thought, "Boy, I should try that." When everybody had that anxiety attack that movies were going to take over from literature. Mailer went out and made his movie, and Dennis Hopper looked like the king of the universe for a few months. But the world wasn't like that when I was young. I wanted to be a newspaper man. But I didn't believe I would ever write serious fiction and be successful at it. I figured the best I'd ever wind up being was some kind of an O. Henry or a Runyon or a Mark Twain at his most casual. It wasn't until I came out of the Army in 1952 when I had some spare time, days off from the newspaper, that I really began to write short stories that made some sense. The movies were always entertainment until I began to see foreign films. Italian neo-realists. That really became a compelling thing. And then I discovered Bergman in the Fifties, and I'd gone to the legitimate theater, and that became very important. I almost became a playwright, but then I decided I didn't want to peg my whole life on being in a world where compromise is essential. I wanted to be in control of the universe, and being a novelist was the only way you could do that.

This may sound curious, now that I'm in the movie business. But I don't treat it all in the same way. This is Francis Coppola's movie, not mine. I have a significant contribution to make to it, but that's something else entirely. It's more for pleasure and fun, and the dollar isn't bad.

But I have a recollection in those days of Bergman: *Wild Strawberries, The Magician, The Seventh Seal.* And Fellini: *La Stada* was a stunning intro-

duction to him. And Buñuel. And Truffaut and some of the Godard. That
came in the Sixties, when I began to write about film.

Where were you doing that?
I was a film critic in Albany for the *Times Union.* I was working part time
from the time I went back to Albany in 1963, while I was writing novels. I
had carte blanche. I was a feature writer, a muckraker, a political analyst . . .

And you could review films?
I wrote a whole lot about slumlords and integration. And then I took a
leave. I was working on *The Ink Truck,* I guess. When I came back I didn't
want to write about politics or poverty anymore so, on a lark, I said I'll go
down to the New York Film Festival. And God, it was stunning! An immersion in movies. I'd see five a day. That was '68 or '69.

Isn't Legs *really a book about stardom, how somebody takes a special
place in the popular imagination?*
Well, that was what started me writing the book, and kept me writing it. I
followed the line of his life very carefully. I had to imagine the dialogue, but
the relationships were fully established. His girlfriend, Kiki Roberts, and his
wife, Alice, and a lot of other women. When I started to write that book it
was not about Legs Diamond. He was just going to be a character. And I
looked at our morgue at the paper. Holy Christ! The things that had happened
to him. He'd been shot five times. He'd gone to Europe, and became an
international celebrity and chorus girls and this and that and the other thing.
He and Kiki, the gangster and the Ziegfeld beauty, were an ideal juxtaposi-
tion. The more I went on, the more I heard people say what a nice guy he
was. And how he'd come in and take over the bar and buy drinks for everybody and sing songs. And go out and have some singer from another bar
come over just so he could sing "It Had To Be You." Or have the band play.
And dancing all the time. And he had parties at his table at the Kenmore. I
mean, he was a bon vivant. He was ubiquitous.

*But there's also a feeling in the book like the Ionesco epigraph: "People
like killers. And if one feels sympathy for the victims it's by way of thanking
them for letting themselves be killed." Take that a bit further, you've got the
concentration camps.*
You *can* take it that way. There's a certain fascination going on right now
with Hitler. The fascination of the abomination. That was definitely in my
mind. I almost used it at one point. I always felt that some day there would

be a film or a novel about Hitler's love affair with Eva Braun, which would be very idyllic. It's the evolution of the mythic elements we deal with all the time. People love killers. Just think of the reverence that history pays to all these conquerors. Napoleon or anybody else. And then you go and you look at a Goya painting and you're brought down instantly to a reality that is so horrible.

How about our own West? This was more relevant to what I was doing, because I felt that out of the Westerns I grew up watching—Doc Holiday and Jesse James and Billy the Kid and the Dalton Brothers—how many times we saw those as kids. And they were telling us something about the mythic element of creating a country. And it came to the point with Billy the Kid where you'd feel bad if he was shot. And he was a little psychopath. You wouldn't think twice about hanging him in reality. The same thing took place as we moved forward into the Thirties when you had George Raft and Edward G. Robinson and Bogey and Cagney playing all these characters who corresponded to Diamond. *Public Enemy* was definitely like him, so was *The Roaring Twenties*. And the feeling was that we were creating these new myths that we would live with for a very long time to come. And Diamond then became really interesting to me.

Because he was the most flamboyant of them all?

He was not as well known as Al Capone, but Capone had none of that charisma. He was just a brute, a pig. Diamond was probably just as much of a pig in his own way, but he had a style he developed along with this cobra quality. Dutch Schultz even called him "The Cowboy." And he did it on his own. He was a pioneer hijacker. He was always, to the end of his life, stealing other people's booze. He was basically a thief who engaged the American imagination.

Just as the movies have liked gangster stories, so gangsters are drawn to the movies. George Raft is a good case in point. And The Cotton Club *mixed the two worlds. Was there ever a time when you felt a little like Marcus, your own character in* Legs, *and said, "Don't tell me that"?*

No, that never happened. I've been close to some guys who were very involved with Diamond in the latter part of his life, and there are stories they told me that'd curl your hair. But they don't absolve themselves, they just avoid telling you the whole detail that would make them vulnerable. I found a guy in Boston who said he'd been a killer for Diamond and who did time for five federal murders. And he was my prototype for the Goose in *Legs.*

He'd just gotten out of jail, and he was working as a janitor. He said that the temptations were very heavy for him to go back into the business of murder.

Do you think that real gangsters got carried away by the screen image and wanted to imitate that?

I don't think so. Real gangsters came up from below. Remember that scene in *Legs* in Germany where a playwright wants to live with a gangster and the gangster shoots between his legs? That had its base in a real anecdote. Just a guy who used to hang around with gangsters and one day somebody did that to him and he wet his pants. They're just fantasizing. They don't know the reality. But then there was a guy in Albany, I remember, my uncle's buddy, he said this guy used to dress up like a gangster, and he would swagger. But he wasn't tough. He wasn't a gangster. He just wanted to have the image of one.

You're doing the script of Legs *for . . . ?*

Gene Kirkwood. And it looks like Francis is going to direct it. At least, that's the way it stands at the moment.

Who would you cast as Legs?

Mickey Rourke is going to play it—as sure as those things can be. But he's dying to play it. He has that charisma that Diamond had. He's quick, he's Irish. If he skinnies down he can be a lookalike to Diamond. I think he's as good as there is right now.

I would think Legs *is difficult to adapt.*

I've been faithful to the book, and Francis tells me he loves it. So he'll do it that way, I presume. There's a more linear presentation in the script than in the book but it isn't a conventional beginning-middle-and-end story. It starts out at the Hotsy Totsy with a shoot-out, and it ends the way the book does, in a surreal way. There's a lot of surreality in it.

Who will play Marcus?

I don't know, I had Nicholson in mind, but he seems a little old for that. Sam Shepard said he might be interested. He came up to Albany one day last summer and we spent the day talking. He's also interested in Francis Phelan in *Ironweed*. He's got that face. I talked to Harry Dean Stanton, too. I met him at a party. And he was pretty well oiled. And he didn't know who I was and didn't know what *Ironweed* was. But I mentioned people and said he ought to play Francis. So I got a call later on. He said De Niro had told him

what an idiot he was. He should have sobered up and talked turkey to me
about it. So he said he was going to go out and get the book. I have since
seen *Paris, Texas,* too. I like it a lot.

Where is Ironweed *now?*
Gene Kirkwood has optioned that too. And I'm going to write it. It's down
the road, but I think his and my attention for the next months will be on *Legs.*

And you're writing Billy Phelan *now?*
More than halfway there. That's for Dick Sylbert and Jerry Wexler.

A pool-hall movie.
It's bowling, cards, pool, the street—a lot of night. Sylbert wanted Polan-
ski to do it. I don't know, can he go to Canada? We might have to do it in
Paris. I hate to do that. So I don't know. Who knows what'll happen to
Polanski by that time?

Have you been tempted to do film originals?
I'm not. Before *Cotton Club* I was talking about a project with Fred Roos.
Bette Midler was interested, a Vietnam kind of story. But after all the stuff
that happened I said I can't.

*Are you doing these scripts to protect your own novels, or to learn more
about film?*
Both. I love the idea of controlling my movies, it so rarely happens to a
writer. I don't know what will come of a collaboration with Francis on *Legs,*
when it's my own material, whether I'll be as amenable to all the changes he
might want to make. Maybe he's happy with the script the way it is. I hope
that'll be settled before we enter on the shooting. He's said he would work
very closely to a script.

Has life been crazy since you got into the movies?
Crazier. My life was crazy to begin with, from the MacArthur award on,
when *Ironweed* was published in January 1983. That's when the world turned
inside out. All of a sudden I'm being interviewed every other day. People are
coming from all over the country and I turn up in every magazine and television show. And the mail has begun to stack up. More letters than I can
answer. I keep trying. A lot of them are just asking me to come out and do
gigs. Come give a lecture. Come read. Come hang out and write a movie,
write the story of my life. There's a lot of old friends, a lot of people I haven't
heard from in years. Great reunions.

Are there times when you hanker for the old anonymity?

I hanker for the time. And, you know, I can't complain, because I did enter into this movie business wide-eyed. And it *is* a time-consuming element. But I've been working on the novel.

But it's had a lot of interruptions?

Oh, yeah. It was a problem novel until I went to Cornell. And I started it anew there. Now it's not a problem novel; the problem is my time. But I've got to get these pictures out of the way and then I'll do it. I know that. The scripts, I mean. And I'm almost finished. I think by the end of the year [1984] I'll finish *Billy Phelan.*

And you're having fun?

Yeah, it's great. You're holding the world. I'm down here a lot, and I love it. So does my wife. The kids are coming down tonight. *PM Magazine* did a thing on the Albany premiere and they came over and took the girls getting dressed and my son walking in with Governor Cuomo. Things like that. The old glamor bit.

Have you been seeing things about yourself in the press that are wrong? Does that show you a bit more about Jack Diamond?

Absolutely. I knew that was part of the whole nature of the myth. He was blamed for everything. He said once, "They'll blame me for the next earthquake in Peru." He couldn't have been that active, not even him. He gave an interview at the end of his life about how they were blaming him. But he was always absolving himself of all that stuff. In his hotel room he had breakfast with a woman reporter and talked at great length about his life. And then at the end, when he was waiting for the trial, he gave an interview with the *Daily News,* and he was excusing himself—he was lying. But he did say, "Look at this stuff in the press they say about me. They've created this mythic Legs Diamond. That's not me." But he had become that.

Are you ever tempted to direct a film?

Coppola said I probably would, but I don't have the talent to do that, or the patience. I don't have the talent to organize anymore. I used to be the managing editor of a newspaper, and that was orchestrating the kind of chaos and diversity that's required on a set. Hell, I wound up being the producer for this world premiere for about a month, and that was agonizing. I just don't feel that my personality is suited to that. Why should I move in at this time of my life, try to compete at the same level of talent and experience

with somebody like Coppola? It's another world, and I'm still learning how
to write a film. And I'm going to have to learn how to write a play, because
I'm going to write one one of these days.

*You had decades of pretty hard times. You're much better off now, and
you've been on a movie where very large sums of money floated past. What's
your attitude to all the money?*

Well, it was so unreal to me. It was like play money when they were talking
25 million and suddenly this film is 50 million, 47, or whatever the hell it is.
Those figures don't have any basis in reality for me. That's why I've got
lawyers now, and an agent. It's a totally new world. To even contemplate
being well-off in this way! It's something I aspired to, and I think I'm OK. I
haven't lost my mind yet. I haven't really lost anything. What I've done is
maintained a kind of stability in the middle of it all.

Are you good at spending money on yourself?

Well, I buy some clothes. I come to New York. We eat out a lot. We went
to Europe, we spent a lot, but most of the places I went were paid for by the
publisher. I've gotten some gadgets. We fixed up the house. I bought Legs
Diamond's house with Kirkwood. It's a little two-and-a-half story house. It
used to be a rooming house in 1931. It was built in 1856. Solid. It was
restructured about seven, eight years ago, and it's very pleasant inside. My
wife has greatly improved it. But it's something I always wanted to do, live
downtown in a little townhouse. I didn't think it was ever going to be possible. But Kirkwood came up to see Albany last St. Patrick's Day and he
marched in the parade. So I took him on a tour and we were on the stoop of
the house where Diamond was shot and there was a FOR SALE sign on it. And
he said, "Why don't we buy it?" And I said OK and we shook hands on it
and bought it in a couple of days.

Tough Guy with a Golden Touch

Susan Agrest / 1987

Published in *Hudson Valley* Magazine July 1987: 42–49, 72.
Reprinted by permission.

A pinched nerve in his neck causes a little unscripted agony if he stays in one position too long, but William Kennedy wouldn't miss this moment for the world. His hair greased with Vaseline, sporting a double-breasted black suit, one of his father's neckties, and a four-pointed handkerchief tucked in his jacket pocket, Kennedy is an extra in the movie *Ironweed,* the story he wrote first as a novel, and subsequently for the silver screen.

Seated next to him at a table on the Albany movie set is his real-life wife Dana, costumed in a black velvet dress with a sweetheart neckline and "looking 1938 gorgeous," as Kennedy puts it. They play "swells" out for a night on the town at The Gilded Cage in downtown Albany. At the bar is Jack Nicholson, playing *Ironweed* protagonist Francis Phelan. Meryl Streep, as Phelan's skid-row lover Helen Archer, is at the microphone.

In the scene, a down-and-out Archer is trying to recapture the musical promise of her youth. Using her own voice, Streep brightly sings *He's Me Pal,* a pop tune from 1905 that Kennedy's own mother sang around the house when he was a child.

"I think watching these people work is terrific," said Kennedy. "You feel like you're privy to an extraordinary event."

Five years ago, the 59-year-old William Kennedy was scratching out a living as a freelance writer and college lecturer. He had published three novels, but by the time he brought *Ironweed* to Viking for publication in 1983, his commercial success was so uneven that Viking author Saul Bellow had to intervene. He convinced the publishing house to issue not only *Ironweed,* but also reissue *Legs* and *Billy Phelan's Greatest Game* as part of what Kennedy calls the Albany cycle.

"I would never claim to be the making of Bill Kennedy," said Bellow shortly after *Ironweed* was published on Jan. 10, 1983. "But I saved him from temporary neglect."

Ironweed went on to win the National Book Critics Circle Award and the Pulitzer Prize for Fiction on April 16, 1984 (the same day his grandson Casey

Michael Rafferty was born). Four days after its publication The MacArthur Foundation awarded Kennedy a tax-free, no-strings-attached grant of $264,000 for five years. It granted an additional $15,000 per year to the institution where Kennedy chose to work. Kennedy used the money to help found the New York State Writers Institute at SUNY Albany where he was simultaneously granted tenure, a leave, and the freedom to teach when he wanted.

The film *Ironweed,* the story of Albany derelict Francis Phelan's private war, got its start in the summer of 1985. On the eve of the opening of his first major success, the Oscar-winning *Kiss of the Spider Woman,* Brazilian director Hector Babenco asked Kennedy if he would like to meet him in New York City because he wanted to make a movie based on the novel.

"We hit it off the first day," recalls Kennedy. "He's a very literary man. He told me how much he liked the book, and how he identified with Francis in a certain way: that he had been on the road a certain portion of his life traveling around Europe as a young man, lost in the world. So he felt he understood the process of Francis' life and wanted to make it.

"We were in the middle of lunch and I said, 'I don't even know why I'm thinking about it, you should make the movie.' From that day forward we were making *Ironweed.*"

A Taft Entertainment Motion Picture/Keith Barish Production, *Ironweed* is due to be released at the end of the year. It will be true to the novel, Kennedy promises. Both he and Babenco worked on the script before Babenco took it to Nicholson, who had already read the book and "loved the character," Kennedy said.

Actor Michael O'Keefe (*The Slugger's Wife*), a native of Larchmont (Westchester) who plays Francis' son Billy, had also read Kennedy's novels. He became a fan of the author's long before he tried out for his part.

"The last thing you imagine about [a great writer] is that he is human and nice and fun to be with. He's just a great guy, who happens to be a great writer, and I don't use that word lightly," says O'Keefe. "Someone able to mingle with the common man as well as he can and yet write about the ineffable is a genius."

Kennedy, a man with an easy, expansive smile, appears to have the kind of happy disposition that enables him to suffer just about anything or anyone gladly—save malcontents. He has an unparalleled talent for the art of living, an absolute lust for life. One of his favorite expressions is "Life, what a sport!"

While most people spend enormous effort trying to physically or mentally escape everyday life, Kennedy embraces it. "The quotidian . . . if you don't have the quotidian—the day-to-day life—you don't have anything," says Kennedy. In his novel *Billy Phelan's Greatest Game,* a character named Martin Daugherty looks at his wife with whom he'd been talking and thinks: ". . . the talk had calmed him, and real and present things took his attention: his wife and her behind, jiggling while she stirred the eggs. Those splendid puffs of Irish history . . . roundaceous beneath the black and yellow kimono he'd given her for the New York vacation. . . . The phone rang and Miss Irish Ass of 1919 callipygiated across the room and answered it."

"In interviews Bill says he's an unautobiographical writer," notes Tom Smith, Kennedy's close friend and associate director of the Writers' Institute, "but one thing he does have in common with his main characters is this tremendous energy . . . this whole sense of the cycle of life that Bill carries with him. He seems to have this hidden agenda within himself to keep the party of life going."

Parties, singing, dancing, playing his ukulele or his banjo, good conversation, good food, and good wine, make up Kennedy's present tense when he's away from his battered typewriter. "He is master of the revels," says Smith. "It's the sense of life as theater, that any event needs a dramatic plot, has a length and energy of its own."

His anchor in day-to-day living gives Kennedy perhaps his greatest gift— the unusual vision that allows him to see the multidimensional facets of "place," most especially in his home town of Albany. In his non-fiction work, *O Albany* (Viking 1983), Kennedy described himself as someone "whose imagination has become fused with a single place, and in that place finds all the elements that a man ever needs for the life of the soul." All his novels to date are part of "an Albany cycle."

While of course his writing demands solitude and discipline, for Kennedy it's both work and play rolled into one. "[The] real game for me is writing," Kennedy told *Fiction International* in a 1983 interview. "What else is as great as creating a world out of nothing?" In his first published novel, *The Ink Truck,* the protagonist—a syndicated news columnist named Bailey— rails at the newspaper's boss, Stanley: "You never learned to value [your imagination], use it, wash and polish it until it was the shiniest imagination on the block."

As a writer, Kennedy's outlook was shaped in part by his former teacher

Saul Bellow, the prime mover in getting the literary world to give Kennedy proper recognition. "Bellow talked about 'character.' I stewed on that for years—he never would tell me precisely what that meant," Kennedy told *Newsweek* early in 1984. "He said, 'Talent goes a certain distance. The rest of the writer's life has to be carried forward by character.' For me character has come to mean pursuit of the art—refusal to yield to failure, refusal to accept any kind of rejection and let that define your life. Character means you believe in something sufficiently that you give it the utmost respect—be it a friendship or pursuit of an art form."

Smith remembers that even in the years that Kennedy was in the literary wilderness and on the edge of penury, "he spiritually felt akin to Joyce, Faulkner, Grass. He lived life at that level—with no pretense and no apologies either."

Kennedy gives the same uncompromising spirit to his characters. Indeed, in his novels Kennedy uses the term "warrior" to describe several of his protagonists. "Warriors are always fighting the good fight," says Kennedy. "These characters are always working towards being something valuable in life. [They're trying] to sustain a serious attitude toward survival. It's always a war—you're at war with somebody or, as in Francis' case, a war of the spirit." As Bailey in *The Ink Truck* observes: "Trouble. If it doesn't kill you, strengthens you. . . . Beaten almost to death, covered with blood, hay dust, gypsy spit and kiddie pee, Bailey smiled."

Kennedy peoples his novels with characters continually able to redeem themselves. He feels a kindred spirit, he says, with the scholar and mythologist Joseph Campbell, whom he quotes in *The Ink Truck*. "Within the soul . . . there must be—if we are to experience long survival—a continuous 'recurrence of birth' . . . to nullify the unremitting recurrences of death. For it is by means of our own victories, if we are not regenerated, that the work of Nemesis is wrought." This theme is one of the strongest currents running through all Kennedy literature. Says Kennedy, "The whole notion of regeneration has always been very important to me. I just know that if you don't change, if you become static, then you die."

The same characteristics that have won Kennedy praise have also drawn the ire of critics. To some, Kennedy's emphasis on the material world often turns too graphic. Both in *Ironweed* as well as in his other works, the protagonist seeking redemption has dropped so far down that Kennedy has been criticized for dwelling too much on life's underbelly. And other critics charge that his books are somewhat shapeless.

How well his work holds up will be seen next year, with the release of the movie *Ironweed* and the publication of his next book. Kennedy's newest warrior is Daniel Quinn, a journalist and soldier. He will be featured in the novel *Quinn's Book,* expected to be published by Viking in the spring of 1988.

"It's basically a love story that takes place from 1849 to 1866," explains Kennedy. "The two principle characters are Maud and Quinn, and they move through a number of major events in American history—the Irish immigration, cholera, pre-Civil war, the war itself, the rise of Fenianism and other 'isms,' the rise of American journalism. It's not an odyssey in the sense *Ironweed* is, of a single man's psychology, but of Quinn and Maud through this age."

The Hudson River, which hasn't played a major role in Kennedy's work or life to date, will be prominent in *Quinn's Book.* "I would love to own a house on the river and be close to the water," he says, adding on a teasing note, "you'll be surprised what happens with the river in *Quinn's Book.*"

In fact, except for *Legs,* Kennedy's novelization of the life and times of gangster Jack "Legs" Diamond, which takes place in both Albany and the Catskills, Kennedy's novels have taken place exclusively in the urban environment he was born and raised in.

The only son of a secretary and a civil servant, his parents moved from Arbor Hill in Albany when he was a toddler. He would have three addresses as what Albanians call a Northender by the time he reached manhood—620 Pearl Street, 607 Pearl Street and then 620 again.

Kennedy found comfort in his physical surroundings early on in life. "It was a terrific homogeneous place . . . a padded crib!" was how Kennedy described his neighborhood in *O Albany!* He went to PS 20 and then to Christian Brothers Academy.

Although a child of the Depression, Kennedy's mind and soul were well nourished. His parents were working-class Catholics who had a "generally harmonious life," notes Kennedy.

"I grew up in a house where there were tensions but not anything that would worry anybody seriously—no significant breaches in relationships, [but] always problems [of] money, personality. It was a large family—not kids but lots of uncles and aunts, lots of solidarity between my parents.

"I was the only child, not only of my parents but of the whole family. My uncle married late, and my two aunts didn't have children. My mother was beautiful and my father was a dude. They always danced and would win prizes. In those days people would go out to the parks to dance, to the lake to swim."

His father was a bowler and a gambler and a dabbler in local politics who took his son with him when he bowled at the Knights of Columbus or visited the political clubs. Kennedy still has a taste for politics, most notably in his fiction. "I've long since taken myself out of [political] activism as a way of life, because to me that would make me partisan, and my writing dismissible," says Kennedy.

My mother could recount the banal events in our lives in ways that were just wonderful," he recalls. "My uncle Pete was an original. He was a man who was marginally educated but extraordinarily smart—just so intuitive about life, like my mother. Pete could have been a writer. His observations of human behavior and the way he could tell a story. Whenever he came into the room, the room lit up for me. He was a hero, a secondary father in a totally different way.

"Pete was a maverick, a hipster. All he did was illegal stuff. He was legal for about six weeks—he became a painter, but he couldn't handle it!" He modeled Billy Phelan after his Uncle Pete, and there are a multitude of references to him in Kennedy's work.

Kennedy fell in love with reading in his youth, and frequented the Albany public library. In *O Albany!*, he notes the branch on North Pearl Street became "my personal point of entry into the beauty and magic of . . . good books. The trashy ones I collected on my own, stored them in the attic, and entered *their* magic with the firm intuition from my uncle that trash was also good for the soul."

Kennedy still is a frequent visitor to local Albanian libraries. He uses them for research and still hunts down "good books" there. (The glass-topped coffee table of his Dove Street townhouse recently snapped under the weight of the books he had piled on it.) That may be why he reacted so angrily when in November 1986 the Troy Public Library bestowed the "Silver Turkey" award on *Ironweed* (where, ironically, a scene from the movie in which Helen goes to the library to get warm was shot).

"They live by writers! That [librarians] would stoop so stupidly low to mock publicly some great writers . . . it's like the *Gong Show!*" Kennedy fumes, still smarting at the incident. "I think those librarians have no taste and no intelligence. I've been insulted by a lot more vitriolic criticism and never responded . . . getting a bad review in Troy is a heroic achievement!"

He left North Albany for the first time to attend Siena College in nearby Loudonville, where Kennedy's own high style and sense of elegance first became noticeable. It was a glamorous era in America, when the likes of Rita Hayworth and Tyrone Power were doing Chesterfield ads, and Kennedy took a shining to it. His auburn hair was deeply waved, the lapels of his jacket wider than anyone else's. He wore a bow tie, not a standard neck tie. Today he's also a snappy dresser, and one thinks of him in his houndstooth jacket on winter days, in his white linen jacket on summer nights, in casual awning-striped shirts. With Kennedy, style and substance are inseparable in his own life and in his novels—with style often defining the substance.

It was also at Siena where the author began to write seriously. Determined to become a newsman, he majored in English, taking many journalism courses. He became the executive editor of the school paper, then called the *Siena News,* now *The Indian.* He also wrote fiction for a school magazine. As a student, and for the balance of his journalism career, language was paramount.

"I wanted to be Damon Runyon," he told students on a trip back to Siena in 1986 at the invitation of *The Indian*'s editor. "The thing that was most impor-tant to me was the language—the importance of the momentary word to catch the mood, the nuance. Make it funny, make it dramatic. I always wanted to use language to the hilt."

After college he became a sports writer. Then he was drafted at the begin-ning of the Korean War, stationed first in Fort Benning, Ga., and later in Frankfurt, West Germany. He returned from the Army to become a general assignment writer for the Albany *Times-Union,* leaving after three years to become assistant managing editor of a newspaper in Puerto Rico.

In the last week of December 1956, he met a Puerto Rican beauty from New York City by the show-biz name of Dana Sosa (see Ana Daisy) who was visiting her parents, who had retired to Puerto Rico. Instantly smitten, he asked for a date on New Year's Eve. She told him it was customary for Puerto Ricans to spend that time with family, so he settled for a date after midnight.

After a whirlwind 19-day romance, as they were sipping anise and soda at Cecelia's Place in Isle Verde, Kennedy blurted: "Let's get married." "Yes, let's do it," replied Dana. They were married on Jan. 31, 1957, in a church wedding in Puerto Rico with both families in attendance.

From that moment on, Dana would devote her life to Kennedy. Working as a model (she is on the cover of the Jan. 17, 1961 issue of *Look*), dance instructor, boutique owner, and various other jobs, she helped to keep the family financially afloat during the lean years.

The Puerto Rican paper Kennedy worked for folded while he was courting Dana, so after the wedding they went to Miami, where he covered the Caribbean beat for the *Miami Herald.* He also began working on his first novel, *The Angels and the Sparrows.* While it was never published, it was the beginning of the fictitious Phelan family that appears in both *Billy Phelan's Greatest Game* and *Ironweed.*

Within a year, he had returned to Puerto Rico to co-found another newspaper, the *San Juan Star.* Managing editor by day, struggling novelist by night, in 1960 he decided to take a writing course at the University of Puerto Rico at Rio Piedras. The teacher was visiting professor Saul Bellow.

In 1963, Kennedy returned home for what he thought would be a simple visit to his father, who was ill. Except for a few brief vacations, he hasn't left Albany since. He went back to his old employer, The *Times-Union,* but Kennedy's heart was no longer in journalism but in fiction.

When he made the transition from reporter to novelist he took several key elements from journalism with him. For one, Kennedy is master of the topic sentence, particularly for the story's lead. The opening sentence of *Ironweed,* for example, deftly establishes protagonist Francis Phelan's place in life and the upcoming confrontation with the ghosts of his past: "Riding up the winding road of Saint Agnes Cemetery in the back of the rattling old truck, Francis Phelan became aware that the dead, even more than the living, settled down in neighborhoods."

In addition, Kennedy's choice of subjects is based strictly on journalistic sensibilities—the placing of his subjects in extreme circumstances. In journalism it's called the *"newsworthy event."* But as a novelist, Kennedy is neither reined in by the event nor burdened by the duty of getting in all the facts. Instead, he's able to give his characters the mythic dimensions he loves.

"In fiction," says Kennedy, "you have the freedom to bring in the unknown. In creating a human being, a character, you take off from the complexity of life." Citing his novel *Legs,* he says, "to write about Diamond I had to respect someone who was a mean, cruel son of a bitch. Yet he fascinated America. My role was to find out why he was so revered. Why people treated him like they treated Lindbergh and Al Jolson. Why people courted his presence." When Legs is murdered toward the end of the novel, Kennedy demonstrates just how far fiction can stray from the narrow path of reporting: "Jack (Legs) Diamond, aged thirty-four years, five months, seven days, and several hours, sat up in bed in his underwear and stared into the mirror at his new condition: incipiently dead. 'Those simple bastards,' he said, 'they finally did it right.' "

And, of course, his journalist's skill as a wordsmith is burnished in his novels. Working first from handwritten notes he keeps in Meade and looseleaf notebooks, Kennedy wrote *Quinn's Book* on both his aunt's ancient L.C. Smith typewriter (that he keeps in his Victorian-era home 12 miles from downtown Albany in Averill Park), and on his old college typewriter that he keeps at Dove Street.

Until 1983 Kennedy's writing momentum was frequently stalled, and his publishing history was spotty. *The Ink Truck,* first published in 1969, went out of print almost immediately. It took him six years and eight versions to produce *Legs.* "*Legs* taught me how not to write a novel," laughs Kennedy. Published in 1975, sales were moderate for the three years of active sales it had. *Billy Phelan's Greatest Game* took Kennedy two years to write. It had only one year of active sales when it was first published in 1978. By contrast, Kennedy finished *Ironweed* in just seven months.

It has taken Kennedy 10 years to write *Quinn's Book*—five years seriously. "Creation of fiction is a process of evolution, trial and error, a test of your own imagination, your own drive," he told students at Siena this winter. "I started in the summer of 1977. I wrote notes all summer long [but] couldn't get going on it. . . . I came back to it in 1981 and wrote another beginning, but it was still the same story. Wrote 125–150 pages. It was rotten and I threw it away. But I was obsessed still. . . ."

Writers, says Kennedy, are the product of their own imagination, of their own experiences—and of other writers. Kennedy himself says he learned about literature by reading. He admires many, many writers. In addition to Bellow, his mentor, he admires Runyon for the way he "could turn a phrase." Kafka, he told the students at Siena, "was so weird I knew he was talking to me."

He shares his love of the surreal and myth-making with Gabriel García Márquez, author of *One Hundred Years of Solitude,* whom he met while Kennedy was still a journalist and with whom he is still friends. "I had [works by artist Salvador] Dali in my house," says Kennedy, searching for the exact point in time "that love of dream, of the irrational, and that element of total surprise" began to captivate him. "A man could act on dreams as he acted upon thought," wrote Kennedy in *The Ink Truck.* "A man could act upon delusions as he acted upon dreams. They would have only private validity. No one would be able to accept them; but neither could anyone negate them." *Legs* has surreal elements, and by the time he wrote *Ironweed* Kennedy himself became a master of surrealism art.

This past January, Kennedy and his family visited Márquez in Cuba. They chatted with Castro, and Kennedy paid homage to another literary hero of his—Ernest Hemingway. An admirer of Hemingway's sense of realism and use of interior monologue, Kennedy went out in the middle of the night to Cojimar, where *The Old Man and the Sea* is set, visited Hemingway's Cuban estate Finca Vigla—now a museum—and ate at Hemingway's hangout, the Cafe Florida.

That Kennedy would invest his time and effort in a special place for writers is therefore natural. The Writers Institute, founded with The MacArthur Foundation grant, today receives funding from SUNY and directly from the state. The institute grants awards to authors and poets, brings in internationally reknowned writers as guest lecturers, and sponsors residences for students as young as high-school age.

Kennedy is also increasing his involvement in film-making. "In a way, movies have replaced journalism for me," observes Kennedy. "There's kind of a kinship there. It's almost like working for the AP." His first screen-writing experience, with Francis Ford Coppola, was *The Cotton Club,* a production bedeviled by delays and rewrites. Recalls Kennedy, "It was wacko, and had very little to do with writing, although we wrote a great deal—as if we were writing *War and Peace."*

Like Steven Spielberg, Kennedy admires most of the movies of the 1930s when the likes of William Faulkner and F. Scott Fitzgerald were trying their hands at screenplays and writers were king in cinema. "Because great writers wrote the scripts they could hear people speak authentically—and they could be funny," Kennedy says. Always a movie freak, today he is the proud possessor of more than 400 videos and holds "film festivals" in his Averill Park house.

He also bought his Dove Street townhouse with the intention of filming the movie *Legs* there. The 19th-century row house had by 1931 become a rooming house—the very rooming house "Legs" was killed in. "I bought this house in conjunction with a movie producer, on an impulse when we were thinking about making *Legs,"* explains Kennedy. Movie plans on *Legs* are amorphous right now, but these days Kennedy spends much of his time living and writing at his comfortable office-cum-*pied-a-terre* on Dove Street.

Kennedy is a family man, and he enjoys collaborative efforts with his family. His son, Brendan, who turns 17 years old this month, is seriously considering going to college to study filmmaking. In the meantime, he's completing high school, and enjoying his own celebrity status after publishing his first book last fall. Co-authored with his dad, *Charlie Malarkey and the Belly Button Machine* had its origins when Brendan was four, lying in bed, his pj's wrinkled-up, and belly-button exposed. Father and son would concoct stories. Kennedy put their ideas to paper, and both refined the book as Brendan got older. For years Kennedy tried unsuccessfully to get it published. Last year, not surprisingly, they made it. Both of Kennedy's daughters— Dana, 29, and Kathy, 28, worked on the *Ironweed* set. (Kennedy also has two grandchildren.) The family is contemplating, not totally frivolously, forming a production company of their own. Kennedy is not finished yet with surprising himself and the public.

Francis Phelan Goes Hollywood

Patrick Farrelly / 1987

Published in *Irish America* November 1987: 25–30. Reprinted by permission.

". . . and Spiff Dwyer in his nifty pinched fedora and young George Quinn and young Martin Daugherty, the batboys, and Martin's grandfather, Emmett Daugherty, the wild Fenian who talked so fierce and splendid and put the radical light in Francis's eye with his stories of how moneymen used workers to get rich and treated the Irish like pigdog paddyniggers, and Patsy McCall, who grew up to run the city and was carrying his ball glove in his left hand, and some men Francis did not know even in 1899, for they were only hangers-on at the saloon. . . ." *(Ironweed)*

In St. Agnes' Cemetery on a hill above Albany, Francis Phelan "became aware that the dead, even more than the living, settled down in neighborhoods." In front of him lay his father and mother, side by side with a host of characters from Francis' past. As he views the graves, remembering each individual from a time gone by, they also evaluate him, and recall incidents from Francis' earlier days in Albany. It is All Hallows Eve in 1938, that "unruly night when grace is always in short supply, and the old and the new dead walk abroad in this land."

In this way, we meet Francis Phelan, an alcoholic bum and wanderer, now returned to his home town of Albany to confront the ghosts of his past, and make peace with the present. In William Kennedy's Pulitzer Prize-winning novel, *Ironweed,* we enter the world of the Irish working-class in Depression-era Albany. We follow Francis Phelan as he wanders through a wasteland of outcasts, soup kitchens and flophouses, and as he remembers his former life as a proud father, a major-league third baseman and a union activist.

It has been called "the greatest Irish American novel of the century" and now it will make its screen debut this December, starring Jack Nicholson and Meryl Streep and directed by Hector Babenco who made the highly acclaimed movie, "Kiss of the Spider Woman." Not surprisingly, it is one of the most eagerly awaited screen adaptations in years.

Already the secrecy surrounding the making of the movie, mirrored in the refusal of stars Jack Nicholson and Meryl Streep to give any substantive interviews about their roles has added to the sense of expectation.

In an exclusive interview with *Irish America,* author and screenplay writer William Kennedy underscored the difficulty of translating his Joycean narrative to the screen. He admitted that apart from the novel's constant drift into the world of the imagination, capturing the reality of the struggles of the poor Irish of the Albany of the early 20th century was equally demanding. The Albany of *Ironweed* is a central character to the novel, just as Dublin in Joyce's *Ulysses.* What was needed, Kennedy says, was "an extraordinary director."

In Hector Babenco, Kennedy felt he found just the right person for the job. Babenco, an Argentina-born and Brazil-based film maker first read *Ironweed* on a beach in northern Brazil, and became obsessed with making it into a movie. Already famous for "Kiss of the Spider Woman," a surrealistic drama set in a prison, which won a Best-Actor Oscar for William Hurt, Babenco explained later, "I started to feel it was boiling inside myself, asking to be translated to the screen. The only way to remove the tumor was to do a movie."

About two years ago, Babenco set off to visit Kennedy in Albany. Kennedy hadn't seen "Kiss of the Spider Woman," so Babenco organized a screening for him. "It was an intelligent film in the midst of this vast Sahara of unintelligence," Kennedy remembers. "Afterwards over dinner, I said, 'I don't know why we can't make a deal right now.' I told my associates in Los Angeles and they said, 'Okay, make the deal.' We just shook hands on it." Later Kennedy and Babenco spent a few weeks working on a first and then a second draft of a screenplay.

In "Kiss of the Spider Woman," Kennedy was impressed with the "second dimension—the surrealistic quality of the movie within the movie." He explained: "It was done very skillfully, in a way that showed that he understood the nature of the duality that exists—as it does in my books—between the real world and the world of ghosts. That magic realism that one associates with Latin American writing these days—that was the major thing that convinced me to go with his direction."

In true Latin American fashion, echoing the style of Nobel Prizewinner Gabriel García Márquez, Babenco had a more clear-cut view of his film. "I never thought of two levels of reality. Both of them were total reality for me." In joining Babenco's Latin sense of reality to Kennedy's Irish journey into the netherworld, the stage was set for a unique, if not historic, collaboration.

A whole range of actors were considered to play Francis Phelan: Sam Shepard, Paul Newman, Robert de Niro, Gene Hackman, Robert Duval and Jason Robards were names that Babenco and Kennedy considered at different times. Jack Nicholson was also interested. Babenco met him and showed him the script. Nicholson was already well acquainted with the book and immediately told Babenco, "Yea, I would love to do it. Just see now if you can make it work." With Nicholson's name associated with the project, Babenco approached an independent producer, Keith Barish, who went out and raised the money.

Barish had produced the award-winning "Sophie's Choice," and that connection now resulted in Meryl Streep, the star of "Sophie's Choice," accepting the part of Francis' alcoholic lover, Helen Archer.

With Barish and Babenco, Kennedy had a collaboration that could have been made in heaven. Written into Kennedy's contract as scriptwriter was a clause giving him complete control over script changes. "They could not change the script without consulting me. That was the way it was, and when changes had to be made, I made them," says Kennedy.

Film versions of famous novels have often resulted in bitter recriminations between writer and filmmaker. Kennedy's previous work on the Francis Ford Coppola film "Cotton Club" had left him well-prepared for the pitfalls of the movie business. "I understand the nature of the compromises that have to be made," he says. "What I am trying to do is create a cinematic work of art, not something that will be the same as the book. Some writers find that hard to accept. The book needs to be transferred to the screen in a way that sustains it as a work of art."

As was not the case with "The Cotton Club," Kennedy found no animosity between the director and the producer. Babenco had the full support of Barish. Kennedy was relieved to find such a supportive working environment. "It is very unusual in a project like this that the director is given carte blanche and the writer is given the freedom I had," he says.

In the motion picture to be released in December, Jack Nicholson is transformed into Francis Phelan, perhaps one of the most difficult roles of his career. Meryl Streep plays Helen Archer, Phelan's companion in adversity, a woman haunted too by her past, and like Francis, struggling to survive.

Jack Nicholson has played Irish American parts before in his illustrious acting career, most notably, Randall Patrick McMurphy in "One Flew Over the Cuckoo's Nest" and Eugene O'Neill in "Reds." Kennedy was especially pleased with the choice of Nicholson as Francis Phelan. "Nicholson was ideal," he says. "He was Irish to begin with. He was tough, he was funny, he was the right age. He is a first-rate actor and he is the top of the world." Although Kennedy had yet to see the final cut when he spoke to *Irish America,* he had little doubt about the final verdict on Nicholson.

"He is different in this film than in anything I've seen him do. He is deeply and profoundly troubled and he still cracks jokes—he makes you laugh and he makes you weep. I think with him it was intuitive, part of being raised an Irish Catholic, which Francis Phelan is. That doesn't mean that Paul Newman or Gene Hackman would not have been terrific, but I think that Nicholson is just perfect."

Had Meryl Streep too glamorous an image for the role of Helen, as has been suggested? Kennedy is emphatic. "You will not think of her as glamorous in this movie—a destroyed beauty, but not glamorous. She is wonderful in the role. She is a comedian, she changes her voice, her walk; it's almost a mutation, what she does on screen."

For William Kennedy, the making of the movie is a dream come true. Kennedy's own life reads like a Hollywood script, a long, hard struggle with adversity that has finally brought him wealth and recognition.

A few years ago in an interview with the *Washington Post* Kennedy remarked that "the reversals of my life have been extraordinary, almost everything has turned inside out." Born nearly 60 years ago to working-class Irish natives of the north end of Albany, Kennedy had ambitions to be a writer from an early age.

In his youth he was taken round the political clubs and meeting halls by his father, a ward heeler in the political machine of Daniel P. O'Connell. Kennedy developed a taste for the poolhalls, bars and bowling alleys that dotted the seedy streets of downtown Albany. It's here that Kennedy's fascination with characters on the fringes of "normal society" developed; people who struggled with deprivation and adversity—with only street cunning and wit between them and the abyss. In this netherworld, Kennedy could see heroic struggles being fought, struggles that have re-merged in the characters of his fiction.

After his military service, Kennedy got a job on the staff of the Albany *Times-Union* as a general assignment reporter. He quickly became bored with both Albany and the *Times-Union* and accepted an offer to work as an assistant managing editor of a new English-language newspaper in Puerto Rico. While there he took a creative writing course under the novelist Saul Bellow. It was to be an important friendship.

His attempts at fiction were set in Puerto Rico but repeatedly he found himself writing about Albany. In 1961 Kennedy returned home to take care of his gravely ill father. Instead of the planned temporary visit he found himself both rediscovering and being seduced by Albany.

He eventually returned to the *Times-Union,* this time on a part-time basis to leave room for his fiction writing. William Kennedy's first novel, *The Ink Truck* was published in 1969. Based on a strike that happened when he worked at the *Times-Union,* it received some critical attention but little commercial success. Kennedy followed it with two novels, *Legs* (1975) and *Billy Phelan's Greatest Game* (1978).

Both novels drew on Kennedy's knowledge of and fascination with the underbelly of Irish American life in Albany. *Legs* chronicled in fictional form the last year and a half of life of the notorious gangster Legs Diamond, as seen through the eyes of his lawyer and confidant Marcus Gorman. *Legs'* appeal to Kennedy is summed up by Gorman's description of him as "not merely the dude of all gangsters, the most active brain in the New York underworld, but . . . one of the truly new Irishmen of his day: Horatio Alger out of Finn McCool and Jesse James . . . a pioneer, the founder of the first truly modern gang, the dauphin of the town for years."

Billy Phelan again takes us into the underworld, this time where it interacts with the Irish political machine, when the son of the political boss McCall is kidnapped. Billy, a small time gambler and man-about-town, is embroiled in an affair which leaves him ostracized by his political patrons when he refuses to become an informer. Based on a real event, the kidnapping of the nephew of Dan O'Connell, the Albany Democratic party boss, *Billy Phelan* is a fast-paced thriller in which the lead character tries to maintain his integrity despite becoming a pariah in his own community.

Legs and *Billy Phelan* received critical acclaim but neither sold well. Viking, the prestigious New York publishing house published *Billy Phelan* but as Kennedy explained, "Billy was very badly published—just shoved out there." Viking accepted Kennedy's next novel, *Ironweed* but with little enthusiasm. Fearing that it would suffer the same fate as *Billy Phelan,* Kennedy submitted it to numerous publishers, but every time the same word came back, "who the hell wants to read about bums?"

An old friend of Kennedy's described the situation at the time thus: "When

I think of it objectively, I'm awed by it. Rejected at the age of 50 and dragging his family down with him. In his mind, he had become like one of his characters, a bum, a literary bum. In the middle of it all, he suffered horrendous financial difficulties. But through it all, he would climb up there and just plug away."

Just when Kennedy was at his lowest ebb help arrived in the form of his old tutor Saul Bellow. Hearing of the rejection of *Ironweed* the Nobel Prize-winner wrote to Viking declaring: "That the author of *Billy Phelan* should have a manuscript kicking around looking for a publisher is disgraceful." The tide was about to turn. Later in the *New York Times* Bellow summed up Kennedy's talent. "There are no dead sentences in his work. His language is vigorous, full of energy. At a time when so much cold porridge is served up in the literary world as hot stuff, here is the real hot stuff."

What was to happen was enough to make anybody's head spin. Titling them *The Albany Cycle*, Viking reissued *Legs* and *Billy Phelan* for simultaneous publication with *Ironweed*. Kennedy won a MacArthur Foundation grant worth $264,000 and finally came the Pulitzer Prize. Kennedy was the toast of the literary world, his work suddenly evoking comparisons with Faulkner, Joyce and Scott Fitzgerald.

In movie circles, talk of all three books being turned into films spread— with big-name directors and actors associated with each title. William Kennedy started to enjoy himself enormously. Profiles of him began to appear everywhere and "60 Minutes" featured his story.

Summing up his new-found fame, Kennedy has said, "I like it. I like it a lot. Being poor and unknown is difficult. But this—this is easy." Fortitude and a stubborn belief in himself had paid off. Kennedy had once defined the essence of the characters in his novels as a "refusal to yield to what appears to be fate. If you don't die and you don't quit, then there's a chance." Now at the age of 55, he had proven just how valuable that trait was within himself.

As a journalist with the *Times-Union,* Kennedy often wrote movie reviews. As a film buff, the idea of his novels appearing in cinematic form excited him. However, his first experience of movie-making came in a most unusual and ultimately almost bizarre way.

Francis Ford Coppola, the legendary director of "The Godfather" and "Apocalypse Now," had been sent copies of *Legs* by actors Mickey Rourke and Richard Gere, just when Coppola was working on "The Cotton Club," a movie based on the famous Harlem nightspot. After reading *Legs,* Coppola phoned Kennedy and asked him to work with him on the screenplay of "The

Cotton Club." He saw Kennedy's evocation of the period and his use of
dialogue in *Legs,* as what he needed to infuse into the movie.

For Kennedy it was a baptism of fire. Coppola wanted to completely rework
a movie to which millions of dollars had already been committed. Brought
in at a late stage to save the project, Coppola was unhappy with the script
and sought Kennedy's help in reworking it.

Kennedy was placed in a suite in the Park Lane Hotel, in Manhattan and
surrounded with the music and movies of the 20s and 30s, he set to work.
Meanwhile, the cast and crew waited around, for a script to be produced by
Coppola and Kennedy. A frenetic pace was set, the two working straight
through for 34 hours at one particular sitting and within a period of five
weeks 28 scripts were produced.

Remembering the experience Kennedy later described how Coppola
"would stretch the script out like a roll of paper towels" and start hacking
away at sequences. "People were murdered and then later you were having
lunch with them," he recalled. In one weekend Kennedy did five rewrites.
"By two a.m. on August 22, it was as logical as it was ever going to be. By
seven a.m., it was out and duplicated. And, by eight a.m., Coppola was out
on location shooting it."

With his "Cotton Club" experience behind him, Kennedy's next major
project was his own book. In the spring of 1987 as filming began, the streets
of Albany were "dressed up" with over a thousand tons of dirt and 300 tons
of stone and gravel. The local people were clad in period costumes ready to
play workers and strike breakers in one of the pivotal scenes from Francis
Phelan's past.

After nearly two years of preparation, director Hector Babenco and writer
William Kennedy had finally decided on how to depict in film all the cast of
Irish characters that appear, ghost-like, to haunt Francis Phelan as he walks
the streets of his home town. As the cameras rolled the retelling of a great
chronicle of Irish American life began anew.

That tale begins when Francis Phelan returns to Albany in the fall of 1938.
He has been away for over 20 years, having fled his family and hometown in
1916, after accidentally dropping his infant son, Gerald, in the kitchen of his
home. Filled with grief and guilt at the death of his son, he had taken to the
roads, leaving his wife Annie to bury the child.

In St. Agnes' cemetery, Francis moves instinctively to the spot where Gerald is buried, although he had never seen his grave. He stands transfixed

before the little mound, ready at last to make peace with his son. "Twenty two years gone, and Francis could now, in panoramic memory, see, hear, and feel every detail of that day, from the time he left the car barns after work, to his talk about baseball with Bunt Dunn in King Brady's saloon . . . his memory had begun returning forgotten images when it equated Arthur T. Grogan and Strawberry Bill, but now memory was as vivid as eyesight."

That desertion by Francis of his family was the last in a series. In 1901, during a trolleyworkers' strike, he killed a strike-breaker, splitting open his skull with a stone, thrown during a street confrontation between strikers and scabs. He took to the roads then, returning years later, when the heat died down, to marry Annie and start a family, only to hit the road, once again, to play minor league baseball, eventually becoming third baseman for the Washington Senators.

When Francis returns to Albany in 1938, he does so because the Irish political machine is offering bums $5 for every time they register to vote. Francis votes 21 times before he is caught. Now he finds some work shoveling dirt in St. Agnes' cemetery to pay off the money he owes attorney Marcus Gorman (whom we met in *Legs*) for getting him out of jail.

Along with Francis is his longtime companion, Helen Archer. A gentle and vulnerable woman, Helen in her youth studied music at Vassar but lacking the toughness to survive adversity, slid into a life of alcohol and wandering. Protected by Francis and haunted by the failures of her life, she roams his netherworld.

Also trailing Francis are the ghosts of his past; the men he has killed and a cast of other tragic characters whose lives have intersected with his. Francis's world moves constantly in and out of his waking dreams as he tries to reconcile himself with his life and overcome the shame and guilt of his flight from responsibility. Now Francis returns to Albany to confront the sins of his past, and ultimately, to find forgiveness and reconciliation with his family.

"Ironweed" drifts easily from the grim reality of the streets of Albany to the illusory world of Francis and Helen's imaginations.

The end of the film, like the novel, is ambiguous. Does Francis Phelan return to his family or does he once again hit the road. That's left to Jack Nicholson to answer. "That's the one question I won't answer," he told a reporter after the shooting was finished, "because I'm the only one that knows. The writer doesn't know, the director doesn't know. You gotta be him to know—you gotta be me to know."

Irrespective of what ending you choose, there is no denying that right now,

William Kennedy is an anxious man. Like a first-time father pacing up and down outside the delivery room, his role, apart from offering words of encouragement, is over.

Indeed, all the cast of his early-century Albany are now in the cutting room, awaiting final cut. "The film is definitvely from the script," he says confidently. "It is not a foreign object to me. There could be cuts that will distort or remove certain elements along the way. But at this stage it looks wonderful to me and conforms to Francis Phelan, the family's story and so on."

On the ghost figures and Francis' imagination, Kennedy is keeping mum, unwilling to reveal the gameplan. "I'd rather not talk about how it was done, but basically, it works very well," . . . like the novel itself, one might say, which, if so, will surely make it an Oscar frontrunner for 1988.

On an Averill Park Afternoon with William Kennedy

Edward C. Reilly / 1988

Published in *South Carolina Review* 21 (Spring 1989): 11–24.
Reprinted by permission.

Viking advanced half the fee for the work, the author finished it as promised, Viking decided against publication, and thirteen rejections later William Kennedy still searched for a publisher for *Ironweed*. In a letter Nobel Prize winner Saul Bellow excoriated Viking, Viking's editor Corlies "Cork" Smith chanced it, and the rest is publication history and legend. For Kennedy, who for twenty years wrote for the joy of creating, 1983 became a miraculous year when *Ironweed* was published. *Ironweed* won the National Book Critics Circle Ward and the Pulitzer Prize for Fiction; *The Ink Truck, Legs,* and *Billy Phelan's Greatest Game* were reissued, re-reviewed, and finally acclaimed; film rights followed; Kennedy received a MacArthur Foundation grant, established the Writers' Institute at State University of New York at Albany, and became a grandfather. A truly remarkable year. But Kennedy is a remarkable man.

My interest in Kennedy and his novels began while browsing in Waldenbooks and seeing the realistically sad picture of a man on the cover of *Ironweed*—Kennedy says the picture awed him as he leafed through Margaret Bourke-White's *You Have Seen Their Faces*. This time I judged a book by its cover and was not disappointed. After *Ironweed*, I read *Legs, Billy Phelan,* and *The Ink Truck* in that order and knew Kennedy was a major voice in contemporary American literature. After teaching his novels—the students were even impressed, also a rarity—and publishing several critical essays about those novels, I decided Kennedy deserved a book-length study. G. K. Hall was interested, and so was I. I also wanted to meet and talk with Kennedy and did on March 14, 1988, at his Averill Park home.

On March 12, a rainy Saturday night, I arrived in Albany and by chance ended up on Dove Street, where I located 67 Dove Street, the rooming house in which Jack "Legs" Diamond was murdered. Using the information and maps in *O Albany!*, I spent Sunday literarily touring Kennedy's Albany—

Lombardo's Restaurant, the Miss Albany Diner, Saint Agnes Cemetery, and Kennedy's North Albany neighborhood with its Sacred Heart Church, Public School 20, and 607 and 620 North Pearl, where Kennedy had lived with his parents. I felt Kennedy's sense of place when reading his novels, but I never realized how accurately keen that sense of place was until I was in Albany and walking down some of the same streets and perhaps seeing some of the same places as had Bailey, Legs Diamond, and Billy and Francis Phelan.

When I called Kennedy late Sunday afternoon, Brendan, his son, said his father was not home but to leave my number. I told Brendan that I wanted him to autograph my copy of *Charlie Malarkey and the Belly Button Machine,* to which he replied, "I'd be glad to." (No wonder Kennedy identified Brendan in the dedication to *Billy Phelan's Greatest Game* as "a nifty kid.") Kennedy returned my call, said he was in Albany for the St. Patrick's Day Parade in his North Albany neighborhood where he met old friends, drank a wee bit of the Irish, had a wonderful time, and must do that more often.

When I arrived at Kennedy's home, we coffeed at his kitchen table with Dana, his wife, adjourned to his upstairs study, where pictures cover the walls, books fill the bookcases, and memorabilia abound—a recent acquisition is the pair of shoes Jack Nicholson wore in *Ironweed*—and where we talked. The phone rang often, Kennedy's daughter and his two grandchildren were downstairs, and Dana was being a housewife and grandmother. At one part of the interview when we were interrupted by an important telephone call, Kennedy apologized and good naturedly said, "it's like Grand Central in this house. So much going on all the time. My daughter's here with my two grandchildren, and the phone never stops ringing. It's kind of quiet today." After the interview, Dana prepared lunch—an appetizing pasta dish, some savory sauteed green and red peppers, wine, and dessert. Kennedy was dieting, and Dana said, "When Bill diets, the whole family diets." We ate, we drank, we talked about politics, books, movies, and the fact that yes, Diamond's name was Diamond and not Nolan as is sometimes reported—his tombstone reads John Thomas Diamond. The Kennedys' warm hospitality and their house full of noise and children and whatever reminded me of the home scenes in *Bill Phelan* and *Ironweed,* as well as my own Irish background and large Irish family. It was a pleasant and memorable Averill Park afternoon with the Kennedys.

Reilly: Were the *O Albany!* essays from the 1963–1964 Albany *Times-Union* articles?

Kennedy: That started them. I had always wanted to reprint those essays because I felt that they had a permanent value to a lot of people from Albany. They appeared over a period of about three months and in 1964, I think, in the beginning of 1964. Then the newspaper never republished them, and I always thought well, someday, maybe I will. The word got around. Somewhere around 1981, I think it was, and 1980—I don't know, I was in—I had finished *Ironweed* and a friend of mine came to me and said she'd heard about my interest in publishing the thing. Did I have the articles? This was Sue Dumbleton, who became editor of the book, and her husband is a colleague of mine at State University, Bill Dumbleton. He's now chairman of the English Department, and she teaches literature over at the pharmacy college. But she has started this publishing venture called Washington Park Press and so, you know, for a token amount of money—$500 advance—I was going to write this book just for the hell of it, you know, just to get those articles on the record. And we both read the articles over again and, obviously, twenty years had elapsed and a lot of things had changed including my prose style, and I couldn't abide most of them, and I obviously had to do a lot more reporting. So I started and did a lot of reporting and wrote the thing as fast as I could really in 1982, and that was the last thing I did before I went to Cornell. I delivered the manuscript to my editor at Viking [Corlies] "Cork" Smith, and I went off to go teach up at Cornell.

Well, Cork did not read the thing for a while. He was uncertain about the book. He thought he was having it forced down his throat because it was, you know, a local venture and so on. But then, I don't know, a month and a half or two months went by, and he finally read the book and loved it and then went to bat for it in a conference, and the publisher liked the idea too. So they decided to go with it, and obviously, you know, Washington Park Press was also going to publish it in a smaller edition. Then they finally got together, and it was just one big edition which both publishers get credit for doing it.

Actually, Sue was the editor of the book, and she worked very closely with me on research and handling of the manuscript and so on. The book was a labor of love. I didn't expect any money out of it. I didn't know what to expect, but the accumulation of work that I had done as a journalist over many years just seemed to fall into place when I began to pay close attention to the structure of the book. You know, like the Nighttown series and sequences—the things I had done on the Kenmore Hotel, my long-standing love for Keeler's Restaurant, which is gone and only a memory, and then tying that all in with the night world of gamblers and Legs Diamond and so on. So that kind of came to pass, and then all the work I had done on the slums in the South End during the 60's, the late 60's that created that "Boulevard of Bluest Dreams" and all the civil rights movement and activity that went on in that period.

Then, of course, my continuing interest in the politics of the town—Dan O'Connell and Erastus Corning. That was the most fascinating of all pieces. And then typing that into the Mall and the Renaissance of Albany because of the building of the South Mall by [Governor Nelson] Rockefeller. And so those sections became very important. The one about Dan O'Connell's going to the political meeting at the Polish Hall, that was something I had written for a book that I was going to publish in the 60's, a book that was called—first it was called *The Slum Book* and then it was called *Sweet as the Flowers in Springtime*. And it never came to be. It was like the origin of *O Albany!* in its own way, but it also had *Ironweed* in the middle of it, or what was then *The Lemon Weed,* which was the series of articles I wrote about the slums— not the slums but about the winos. That was in '64, I think. I have those specific dates I can get you on that.

But the whole thing became an amalgam of everything I'd ever done, and so I had a very good feeling about the book. It came out extremely well and handsomely packaged, and we were able to put that whole section of photographs in the middle of it, and they spent a lot of money preparing it. They figured they would make some money on it, but they sold like 25,000 copies hardcover—24, 000, I don't even know. The book has at least sold like 40,000, 50,000 copies, and for a regional book it continues to sell. I don't know exactly whether the hardcover is still in print or not, but the softcover is.

Reilly: Did you change the title of the book? One source listed *O Albany!, an Urban Tapestry?*

Kennedy: *That* was never my title. That was Cork's, and the other people at Viking wanted to differentiate this from fiction. They wanted it to be clearly a non-fiction work, so they put that in there. But I never liked it. My title was the subtitle, "The Improbable City," political wizards and all that stuff. That was the subtitle and when we came back to the paperback, we dropped the "Urban Tapestry." It shouldn't have been there to begin with. That was a marketing decision that was a *fait accompli* when I discovered it on the cover.

Reilly: In the *O Albany!* essays is a great deal of new journalism. Would you agree with that? The journalistic techniques?

Kennedy: Sure. Oh, yeah, I would agree with that. I usually teach that. And I practiced it all my life, long before it was called that (laughs).

Reilly: But there are also fictional overtones. You know, like the ending of "The Democrats Convene," when Dan O'Connell leaves the Polish Hall and "Then the evening turned emerald green."

Kennedy: Oh, yeah, right (laughs).

Reilly: That's a beautiful ending for that essay.

Kennedy: Well, that was a little literary license there on top of what was just—there was no invention there. I mean all those facts are reported facts, but that kind of embellishment of the finale—on Gander Bay "there would be no storm"—is just writer's conclusion, you know, a little literary license to make a point.

Reilly: I think there's a two-part theme in *O Albany!*, too. One is beginnings and endings, or closings and endings, and then I think the major theme is restorations, recyclings—the closing and ending, for instance, of Keeler's and the Rain Bo Room, some of the neighborhoods declining. Always at the end of the essays are ren . . .

Kennedy: Renewal. Yeah, it's a constant regeneration of the city by various ethnic groups and the political powers—Dan O'Connell passing, Erastus Corning passing on, and Arbor Hill going through its escalations and decline and profound slump. North Albany is just continuing to change now. I never got into the modern situation in North Albany. It's becoming largely a black neighborhood now.

Reilly: There's a kind of universality, too, in that Albany is going through changes just like other cities.

Kennedy: Well, that was my point that here we have a microcosm of America with all the ethnic parallels to big cities that we've heard about, but nobody had heard about Albany. But everything that's happened in this country, except for the Oriental migration and Hispanic migration, it all happened here. Even the old west. I mean, you had frontiers, Indian fighting, and wars with the Indians, and cowboy towns, and the wild west of West Albany—it was a cattle town. So, you know, the playing out of the whole Albany plan was the precursor to the formation of the Declaration of Independence. It was all happening here. [General Philip] Schuyler's significance in the Revolution, the Battle of Saratoga, the turning point—so *many* things, so *many* allusions, [General John] Burgoyne's becoming a prisoner of Schuyler here in the south end, the Pastures.

Reilly: So Albany is in both the nation's and the human continuum?
Kennedy: Yeah, right.

Reilly: In your essays you use the world *magical* often. For instance, you said "Albany is a magical place," and when you began writing about the Phelans, you said it "freed" your imagination. It was "magical." Is that more *mystical?*
Kennedy: Well, I had once wanted to do a series of articles called "The Magical Places," and I only wrote one (laughs) which was the Union Station piece ["The Romance of the Oriflamme"]. That appeared in the *Times-Union,* and I added to it—discovered who built it and that sort of thing. I added much in later years. But, by and large, that essay was there, and that was the notion—the magical places in the sense that magic was in nostalgia for me, I suppose, the feeling of going back and being able to reconstitute a time that was lost but could be reimagined and reconstituted as literature. And that was very appealing to me. You know, just reading the works of Faulkner and Joyce, and Dublin and Yoknapatawpha, and the power of the imagination to bring back bygone time, bygone life, and transport the reader. And when I was doing it, I felt some kind of magic was happening to my brain. And the discovery of your own imagination, it seemed like something mystical, something you couldn't understand that was happening to you. I understand it now, but I suppose it's a lot different. Now I know that you feed the imagination and it goes to work.

Reilly: Well, that mystical magic is also in your fiction—the mystical moments, even in *The Ink Truck* with its surrealism.
Kennedy: It was always very important to me. The surrealists were far more interesting than the realists, especially when I wrote *The Ink Truck.* I decided that I didn't want to go quite so far out again and leave realism behind. I think that literature should have that grounding in the real world. Otherwise you begin to move into a kind of fantasy world that is equatable with science fiction or fantasy fiction.

Reilly: I think it's your sense of history and place that gives your works the realism and thus complements the mystical elements.

Kennedy: Right. The mystical part is just the element of dream in everybody's life, the element of the improbable that is always with us. No matter what way you turn, there's some new manifestation of strangeness, mystery, that confounds the imagination, confounds the logic and reality of our lives as does dream, and therefore the mix seems absolutely essential in order to keep on track to what it means to be alive. That's all. Those two things have to be addressed, and I keep trying to find the ways to address them.

Reilly: Are they evident in *Quinn's Book?*

Kennedy: Oh, you'll see a lot of it in *Quinn's Book*. Absolutely. It's not, you know, the ghosts are (laughs)—well, there's a ghost in it (laughs)—but a lot of bizarre things happen. But there's nothing that hasn't been vividly documented in history including the cataclysms in the beginning of the book. They're taken from history. maybe I've amalgamated them and made them happen on top of one another in ways that history had not seen fit to do, or Mother Nature had not seen fit to do, but I'm not being false to possibility. They all took place—the fire, the insane crossing of the river there in the middle of that ice floe, the bridging of the river with that iceberg and the explosion of that iceberg, the breaking up of the ice. Those are real historical moments that I just discovered and probably embellished to a degree that makes it more dramatic. People falling into the river from the bridge, those things happened. The pier being washed away by the ice, those things happened. So I feel that that surreal or mystical or magical quality of everyday life must be addressed in fiction if it's to be true to what it means.

Reilly: The ending for the shooting script for *The Cotton Club* ends differently from the movie itself. Was that ending your doing?

Kennedy: I don't remember how the shooting script ended.

Reilly: Dixie's and Vera's cars are parked in different directions. They say they love each other but then drive off in opposite directions, and the movie's ending contains a bit of magic—a kind of floating along, dancing down to the train station to board the 20th Century Limited.

Kennedy: Well, we wrote two endings for the film. One was the happy ending, and the other was the far more logical ending (laughs). But that was not a film that you expect to have a downbeat ending, especially when Dutch Schultz had been eliminated. In one script there were two endings. You read and it said "The End," and you turned the page and it had another thing that said "The End" again (laughs). I think I have that in the main script some-

where. I don't know, the shooting script—was that a published version? did
you see it in a bound edition?

Reilly: No. It was just a—

Kennedy: Just a thing like that with folders (points to file folders)?

Reilly: Yes. Script City was the publisher?

Kennedy: Well, it was actually published. There was actually a script published. It was pirated. Nobody ever paid me a nickel for it. Nobody ever paid
Francis [Coppola] that I know of. They published it. How they did it and why
they got away with it, I don't know.

Reilly: I know St. Martin's Press published one script.

Kennedy: That's it. That's what I meant.

Reilly: That's the pirated edition?

Kennedy: St. Martin's Press got it from somebody. I don't know where,
but I know whom they didn't do business with. They didn't do business with
the authors. They didn't do business with Mario Puzo. They didn't do business with Francis. And they didn't do business with me.

Reilly: Did Puzo write the story?

Kennedy: Puzo wrote four scripts which were not used. He started the
project, and that's why he got credit for "story by." That's minimum credit
that you receive from the Writers' Guild, who force the producers to give
credit to the first writer who originates the movie no matter what happens to
the script. Puzo's scripts were set aside when nobody would make the movie.
That's when they brought Francis Coppola in, and he wrote two scripts. His
first script didn't work, but the second script did. And that's when the movie
started to move, and it was very different from Puzo's. Then when I came in,
I started from Francis's second script. I never even read the first or I never
read Puzo's. I didn't read Puzo's until like a year and a half later when the
film was on the way to being edited and so on. And then up came the issue
of credit, and we had to go to arbitration for whose screenplay was on the
screen. The way it came out was the way it should've come out, and Puzo
got credit for being the original author. But he had not created the story.
Actually, Francis and I created the story of Dixie Dwyer. Francis started it,
and then we changed it over and over and over again (laughs). It's the most
bizarre piece of writing I've ever done.

Reilly: Did you see Jim Haskins' book *The Cotton Club*?

Kennedy: Oh, yeah. We worked from that. We had mountains and volumes of research. But that was factual—that was a picture book with captions and some reminiscences. It was a good book. I enjoyed that. Oh, and we had interviews galore with Cotton Club people. There was a parade of old timers, and Harlem gangsters' sons, who turned out to be doctors, came in to talk about their fathers. We had a black woman who did a lot of research in all directions on the Cotton Club. And there was guy who was a Cotton Club *"boy,"* a dancer. He was sort of an advisor on the project.

Reilly: I thought the characterization of Owney Madden was well done. He had a cobra-like personality like Jack Diamond. I guess Dutch Schultz did too.

Kennedy: Schultz was nowhere near as appealing a character as Diamond was to me. And that's the way we played him. Schultz was that way in life. He was smart, a smart business guy, and *ruthless.* Diamond was not such a businessman. Diamond was more of a cowboy, but organized and very smart as well. But smart! I have a feeling that Diamond was intuitive, and that Schultz was like Al Capone, an animal. Different kinds of cats. Diamond was no prize either.

Reilly: That scene in which Schultz's wife tells him to "spill gravy on your suit"—is that fairly accurate?

Kennedy: (Laughs) That's the way I felt about him. He was always a mess—everything you hear about him (ad-libs from the film's dialogue) "They don't recognize me." "Spill a little gravy on your tie. They'll recognize you."

Reilly: Most people remark that *Ironweed* is too depressing, both the book and the film. But I think both contain a great deal of humor, especially in some of Francis's lines. For example, his reply to the man who asked him why Francis asked his wife about buying a turkey—

Kennedy: "My duck died." Well, I don't think *Ironweed* is a depressing book. I think that the charge *Ironweed* the movie is depressing is not true either, but it's probably more true because there isn't much of the leavening of the humor in the Katrina section, for instance, or all of that kind of crazy bum dialogue that lifts the novel into a realm of wackiness, a bumdom that is very comic. I mean there's some of it there in the movie around the fire.

Reilly: There's also a great deal of humor in the *O Albany!* essays.

Kennedy: Oh, well, I can't do without humor. There's a world of humor in *Quinn's Book.* It was always one of the great things of my life to find a

writer who would make me laugh. I started very early, in preteens, reading
Damon Runyon. That was one of the funniest newspaper men that ever lived.
And it went on that way—Ben Hecht, an irreverent character; Red Smith,
who was a sports writer, he was God almighty as a newspaper man because
he was so funny. He was a literate, funny, intelligent writer—very lyrical
prose, writing about the stumble bums and dummy baseball players, and yet
creating a kind of mundane poetry and wit out of it. It was always Meyer
Berger's sense of journalism with clout, with power of the dramatic phrase
and the dramatic turn of events and structure. Those things—the literary quality and the wit—were always part of my drive. Even in college I was writing
funny columns and trying to make people laugh and also trying to be as
dramatic as possible within a certain framework. That's why when I went
into the newspaper business I much preferred writing feature stories to covering ordinary news. I wanted the high drama, the complicated character, whatever. I was already at that point of looking for literary dimensions in the raw
material of the news.

Reilly: Many reporters—Dreiser, Hemingway, Dos Passos, yourself—
eventually leave reporting for fiction.

Kennedy: Well, it was a dream for years and years and years, and the
cliché is that every reporter had an unfinished novel in the drawer. And it
was really true in Puerto Rico when I was there. We had a dozen aspiring
novelists. playwrights, movie screen writers, whatever, poets. As far as I
know, I'm the only one who has ever published anything (laughs). There
might have been another one. Oh, yeah, we did have one guy who was a
movie critic. He was a first-rate novelist, but he was already published. Pedro
Juan Soto, a good guy. I must call him.

Reilly: In one interview you mentioned that you had to have "some Cheever input" every now and then.

Kennedy: Cheever, to me, writes the most elegant prose of probably any
American in the last twenty or twenty-five years. I don't know—that's an
arbitrary reading but nobody was quite so funny. He was a very funny writer
and elegant in his language. He *really* understood the language and told stories so strangely and obliquely and with great flair. Those short stories stand
apart from almost anybody else's achievement in short fiction in the last half
century. You go back to Sherwood Anderson and to Hemingway; and of
course, Faulkner's short stories are more or less extensions of his fiction—
generally, his novels but not entirely. A few people, John O'Hara, a hard-

boiled sort of stuff, a wonderful short story teller, but then you come to Cheever, and that's a formidable achievement—that book of his collected stories. I always credit that book with being the beginning of the Renaissance of the short story in contemporary times because it became a best seller and therefore respectable for publishers to think about the short story again.

And out of that has come, you know, the whole minimalist crew. For instance, Ray Carver, what wonderful short story writer. And Richard Ford, another terrific short story writer. Amy Hempel, wonderful. These people who are just so gifted with minimal eloquence. Scratch that phrase. They're gifted with the eloquence of telling a great deal in short compass and giving power to a few words. Uh, I wouldn't exactly put Ford in that category, but so many good writers are coming along now and working in the short story, which is the way it was when I started to write. I wrote a lot of short stories that didn't go anywhere, and after a while I gave up. I did publish a few, but I realized that wasn't the way to go. I was working from a distant outsider's perch looking longingly at the literary culture without being able to enter it. And then I just decided to hell with it. I'll just go for the novel. I quit short stories and wrote two novels. Then went back and wrote some more short stories without success (laughs). It hasn't been my medium, and every time I'd start a short story, now anyway—*The Ink Truck* was a short story. The thing I'm just writing now, beginning to write, I thought of as a series of short stories, but no matter when I do that, it always turns into a novel. There's too much complexity, too many factors at hand to do a single story.

Reilly: A reviewer faulted your treatment of women in *Billy Phelan's Greatest Game.* Although your novels depict a man's world, there are some strong feminine characters.

Kennedy: Yeah, well, that was kind of silly because that's a man's novel. There are two characters in there, and one of them is a very strong woman who is very briefly in it. The other one—I have to mention Annie—but Peg is the other character. And then Billy's girlfriend, Angie. Those are the only characters that really enter that world, which is really a night world where women didn't appear. You either went home and there were women waiting for you who were running the house or working or whatever, but they didn't intersect with that world unless they were somehow on the fringe of the show business element or, you know, ladies of the evening. That was the kind of world that those men inhabited. I remember it very well, and it wasn't a world where women functioned.

Reilly: I think Helen Archer is a strong woman, what she does in life, and she's just as strong as Franny.

Kennedy: Well, I tend to agree with that. I think her monologue gives the context for the entirety of her life. There's reflection on it by her and behavior as a consequence of that. You get a sense of an odyssey. You get a strong sense of personality, and I think that's probably the most complete female character I've ever dealt with. Annie is important. Katrina was important. Katrina was unusual, a rare bird, anomalous almost. I *love* Katrina. I feel I have another book to talk about Katrina. *The Flaming Corsage,* the story of Katrina, Melissa, and Edward Daugherty. I've been noodling around with that for ten years, eight years, nine years, ever since I finished *Ironweed.*

Reilly: *The Angels and the Sparrows,* that was where Billy Phelan came from?

Kennedy: Not Billy. That was from where Francis came. The Phelan family was created there. Billy was not in existence at that time. Francis was created, and I couldn't forget him, and he was very like the Francis we come to know, but we see him at an earlier time. We see him in '34 when he returns to Albany for his mother's funeral and what happens to him as a consequence of the return to the house. He alludes to it in *Ironweed,* and Billy alludes to it in *Billy Phelan's Greatest Game.* I'll probably write about that in a new novel. I think that's part of the story.

Reilly: Is there any symbolic significance to the title, *The Angels and the Sparrows?*

Kennedy: Well, it's a quote out of Freud. I can't remember the source now. It's one of Freud's essays: "Let us leave the heavens to the angels and the sparrows." I should get that and quote it.

Reilly: So Franny Phelan was created before *The Lemon Weed?*

Kennedy: Oh, yeah, right. Francis wasn't that kind of character at that time. He was on the bum, he was a drunk, he was aggressive and hostile, and nasty, but he was single. He had left home and gone on the road and remained a kind of bum and then comes home. When he comes home, he gets very drunk and winds up at the Mission, which I had written about in the early '50s. So that creation of the Mission relationship to the family and drunkenness was there. When I began to write *Billy Phelan,* I decided that Billy would be Francis's son. There's no historical precedent. I don't know where this comes from. There's nothing in the family like that. There's no character like Francis in the family. But in creating him as Billy's father, I had to create Annie. I already knew about Annie and the mother and his sister. And then Francis comes back, and the encounter with Billy coming again as, you know, some imaginative magic (laughs). I don't know where it came from, but it was the thing that created Francis specifically—the conversation with Billy where he discovers that Annie never told that he dropped the child. The whole dropping of the child and the significance of that and the significance of the flight, and Francis became really a fascinating character. While I was writing *Billy Phelan,* I had already decided that I wanted to do *Ironweed.* I wanted to do—I didn't know it was that—but I wanted to give Francis his own book. I incorporated the stuff I had done in '64 on the bums in the south end of the city, tracking them, drinking with them, and that sort of thing— seeing what their life was like and where they lived in empty houses. That was a very indelible bit of reporting for me and so it all fused. Billy Phelan's world fused with the world of Francis, and then the world of Francis fused with the world of those bums and fused also backwards to *The Angels and the Sparrows.*

Reilly: About Catholicism, the power of the Church—all your characters are not brainwashed by the Church, but something strong exists within them. Francis never remarried, even Jack Diamond. Was that your—

Kennedy: No, he was a Catholic.

Reilly: No, I meant Diamond's tolling his beads.

Kennedy: There are photos of his rosary on the bed. His wife was very religious. She gave money to the church in Cairo down in Greene County. Priests were around them often. The Church denied him a Catholic burial, so he was obviously Catholic.

Reilly: Still, the idea of not divorcing, was that more or less a sign of the times about which you were writing?

Kennedy: Well, I don't know. Jack didn't have much of a problem. I think he was married twice actually. He married a girl in 1914 or somewhere around then also married Alice.

Reilly: Most of your books are set in Albany's past and *Quinn's Book* goes back even farther?

Kennedy: *Quinn's Book* goes back to 1849 and beyond. There are allu- sions to the whole of the city, its history under the patroons, taking the gene- alogy of one Dutch family and moving it forward from the time of the colo-

nists in through the Revolution and on up to the times of pre-Civil War. And
Quinn enters the picture. The past is a genuine fascination for me. I've never
thought of myself as an historian, and I still don't although I am becoming
more and more of one (laughs) in spite of myself. I've never thought of
myself particularly as Irish either and that becomes more evident as time
goes on. As I've mentioned in *O Albany!,* my buddy, Jerry Mahoney, is
skeptical about it (laughs), wonders about it—suspiciously. But I have no
problem with that because if you're not Irish, what else are you? You have to
acknowledge the roots where you came from.

Reilly: *The Ink Truck* was set in the '60s?

Kennedy: The '60s, yes. That newspaper strike was the embryo. The silli-
ness of the strike and the absence of achievement as a result of the strike, the
threats of the violence—they shaped the making of that book. It was ultimately not at all like the strike itself. But the parallel characters—including
Bailey, Stanley, or the gypsies—were fictional. There were no gypsies. I did
love the gypsies. I wrote about the gypsies in the '50s, the gypsy queen. I
covered them one day when they came here to convene to elect a new queen.
I wrote a piece that was very indelible to me, like my story on the Rescue
Mission and the bums, those worlds.

Reilly: Well, with the exception of *The Ink Truck,* do you think you'll ever
write about more modern times in Albany?

Kennedy: Yeah, I think that the new book will bring me into the '50s and
maybe the '60s. I'm not exactly sure where I'm going to start. I think it's the
late '50s. It's possible. You know, every time I try—I've tried—I've tried to
write about the '50s.

Reilly: *Ironweed* and *Billy Phelan* end on the same day, what, a two or
three day time frame? You could go anywhere from there and keep building
plots from there.

Kennedy: Well, the way that happened, *Billy Phelan,* when I was writing
that I wanted to set it in an election year because I wanted to have the governor, the candidate [Thomas E.] Dewey, attacking the Machine. I wanted to
establish the whole idea of how the Machine squelched the American Labor
Party. They actually didn't do that until the '40s, but I brought it back into
the '30s and also set it in a time of registration so it could be a reason for
Francis to come home—to get paid for voting. I mean one thing led to another, I guess, because I really wanted to write about politics. That was the

first notion, so, therefore, it wound up being in that period. I think I was fairly historically accurate in that it was the last two weeks in October. When I got that far, I carried it on through to the kidnapping which really took place in a totally different time of the year five years earlier. Billy's book was Halloween and All Saints' Day, and then bringing Francis in as sort of the finale of that was the thing that was ready-made. It was preconceived, so I had that to work with. It was All Saints' and All Souls' Day. There's definitely a religious thread in the books. It's a pattern because life does revolve around the Church in many ways for Catholic people. The Irish are notorious for it—the relationships to priests, nuns in the family, and all that sort of thing. Whether they practice it, whether they believe it or not, it's up to every individual to analyze after that. But there's no doubt that the prevalence of religion and things ecclesiastical are in people's lives, and that's what I keep referring to. It doesn't die. There's no question about it.

What was the second question after that? Oh, the three days from which I could go anywhere, backwards and forwards. Well, yeah, the original concept I had for the Albany cycle was that I would write a novel that would take the whole city of Albany from the patroons' time on up to contemporary times. Well, obviously, it's more than I can handle.

Reilly: What about the future, the films for *Legs* and *Billy Phelan*?

Kennedy: They're both very possible for film. I've just completed a third draft of the screenplay for *Legs*. This one done on my own. The first one I did back in late '84—late '83—'83 I wrote that. And also I wrote *Billy Phelan* about that same time, but I've learned so much since then. They never got off the ground, neither version. But now it seems probable that something will happen with both of the films, and I will write the screenplays for them, possibly even produce the films and in a certain way become a producer. That's a possibility.

The other thing is that I'm starting a new novel which has begun to have serious appeal to me. I started taking notes on it. When I was back in the concluding elements of *Quinn's Book,* I was making notes toward the next project. I've had a lot of interruptions between then and now, but I think by the middle of the summer I'll get back to it when the publicity elements for *Quinn's Book* are taken care of.

I may do a political film, a script for a political film with Costa Gavras, the man who did *Z, Missing, State of Siege*—a first-rate director and probably the most politically oriented director in the world, or one of them certainly. I have an on-going commitment to the Writers' Institute, which is very successful these days in its development in bringing in writers of all kinds to Albany. Now we have a film series developed that will bring in directors and screen writers.

I have two more, three more, novels somewhere in my head. The one that I'm working on has just emerged with subject matter somehow and demanded my attention. It's a potential sequel to *Quinn's*; it's a potential antecedent for *Billy Phelan's Greatest Game*—the Daugherty family, *The Flaming Corsage* novel. And so on. I'll be doing a little essay writing now, and I'm writing a piece for a speech I have to deliver at the New York Public Library in June. It'll be a literary essay on the history of my novel.

I'll be doing some travelling in Europe for the publication of the books over there. The books are now being published in eighteen or nineteen languages. In some countries, it's only *Ironweed*. In many of them, it's all three books. And now *Quinn* is in about five or six countries. England is bringing it out almost simultaneously. We'll be going there in June. We'll be going to Italy in May for *Ironweed,* and France right thereafter for *Legs* (laughs). Then in June going to England for *Quinn,* so I'll have a variety of projects to talk about. Then, of course, the movie is popping out in all those countries at about the same time.

There's always something going on that way. That's a lot, and I don't know which will get priority. It seems that circumstances decree that you give an intense month to a movie script or something. But it's always the principle of literature to which I come back, obviously to reestablish my equilibrium. That's what I'll be doing in the weeks ahead.

William Kennedy's Moveable Feast

Stephan Salisbury / 1988

Reprinted with permission from *The Philadelphia Inquirer* 31 July 1988: 36–38, 43.

Novelist William Kennedy fiddled with the microphone and cast his pale eyes over the big room. He looked pained. TV crews were there. Reporters. Students. Professors. He looked worried. It's one thing to conjure up words from the most private part of your self, set them to dancing in a story and then send the whole out to millions of unknown, unseen readers. It's quite another to put your sandy-haired, raspy-voiced, 5-foot-10-inch self in front of a few hundred people at a *public* lecture. This isn't fiction; this is performance or auctioneering or modeling.

Too late now.

He anxiously smoothed the lapel of his coat and began to speak—but not about deconstruction theory or semiotics or some such literary arcana. Kennedy began to talk about a distant afternoon when his father unwittingly inspired an unusual novel set in an amazing city known as Albany, N.Y.

"Twenty-three years ago, on March 21, 1965, I was in Albany talking on the phone with my father, who was then 77 years of age," Kennedy said, describing the precise moment of the birth of *Quinn's Book,* published this spring, his first novel since the Pulitzer Prize-winning *Ironweed* in 1983. "He was remembering Van Woert Street, the long Irish block with an old Dutch name where he had been raised; also he was remembering his friends the O'Connell brothers, who successfully entered Albany politics in 1921, took the city away from the Republicans, and never gave it back. And he was telling yet again some of his World War I stories that I knew almost by heart."

As Kennedy described this ancient, desultory conversation with his father, he did not look at the enthralled crowd in the sterile conference room on the campus of the State University of New York at Albany. Instead, he stood like a taut wood plank wrapped in tweed behind the podium, his mouth close to the microphone, the 21 pages of his carefully composed talk clutched tightly in his hands. His eyes never left the pages. He coughed. He adjusted his gold-rimmed specs. He fidgeted. He looked as though he were facing a firing squad.

O, agony!

Kennedy pushed gamely on, conjuring up his father and their long-ago conversation: "His memories and stories were randomly told with no perceptible logic as to sequence, yet they coalesced with such significance that I wrote down what I called 'Idea for an Albany Fantasy.' . . .

"The plot included such Albany characters as Philip Schuyler, the great Revolutionary War general; Martin H. Glynn, the Irish newspaper editor who became governor; Aaron Burr, Alexander Hamilton and Gen. John Burgoyne; Herman Melville and Henry James; a stunningly beautiful girl I knew extremely well, and, as I wrote further, 'other outstanding Albany figures, all of them somewhere together, all contemporaries, all eternally living out their same destinies over and over again as they are rediscovered by people like me.'

"Then I concluded: 'This is an exciting idea, suddenly arrived at during phone conversation with my father. It is his fate to live through those days over and over and over again. That's all there is in our past.' "

It was a vintage Kennedy literary performance—full of anecdote, memory, humor, diffidence, Albany, family, anxiety and fantasy, and when it was over and the audience rose to applaud, he emitted a barely audible thank-you, limped away from the podium on a gimpy leg, and breathed a sigh of relief.

Kennedy had survived the lecture hall and the formal public occasion; now he could get on with real business: a night on the town with pals.

Within 10 minutes, Kennedy, and wife, Dana, and daughter Kathy, one of three Kennedy children, were surrounded by friends in Kennedy's offices at the New York State Writers Institute, a program he founded at the university with seed money from a MacArthur Foundation "genius" grant. A small party erupted. Tom Smith, a professor of literature who has known Kennedy in good times and bad for close to 20 years, popped open a few bottles of red wine. Dana, a small-boned, raven-haired woman with a remarkable resemblance to the "stunningly beautiful girl" from the very first notes for *Quinn's Book,* opened her voluminous handbag, pushed aside a flashlight, some boxes and containers, and pulled out a beige mobile phone. "It's my toy," she said, laughing. "I'm never without it."

She began a series of calls, alerting Kennedy to the results of each one: Coppola visit to the institute definitely on; C-SPAN interview set for the

15th; party for Seamus Heaney, Irish poet, ready to go; another interview set
for 7 p.m.

Kennedy, jacket off, burgundy tie loosened, goblet of red wine in hand,
and easily looking two decades younger than his 60 years, took in all of
Dana's information without missing a beat in his conversation. He was talking about Donna Reed's performance in the 1954 movie *The Last Time I Saw
Paris.* "So bitchy," he complained. "I'll never forgive her for that." Toni
Morrison, a colleague at the university and winner of this year's Pulitzer
Prize for her novel *Beloved,* wandered in. Kennedy urged her to come to
dinner at Jimmy Rua's Cafe Capriccio. She demurred. "OK, you dirty rat,"
he snarled, in a poor Scarface imitation. "But if you're on the town, come
over and hang out." Poet Judith Johnson dropped by, wine in hand, and
announced that she had been up for 40 hours straight. Kennedy looked intrigued by the thought.

Vinnie Reda, writer, former student and good friend, sadly said he had to
leave.

"Why?" asked Kennedy, taken aback.

"We're out of wine," said Reda.

"Ha!" said Kennedy. "Look in the cabinets."

Reda opened a cabinet door onto a virtual wine cellar.

"It just so happens," laughed Kennedy.

Dana rushed over. Phone interview. Kennedy disappeared for a few minutes. More people. More phone calls.

As the chaos increased, Kennedy began to unwind.

"It's like this all the time," he said. "My house is far worse than this."

"Bill Kennedy's moveable feast," Tom Smith called it later. "It's a circus,
and that circus is a mobile circus that goes on all the time."

"Hey," Kennedy said, jumping up for the umpteenth time, straightening
his burgundy tie and buttoning his brown-and-white tweed jacket, "let's get
going."

Back in 1965, when Bill Kennedy was having that long, seminal conversation with his father, there was nothing in his life that foreshadowed the great
acclaim that lay down the road. Raised in Albany's Irish North End, the only
child of older parents, Kennedy stayed in town and attended Siena College.
He worked on the Albany Times-Union for a few years in the mid-1950s and
then decided Albany was not the place to be. He took a job on an English-
language paper in San Juan, Puerto Rico. It was there, on Dec. 27, 1956, that

he met Dana Sosa, a beautiful ballet dancer and actress, fell in love instantly, and on Jan. 31, 1957, they were married.

The next few years saw quite a bit of moving around. They moved to Miami, where Kennedy covered Cuba and the Caribbean for the *Miami Herald*. They moved back to Puerto Rico, where Kennedy helped found the *San Juan Star*, another English-language daily. And finally, as he became more and more obsessed with his own past, the past of his family, the past of his home town and the idea of writing fiction, they moved back to Albany, where he worked for the *Times-Union* and tried to write novels.

None was any good, but that didn't really matter. This was an apprentice stage. Kennedy would write constantly, and after the writing was over, he would surround himself with people. It's exactly the way he is now.

Tom Wilkinson, assistant managing editor of the *Washington Post,* was a reporter at the *Times-Union* when Kennedy was there in the 1960s. He remembers "this amazing collection of people" who were always popping in and out of the Kennedys' rambling white farmhouse in Averill Park, a few miles east of Albany, where they still live. "He was kind of struggling with novels back then. I mean, he was working at the newspaper so he could eat, although he really loved journalism. And he would write all the time. He was a guy who was in love with writing."

By the mid-1960s, Kennedy had made the commitment to fiction and was working only part time at the *Times-Union*. Dana was running her own ballet school in town. Somehow they made ends meet. "I quit newspapers at a moment when I was on a sort of escalator in journalism, moving toward what I had dreamed of all my life, which was to be some kind of daily columnist," Kennedy said, after settling in at Cafe Capriccio with his friends. "I was going to become Damon Runyon or somebody, I don't know, just go in there and write about anything or cover anything or anybody I wanted. But it's a very limited field in terms of the kind of language you can use, the kind of insight you can bare, and the kind of subject matter you can cover. I was far more interested in what was going on inside people. So I quit."

His first novel, *The Ink Truck* a fantastic tale of a heroically deranged columnist in the final days of a disastrous newspaper strike, was published in 1969. The novel received good reviews, sold a few thousand copies and went out of print. His second novel, *Legs,* based on the legendary gangster Jack "Legs" Diamond, who charmed and blasted his way through Albany and the Catskills in the early 1930s, was published in 1975. It received good reviews, sold a few thousand copies and went out of print. His third novel, *Bill Phelan's Greatest Game,* based on the actual kidnapping of Democratic party boss Dan O'Connell's nephew in the 1930s, received good reviews when it came out in 1978, sold a few thousand copies and went out of print.

Then came *Ironweed.* Set in Albany in 1938, a week after the action in *Billy Phelan, Ironweed* focuses on the lives of, well, a couple of down-and-out bums. Bums in Albany hardly seemed the stuff for publishing success, let alone literary superstardom. Kennedy's editor at Viking suggested that another house might do a better job by the book. But when Kennedy peddled the manuscript, more than a dozen publishing houses flat-out rejected it. By 1981, Kennedy was in utter despair. Then out of the blue, an angel descended in the unlikely guise of Saul Bellow.

Kennedy had studied writing with the Nobel Prize-winner in Puerto Rico in the early 1960s. Bellow had been taken by the energy and authenticity of Kennedy's earlier work, and he was impressed by the quality of the novels that followed. After learning about the difficulties with *Ironweed,* Bellow wrote a now-legendary letter to Viking, Kennedy's publishers. "That the author of *Billy Phelan* should have a manuscript kicking around looking for a publisher," Bellow declared, "is disgraceful."

Suitably shamed, and armed with a Bellow quote about "these Albany novels," Viking agreed to publish *Ironweed* and make it an event by reissuing *Legs* and *Billy Phelan* and dubbing the whole "the Albany Cycle."

In 1983, when Kennedy had just turned 55, these books hit the racks and created a publishing bombshell. *Ironweed* was hailed as a masterpiece. Kennedy won the Pulitzer Prize. He won the National Book Critics Circle award. He won a MacArthur award. He signed on to write movies—*Cotton Club, Legs, Billy* and *Ironweed.* Albany was in. Bums were in. Go figure.

The books were "well-published," as Kennedy says, but their success stemmed from something more. They struck a chord, perhaps, an anti-glitzy, anti-hip sense of a real American place of dirt and concrete. Like Sherwood Anderson with small-town Ohio or James Farrell with Chicago, Kennedy defined an entire place in his fiction. It is impossible to visit Albany now without taking Bill Kennedy's vision into account. It is impossible to look at the renovated Kenmore Hotel without thinking of Kennedy's Jack Diamond and his antics in the old Rain-bo-Room; it is impossible to look at the renovated Union Station and not think of the disastrous confrontation of strikers, descried in *Ironweed,* that took place in the street outside. "He knows Albany better than Albany knows Albany," says Howard Simons, director of the

Neiman Foundation at Harvard University, an Albany native and Kennedy friend. "He sees it in lights that are amazing."

Creating that fictional Albany, however, was done at great emotional and financial cost. There were some truly "dismal times," as Tom Smith said. Only a rock-bottom faith in the value of his work got Kennedy through.

"He has always had enormous faith in what he was doing and that it was good," said novelist and critic Doris Grumbach, one of Kennedy's oldest friends. "I remember his bringing the manuscript of *Ironweed* to me when I was at Yaddo one summer, and I read it and I thought it was what I think it is now, a small masterpiece, a large masterpiece. I made one suggestion which, without thinking for a moment, he turned down. It turned out he was right not to accept this suggestion. But the rapidity with which he did made me see how sure he was of himself."

Kennedy leaned back at his long table at Cafe Capriccio, a somewhat up-scale Italian restaurant in what used to be an old South End bakery on Grand Street. This is Kennedy's principal hangout these days, a pleasant place with blond wood, operatic arias in the background, French posters on the walls, and rabbit with sun-dried tomatoes on the menu.

The gathering was small by Kennedy standards—Vinnie Reda, Larry and Madeleine Ries, Joe and Vera Gagen, all very old friends, and a visiting reporter. No one broke out in a chorus of "My Gal Sal" or "The Curse of an Aching Heart," as they have been known to do in the past. But as the evening progressed, various pals, friends and a stranger or two stopped by.

Conversation swung wildly between the effects of cholesterol, Frank Sinatra's performances in two assassination movies, *The Manchurian Candidate* and *Suddenly,* and serious literary topics like the poetry of Joseph Brodsky and Seamus Heaney. Kennedy listened and watched and joined in. Clearly this was his kind of scene—comfortable, intelligent and funny talk, no podium anywhere to be seen.

"One reason that Bill stays so close to Averill Park and to Albany, I think, is that he has made those places his personal circle," said Grumbach. "He doesn't have to go anywhere else. He goes, he travels, but when he comes back, the city is his. It's rare for a writer to have a thing like that."

Late in the evening, Jimmy Rua, chef and owner, came out from the kitchen and began talking about his efforts to acquire the nearby Palace Theater, a grand deco movie house, and several adjacent buildings on North Pearl Street. Rua wanted to renovate and convert the buildings into a restaurant and nightclub complex.

Kennedy went after the idea like a terrier. The music in this once-and-future bistro would be diverse, he said—Frank Sinatra, a pinch of Duke Ellington, rag-time, honky-tonk. But what should the name of the restaurant be? Jimmy liked Palace Cafe. Kennedy was vigorously un-impressed.

"I guarantee it'll go right down the drain," he said, shaking his head. "People'll think it's a diner."

He pondered the name for a long time ("Jimmy knows food; he needs somebody who knows language") before letting it go for the next day and night.

As Jimmy left the table, Kennedy took him by the arm.

"Anything that will help bring it back to the way it was, I'll do anything I can," he said. "I'm all for that."

Bill Kennedy has literally made and remade Albany. He fought to make his fiction from this unlikely place, and he succeeded. He fought to save the Kenmore Hotel and Union Station from the wrecker's ball and succeeded at that. He bought the infamous Dove Street boarding house where Legs Diamond was shot to death, so he saved that, too.

He has given a whole city a new sense of itself, and he has done it without changing his life and his basic attitudes an inch. "God knows, I'm very, very fond of that great line from Nabokov that it's a short walk from the hallelujah to the hoot," Kennedy said some time after midnight. "I believe that with a passion, because I've seen that happen to so many people.

"The basic thing is that I wrote the books. I wrote *Quinn* in the face of all the hoopla of *Ironweed,* and I did the best I could to be different, to not repeat myself, to say something that was worth saying and to not be intimidated by the possibility of failure, because I never have been and I don't know as I ever will be."

He paused, fiddled with the salt shaker, smoothed the already-smoothed tablecloth.

"What else can you do in life except face up to alternatives?" he continued. "If you're going to write, if you're going to do anything, you've got to put yourself on the line. And they're going to try and hit you with sledgehammers and they're going to throw palm fronds and roses at you. But whatever it is, you've still got to get up in the morning and go back to work and do what it is you're supposed to do, which is write the next book. That's all I have to say."

Up Front: Upstate Eloquence

Jim Reilly / 1988

Published in *Syracuse Herald American Stars* Magazine 9 October
1988: 3–6. Reprinted by permission.

The party was spinning fast and picking up speed, and William Kennedy was
at the hub of it. It was early 1984, and his book *Ironweed* had proven the
publishers wrong, becoming the darling of critics and readers alike, selling
by the truckful and winning the big prizes, including a Pulitzer. Kennedy
himself had been dubbed a genius, handed a pile of money and laurels and,
in less than a year, gone from obscurity to celebrity.

"It was very unreal," Kennedy remembers, "but it was very sweet."

So here he was being feted by the New York literati and glitterati, welcomed into the literary pantheon and courted like a deb with a golden pedi-
gree: Francis Coppola would like to chat, Bill, and could you do a screenplay
for so-and-so, and how about some time for "60 Minutes"?

In the midst of this most effervescent of a writer's champagne dreams,
Kennedy, a man known for creating or outlasting parties, not leaving them,
pulled the plug, shut off the taps and went home.

Home to Albany, the place that has been muse and matrix for all his books,
from *The Ink Truck* to *Ironweed* to his latest novel, *Quinn's Book,* which
earned qualified praise from most reviewers and made a cameo appearance
on the *New York Times* best-seller list.

Home to the people who'd been there for him when things weren't so
sweet, when a victory at the typewriter was often as not followed by boredom
in the publisher's boardroom, and scant sales in the bookstores.

Home because Bill Kennedy is nothing if not loyal; nothing if not generous, and this cataclysm of good fortune, this flood of good tidings, was something to be shared with people who cared.

So Kennedy gathered kith and kin and headed up the Hudson to continue
the party in his native city, "a magical place where the past becomes visible
if one is willing to track the multiple incarnations of the city's soul."

Kennedy has been tracking those incarnations almost since he began writing fiction in the 1960s, and the city—the place, its people and its past—has

150

repaid faithful scrutiny and the investment of time and talent with a material as rich, malleable and filled with archetypes as Joyce's Dublin or Faulkner's Yoknapatawpha County:

> Billy Phelan, a hustler with a tightrope walker's lust for the edge, a place, a game, a state of mind where you win or lose it all, never mind which—it's the danger that thrills. Billy's heart beats to the rhythm of the streets, but he'll risk banishment from those streets—life itself—rather than rat on a foe to a friend. Billy won't be compromised.
>
> Francis Phelan, ex-ballplayer, stew bum, reluctant killer, defender of the incomplete and incoherent, a man haunted by the past and forsaken by the future, who asks little of the present, except for a jug, a flop and redemption.
>
> Daniel Quinn, cholera orphan, accidental hero, seer of visions and wide-eyed witness to history's magic, mystery and misery, buffeted by people and events, a curious child whose growth into manhood and wisdom cannot quench his passion, which lights the way to romance fulfilled.

Kennedy fled and reclaimed Albany several times before settling for good 25 years ago in a rambling 1840s farmhouse in nearby Averill Park. He paid tribute to the city in *O Albany! An Urban Tapestry,* a substantially rewritten and expanded collection of newspaper articles about Albany neighborhoods he wrote for the *Times-Union* in the '60s. In the book, he calls Albany a place "as various as the American psyche itself," where he found "all the elements that a man ever needs for the life of the soul."

Ironically, Kennedy wrote his first Albany novel in Puerto Rico, where he'd gone to work as a journalist and to escape his provincial hometown.

"It wasn't a good novel; it wasn't a bad novel. It was a near miss," Kennedy said in a series of interviews in and around Albany. "That was when I realized I had to come back to Albany to understand Albany. Because that novel was strong; all the rest of the stuff I'd written was very weak."

That novel, "The Angels and the Sparrows," was the second of Kennedy's two early, unpublished novels. It was strong for the same reason all of his books since have been strong: He was writing about what he knew.

"I knew these people, I knew them intimately," Kennedy said. "I knew the whole society, I knew the fabric. I had the matrix. I had the matrix. And it was in Albany."

Twenty years later, he dedicated *O Albany!* to "people who used to think they hated the place where they grew up, and then took a second look."

The act of returning—to places, to people, to books half done, to times remembered or reconstructed—has been a consistent theme in Kennedy's life.

The past, in particular Albany's and his own, has been the well from which he has drawn inspiration for his writing. All of his novels have been set in the past. The non-fiction *O Albany!* reached back into the past of the city's neighborhoods to bring them alive for present-day readers.

Why this fascination with yesterdays?

"I think my imagination is engaged by things that are finished, that I know how they come out," Kennedy said. "I may be wrong on that. That's a facile answer; it's facile to me. But I know it's also a true answer.

"I can look back and see that the trajectory of history is this. And then I can go back and work out an odyssey within that trajectory of history. What I seem to need is a matrix of time which is completed. I can then project all sorts of possibilities within that framework."

Three of Kennedy's best-known works, *Ironweed* and the earlier *Legs* and *Billy Phelan's Greatest Game,* which Viking cleverly reissued as "the Albany cycle" when it published *Ironweed* in 1983, are set in the 1930s. Kennedy was born in 1928; he'll be 61 in January. Still, he says the people, events and images of the '30s remain alive for him today, in memory.

"I didn't have to create the '30s; I remember the '30s. I remember Billy Phelan's world very well, because it continued to exist into the '40s. Nothing changed in Albany. And when you're 10, you can remember," he said.

What Kennedy didn't remember, his father or his mother or her brother, Pete McDonald, usually did. Uncle Pete was a particularly strong influence on Kennedy; he was the real-life template for the fictional Billy Phelan.

"He was very accomplished at what he did . . . which was playing pool, bowling, being a sport. And being a buddy of mine," Kennedy said of his uncle. "He was just like a second father to me, but a father in a totally different way; a way that fathers are not supposed to be. He was no paradigm of righteousness, no exemplar for behavior. But he was one of the great wits. He was very hip, very intuitive, and he read all the time. He didn't read any good stuff, but he read all the time.

"There's a lot of Irishmen like him. There's a lot of thickheaded Irishmen, too. But Pete was one of those who had the intuition for writing. He had this capacity for telling a great story, he knew a great punch line. He had a great sense of humor. He had a sense of drama. He had it all.

"My mother had that, too.

"My Aunt Katherine, she's another story. She was one of the most wonderful people in the world, and I loved her like a second mother. But she couldn't tell a story worth a damn. She couldn't remember things, she'd forget, and she'd overlap it and tell it four times. But my mother and my uncle were both great storytellers."

In *Quinn's Book,* Kennedy has gone back to an Albany and a time not even his oldest uncles or aunts would have remembered. Here, he made a 90-year leap backward from the 1938 of *Ironweed* and *Billy Phelan* to an Albany at the midpoint of the 19th century, an era of canal boats, horses, floods, cholera and runaway slaves, to tell a wild, funny, occasionally surreal tale of an ecstatic and difficult romance. It is a wonderful story told by a masterful storyteller.

When he first thought about writing the book that eventually became *Quinn's Book,* 20 or 25 years ago, Kennedy said he imagined tracing the history of Albany from the time of the first Patroon, Holland's local governor when the area was Dutch-ruled in the 1600s, to the present. He realized it was too grand a vision to be realized in a single book.

"But that's exactly what I think the cycle will be, if I keep going long enough," he said. "And there's a great Revolutionary War story here somewhere, I feel, that's just undiscovered by me, waiting to be told. If I could just reconstitute that period for myself. . . ."

His hands clasp before him, and his eyes seem to be trying to penetrate the curtain of years time has drawn between him and his material, the raw data of the past, the minds, deeds and souls of the people who lived it.

Kennedy has always been a glutton for information, for history, for news, the stuff of which events and eras are made. When he was writing *Legs,* the 1975 novel about the notorious Prohibition-era gangster that brought him his first taste of national attention, he spent two years in the library, poring over old newspapers and reading books. "Legs" took him six years to write.

"There's something magical about going through old newspapers that books don't give you," he said. "Just the raw data, and the way it's written, is very magical."

He drew on his own memories and those of his father, friends and other relatives, as well as what he'd gathered during his *Legs* research, to write *Billy Phelan's Greatest Game* and *Ironweed.*

Ironweed took him less than a year to write; *Quinn* was another long-term project: The gestation took five years, the writing another five.

At first, *Quinn's Book* was not going to be confined to a single time. Kennedy said he thought about telling parallel tales, jumping between the 19th and the 20th century. But his imagination kept getting stuck in the 1800s.

"When I began to go back into the 19th century, that was when the story"—he snaps his fingers with a pop—"came to life for me. And I just got caught, ZAP! And all the stuff that was happening in the 20th century, paled."

He'd written 150, 200 pages. He put it aside and started over.

Once again, the past had caught this child of the '30s in its multifarious web.

A novel-in-progress, which Kennedy is writing upstairs in his Averill Park study and in his 67 Dove St. office in downtown Albany, is also set in an Albany past, but it comes closer to the present than any of his books so far.

"It's a Phelan novel," Kennedy said. "It's like Billy Phelan 20 years later, but it's not just Billy. It's a whole clatch of the family and a lot of new characters nobody's ever heard of. It's set in the late '50s or early '60s."

Kennedy said the book's structure—"the way the story will be told"—is different from anything he's done before in his novels, but he was reluctant to be more specific. "It's still too embryonic to talk about."

He does have a good idea of the time frame of the novel.

"It's not a sprawling book the way 'Quinn' was, in terms of time—it's far more concise," he said. "I suppose it will be a little closer in terms of time to *Ironweed,* which took place over three days. This one takes place over even less time, but it will reach back into the past, too. . . . ."

Will he ever set his books in the present?

"I may make it into the '60s by the 1990s," he says, laughing.

Kennedy's work is notable for its potent, beautiful language, and for its vivid sense of time and place. The city of Albany has provided people, neighborhoods, a landscape for Kennedy's evocation of a specific place. Its history has provided a context for a specific time.

Details bring a time and a place to life in the imagination, and Kennedy's books are dense with detail, rich with description. His dialogue sounds right; people talk this way. His prose, occasionally blunt for impact but mostly finely turned, gives his stories rhythm and melody. The clarity of his images makes a place take shape in the mind; his language makes the stories sing.

Kennedy's stories ebb and flow around passages where time, place, language and an idea or insight come together seamlessly, solidly.

The books are their own most eloquent witnesses to this. From *Ironweed: The jungle was maybe seven years old, three years old, a month old, days*

*old. It was an ashpit, a graveyard, and a fugitive city. It stood among wild
sumac bushes and river foliage, all fallen dead now from the early frost. It
was a haphazard upthrust of tarpaper shacks, lean-tos, and impromptu con-
structions describable by no known nomenclature. It was a city of essential
transiency and would-be permanency, a resort of those for whom motion was
either anathema or pointless or impossible. Cripples lived here, and natives
of this town who had lost their homes, and people who had come here at
journey's end to accept whatever disaster was going to happen next. The
jungle, a visual manifestation of the malaise of the age and the nation, covered the equivalent of two or more square city blocks between the tracks and
the river, just east of the old carbarns and the empty building that once
housed Iron Joe's saloon.*

And, from *Quinn's Book:*

*They are the famine Irish, Maud, and they are villains in this city. It wasn't
this way for the Irish when I was little, but now they are viewed not only as
carriers of the cholera plague but as a plague themselves, such is their number: several thousand setting up life here in only a few years, living in hovels,
in shanties, ten families to a small house, some unable to speak anything but
the Irish tongue, their wretchedness so fierce and relentless that not only
does the city shun them but the constabulary and the posses meet them at the
docks and on the turnpikes to herd them together in encampments on the
city's great western plain. Keep them moving is the edict of the city's leaders,
and with obscene pleasure the Albany wharf rats and river scum (some Irish
among those preying on their own) carry out this edict by stoning the canal-
boats that try to unload newcomers here. It is no wonder the greenhorns
grow feral in response, finding in this new land, a hatred as great as that
which drove them out of Ireland, that suppurating, dying sow of a nation.*

Some people have been bothered by the ghosts Kennedy occasionally con-
jures in his fiction: Jack Diamond's spirit hangs around to remark on his
bullet-sped death at the end of *Legs;* in *Ironweed,* the dead ponder Francis
Phelan as he walks through the graveyard, and ghosts of his victims haunt
his ramble through familiar Albany streets and rediscovery of painful memories.

Kennedy, who's never encountered a ghost in the shroud, doesn't deny
them their place in his imagination.

"I guess I trace it back to somewhere in the '50s, early '60s, when I began
to write, when I was dealing with dead people," Kennedy says, grabbing his

chin and thrusting himself back in an old, beautifully refinished armchair at 67 Dove St.

"I mean, my antique uncles, aunts, grandparents," he says, recalling his ghosts. "Some of whom I knew, some of whom I didn't, but whose ghosts had pervaded my life. Not really as ghosts, but in the sense that I couldn't forget them. These uncles that I can remember who gave me fire engines and steam engines, which I still have, in the attic. Memories of the generosity of those old people, or the curiosity, the peculiarities—my one uncle telling me that you should never drink anything colder than water that comes out of the tap; that's how he lived to be 80. Or my other uncle saying you should eat a lot of oil, because it was healthy: 'Did you ever see a sick Italian?'

"Things like that these impossible statements about life, that I just never forgot. I can see all those people the same way now . . .

"These ghosts just walk around in my brain, these indelible memories of these people. I don't know why they're there, why they haven't been forgotten, but they haven't, any more than the people I remember from the Army. My memory just retains a great deal. That's what a writer is, really."

His downtown office, once a rooming house, is a place not unfamiliar with ghosts of the past itself: Jack "Legs" Diamond, the Prohibition-era gangster and central figure in Kennedy's second novel, was shot to death in a rented room here early on the morning of Dec. 18, 1931. There are no bullet holes in the walls, contrary to popular myth; the interior is immaculate.

Kennedy bought the place with a movie producer friend a few years ago, figuring it would make a great office and a nice location for the final scene if "Legs" ever made it to the screen. He's got a third screenplay partly done; the first was "strictly amateur night"; the second, which he wrote with director Francis Ford Coppola in four days, "read like it had been written in four days," Kennedy says. Right now, there's a "problem" with the rights to *Legs* that Kennedy doesn't want to talk about. But people are working on it. "There's a lot of interest," he said, "but right now, it remains on the shelf."

Instead, he'll be working on an unfinished screenplay for *Billy Phelan's Greatest Game.* "It may be the next film project," he says, "but in this business, you never know."

For a writer who draws endlessly on the past to feed his present (he is a big fan of old jazz, old Sinatra, and old ideas like class and style), Kennedy is one guy who hates to dwell on old news, at least when it comes to himself.

"So what are we gonna talk about that makes sense, that's new?" he wanted to know, 10 minutes into a two-hour interview. He poured a bourbon for a visitor, a Beaujolais for himself. "I'm tired of talking about myself."

He's tired of telling how many publishers rejected *Ironweed* before it was published (13); about how he didn't believe it when, a couple days later, the MacArthur Foundation called to give him $56,000 a year for five years, tax-free, for being a genius; about how Gov. Mario Cuomo stayed up all night reading *Ironweed* and sent him a fan letter that got in the newspaper before it got to him; what it was like working with Coppola on *Cotton Club* (Kennedy wrote the screenplay with Coppola), or Streep and Nicholson on *Ironweed*.

He'd rather talk about "What's going on with you?" if he knows you, or other writers like Richard Ford or Milan Kundera or Gabriel García Márquez or music or sports or ideas or life or love or just about anything but himself.

Still, there are a few stories too good not to be told.

One is how he came to marry the beautiful and talented Dana, love of his life, mother of his three children, creator of feasts, and the calm, efficient, affirming presence that keeps WJK Enterprises (Kennedy's incorporated self) orbiting smoothly and productively (with help from daughters Dana and Kathy) around Kennedy's creativity. Here's the story:

Once upon a time in Puerto Rico, a handsome young journalist was struck by the beauty of a ravishing young Broadway dancer with raven hair, a flashing smile, Puerto Rican roots and a New York accent, a woman vivacious enough to embody the beauty, warmth and sensuality of Puerto Rico on the cover of Look *Magazine, which she did in 1961. Smitten, he asked for a date. Equally smitten, she agreed. Two dates later, ever more smitten, he proposed marriage. Smitten as passionately, she accepted. Whereupon, she flew off to dance in New York City. Two weeks later, she flew back. A week later, they were married. Elapsed time from "How do you do?" to "I do": 31 days. Happy ending: They celebrated their 30th anniversary this year, still in love. Moral: Seize the day. He who doesn't hesitate, finds love.*

Kennedy may not like to talk about himself, but his friends do. They talk about his generosity, his loyalty, his commitment to family, friends, and art.

Vinnie Reda, for instance, who's known Kennedy since he took Kennedy's writing course at the State University of New York at Albany in 1973. "He was always totally free with his time, and in giving you responses to your work," Reda said. "And he was always generous in never giving up on you if he believed in you.

"Bill has a generosity that extends not only to everybody else, but to his own spirit," Reda continued. "It incorporates everything. I think the phrase that to me characterizes him best is, 'Are you aware of . . . ' He always had to be aware of everything, whether it was politics, or what was happening in music. If there was a song from 1935 you knew that he hadn't heard of, he'd say, 'Get me the lyrics to that.' He'd whip this little notebook out if somebody said something he hadn't heard before, in a *way* he hadn't heard before; if it was a line that was funny, a turn of a phrase, he'd write it down, because he wanted to never not *know*."

Tom Smith, who has known Kennedy for more than 20 years, says this: "The Kennedys always took in people. There was always another bed, and someone who was having a nervous breakdown or was in a bad situation, who just seemed to get absorbed into that household." Smith teaches literature at SUNY-Albany and, with Kennedy, runs the New York State Writers Institute there, which Kennedy helped found. "Bill's helped a lot of people, in a lot of ways."

Among the people who have known Kennedy for a long time, and there are many in and around Albany, a mythology has grown. Everybody has a favorite Bill Kennedy anecdote, a story—several, many—that uncovers another stone in the foundation of his character. Jim Clark and Susan Dumbleton, the latter a friend whose Washington Park Press co-published *O Albany!* with Viking, tell this story:

In the lean years, the years before Ironweed *and the MacArthur and Pulitzer, before honors and screenplays and international film fests and all the rest, money was tight around the Kennedy house. Dana gave dance lessons and ran her own clothes shop. There were parties, feasts and good times, but the wine was cheap. Everybody drove used cars.*

Kennedy bought his cars from Clark, a burly, middle-aged Irishman with blue eyes and silver-white hair, who sells Chryslers and Plymouths for Armory Garage on Central Avenue, a commercial drag that was an eyesore and a money-maker long before Wolf Road's mile became Albany's retail miracle.

One time, Clark and a banker friend helped swing a small loan for Kennedy. No big deal, Clark says, lighting a cigarette a few feet from the lot where he makes his living. "It was tough getting Billy financing in those days."

But Bill Kennedy is not one to forget a friend. Or a kindness, small or large.

So when Kennedy hit it big a few years back, he didn't go out and buy a
Mercedes. He went to see Jim Clark.
"He walked in and he said, 'I'll take one of those and one of those,' "
Dumbleton says.
And Clark got a nice commission off the brand-new Chrysler New Yorker
Bill Kennedy bought for himself, and the Town and Country wagon he bought
for Dana, and the little Turismo he bought for his second-oldest daughter,
Kathy.

Many things have changed since "the world turned inside out" for the
Kennedy's five years ago. For one thing, there's a new pool in the back of
the house in Averill Park, new furniture inside, and no phone in William
Kennedy's study. There's a new well and plenty of water, so there are no
longer periodic bans on flushing during parties. And Kennedy has stopped
worrying about how to pay the bills, and started worrying about finding time
to write and enjoy life between the book signings in London, Paris, New York
and Boston . . . the movie deals . . . the speaking engagements . . . the social
commitments . . . the good causes. He's had to learn to say no to some things
and some people, which is something he never was very good at.

"He has to now, or the world would eat him alive," Tom Smith said.

Kennedy never answers the phone at home anymore, and his family pulls
together—screening calls, mapping out schedules, handling details—to draw
a protective but not impenetrable cordon around him. They can't insulate him
entirely; he'd die of boredom and loneliness in a cloister. But he needs still-
ness and time to work. The irony of the famous writer is that the very thing
which has made him wanted by so many—his writing—is essentially an anti-
social activity, something done in silence and solitude.

This year has been especially disruptive, with promotional tours for *Quinn*
here and abroad, as well as trips to Europe to promote the publication of
foreign editions of *Ironweed* (Italy), *Legs* (France) and the release of *Ironweed*, the movie.

"It's been a year of constant interruptions of the work," Kennedy said,
"and for a lot of good reasons—to help my own books along, for one." He
recently had to turn down the chance to do a "major magazine piece" on
Ellis Island—"I've written a lot about immigration; it's right up my alley"—
because he couldn't afford the time away from other commitments, including
his new novel.

"I can conceive of myself just getting into a hibernating position," Kennedy says, more lamenting than complaining.

"I mean, I function as a writer. It's nice to have; we've got friends in a lot of places now, and we could have a good time wherever we go. But it's debilitating, psychologically and physically. If I don't work, something happens. And I can't go on making excuses for myself. Sooner or later, I've just gotta shut it down and that's it."

Still, there are some things and some people you can't say no to.

This past June, Kennedy gave the commencement address at The Doane Stuart School in Albany. His son, Brendan, was graduating.

Brendan, now an English major at Trinity College in Connecticut, is the only one of the Kennedy kids who has shown a literary inclination to date (daughters Kathy and Dana, who has two children of her own, had production jobs on the film *Ironweed,* much of which was shot in and around Albany).

Brendan and his father co-authored a children's book, *Charlie Malarkey and the Belly Button Machine,* when Brendan was "just a kid." It grew out of bedtime stories Brendan loved.

They collaborated more recently on a sequel, not yet published.

For the past five years, Bill and Dana Kennedy have been living a life most people only dream about or read about in magazines.

And they love it.

"They are indefatigable. They cannot get enough of it," Dumbleton said. "The life and the people and the places and the events, the glamour, the opportunities—every one of them, they grab. They are tireless. They are beyond exhausting."

"I have not abdicated good times," Kennedy says, smiling broadly.

But those good times are not had only among the famous. Back home in Albany, among family and friends, some things really haven't changed.

"Both Dana and Bill are at home in the spotlight. But they can turn it off, too," Dumbleton said.

She thinks one reason Kennedy has handled success so gracefully is because it came to him late in life, when he was in his mid-50s.

"He still knows everybody he knew," Jim Clark said, "he didn't forget anybody."

At home in Averill Park, the kitchen is warm and noisy. Dana brushes a long strand of dark hair from her face and stirs the thick red sauce bubbling in a pot on the stove.

She covers the sauce, turns it to simmer, and sits in the living room beneath a framed picture of herself, in a bathing suit in the blue waters off Puerto Rico, on the cover of *Look* magazine.

She talks about her 30 years with Bill Kennedy, her years before on Broadway, when she replaced Shirley MacLain in "Me and Juliet," danced and sang in "Pajama Game" and "New Faces of '56." She left it all, never felt bitter, and glories in her husband's success.

"Wretched excess," she says with a smile, "I was ready for it."

Several hours later, Bill comes down.

He's written five pages on the *Legs* screenplay. "That's good; you should be happy with that," Dana says.

"Yeah. It's all right," he says. He pours wine all around. It's time to eat.

Later, after the feast and the cognac and talk about writing, after Brendan has gone off to study and Dana and the grandchildren have gone off to bed, Bill Kennedy puts his feet up on a wicker chair in front of the television to watch a PBS program about William Carlos Williams, the doctor who became a well-known American poet and writer.

He takes a spiral notebook and a pen from his shirt pocket. The notebook rests on his knee.

His fingers tap. He frowns, listening. He's waiting for the news, the idea, the thing he doesn't know.

He won't let it get away.

William Kennedy: The Singularity of Fiction

Melissa Biggs / 1988

Published in *The Yale Vernacular: An Undergraduate Publication* 4.2 (January/February 1989): 4–7, 21.

William Kennedy, who was born and raised in Albany, New York, divides his time between an old farmhouse in the hills east of Albany and the brownstone rooming house in Albany where "Legs" Diamond was shot. The always flamboyant, often endangered, mythical characters of his novels, *The Ink Truck, Legs, Billy Phelan's Greatest Game, Ironweed,* and *Quinn's Book* also inhabit Kennedy's wondrous world of Albany. Having written about both fictional and historical Albanians in his books, Kennedy himself has become a legend in his hometown.

M.B.: I've read that your idea of novels working as cycles extends beyond the Albany cycle of *Legs, Billy Phelan's Greatest Game,* and *Ironweed.* Could you explain your idea of a literary cycle?

W.K.: Well, the word cycle was my choice because I knew I wasn't heading toward a trilogy or a quartet or a quintet. I didn't know what I was heading toward, but I was working on the assumption that this was a group of novels, number unspecified, that would be related. It was my idea to do that fairly early on. I wrote two novels that were never published and at the time of the second novel I was thinking seriously about this concept of interrelated stories. Back even to the sixties, my notes all point to that idea of developing cycles. It didn't quite work that way. The first novel I published seemed like a separate work. It had its own dynamics. But thereafter when I wrote *Legs,* I could see that there were connections both backwards and forwards with other local characters. *Legs* was the first novel in which I really used Albany by name and also used genuine historical figures like Diamond himself and his lawyer, who was actually a composite of several lawyers and other historical characters, and real street names and place names, because I was dealing with serious history. I mean I was dealing seriously with actual history that was very well known.

Out of that book came the people of *Billy Phelan.* At that point, I understood the political dynamics of the city, fairly well. I'd been writing about it for some years as a journalist, and then I began to think about it in a different way and I decided to write a political novel. I took some of the characters out of *Legs* and I moved it forward in time. In *Billy Phelan's Greatest Game,* which was that political book, I created Francis Phelan. I had created him back in the earlier unpublished novels. I had created the whole Phelan family. Now I just took him out of that earlier novel and *Billy Phelan's Greatest Game* and put him into a totally new shape and form with new attributes in *Ironweed.*

And so I had three books that were somehow connected. *Quinn* turned out to be a kind of ancestral book, which was the look backward in time toward the origin of the things that I had been writing about. So that was my rationale and remains so today. I'm working on a book now that takes place in 1958 and you'll recognize some of the people.

M.B.: You once wrote that writers are empowered by the spirit of their age. As you set your novels in earlier eras, how do you see the spirit of this age working in your books?

W.K.: In writing that, I was talking about the way writers work and think. Writers are not scholars, sometimes they are, but generally they are not, even when they are scholarly. If they are great fiction writers, a writer like Saul Bellow or such a scholar of the world as Henry James, you don't look to them for scholarship. You look to them for the power of real characters portrayed on the page fully fleshed in their minds and in their bodies and in their spirits and so on. And these people who become writers are somehow imbued unconsciously with what's going on in their age, in their own particular times or in the history that precedes them.

You think of a writer like Faulkner, whom we now think of as personifying the South, portraying the enslavers and the plantation aristocracy and the kind of white trash figures who rise in the world as personified in the Snopes family, and you see in them the decay of the aristocracy and the decline of the families and the changing South constantly portrayed. Well, Faulkner was not a scholar. I mean, he certainly was a scholar of a kind, but what he was talking about was his own time. And now when we look at it we see how true he was to it. But he wasn't a man who was obsessed with reading all of the books about all of the Civil War battles and all of the slavery accounts. He knew it in his bones. And it comes out in the working out of the story and in the minds of the characters—what is going on in the world today.

When I wrote *Quinn's Book,* I looked back to the middle of the nineteenth century. The book starts in 1849 and goes to 1864. It encompasses slavery, the working of the theater, women in the theater, the sensual dimension of woman as public attraction, the sex godesses, the ethnic battles among the Irish and their antagonists, who were many, the rivalries between the Irish and the Blacks, the clandestine groups that existed, the Knights of the Golden Circle, secret societies, the Underground Railroad, the rise of the Dutch aristocracy, the rise of the English moneyed classes which controlled so much of the manufacture and culture of this country.

I looked back at all of these things and when I discovered what was going on in those days, I saw the absolute parallels to what is going on today. I mean if you look at what is in the movies, it is *Mississippi Burning,* and the secret societies and the Klan again and *Betrayed,* the Costa Gravas film. You can look at the clandestine operation that happened with the Contras, the Iran-Contra scandal. Take a look at the constant emergence of the ever more daring or sensual attitude of films and theater. Nudity on the stage began in this country in about 1855 with a woman in a body stocking who looked like she was naked. This actually happened in Albany. Ada Isaacs did ride on the back of a horse in a body stocking as Mazeppa.

M.B.: The way Maud did in *Quinn's Book.*

W.K.: That's just one element of Maud. Maud is a composite. Maud is an invention. I drew on so many of the women of the nineteenth century who were somehow reflective of significant behavior. Anna Cora Mowatt was an actress who became ostracized for her public appearances as an elocutionist or a reader of poetry, something that a proper Bostonian woman could not do. So she was bitterly scandalized, but did a lot for women and wrote very eloquently about her life. Anyway, she was another contribution to Maud.

So the idea of combining the ages, well you can't embody the past entirely; you're not a part of it. All of your thinking is created in this time and place and whatever you're using has to be a metaphor for what you're feeling, what you've learned, what you understand about life. And so I think of *Quinn,* even though it's a novel that ends in 1864, as a very modern novel in style and attitude. Even though it uses an antique language, it's not an antique language that corresponds to anything specific in the nineteenth century. It's not like James. It's not like Poe. It's not like Melville. It's like me.

M.B.: Do you think you have a responsibility as a writer?

W.K.: I don't feel that I have a didactic responsibility. I feel a moral fervor, but I don't consider it a responsibility. I think when you get into that category you become too prone to propagandizing, to decide that you are in possession of the truth therefore you must spread the gospel, like Jerry Falwell or Jim Bakker. I don't feel that writers do that. Writers tell stories about their time in ways that are extremely responsible because they are a) accurate and b) real.

I mean there's nothing more wonderful than reading *The Great Gatsby* or Kate Chopin's *Awakening* or *Bartleby*. And John Cheever's stories and Raymond Carver's stories, what do these tell us about the responsibility of the writer? I mean where is the responsibility in F. Scott's Jay Gatsby? The fact that it's so illuminating. Fitzgerald felt the responsibility to be a great storyteller and to use language to the best of his abilities and to perceive the world around him with as much accuracy and insight as possible and that's why he wrote so well. So I think the writer's responsibility is chiefly to himself, to design himself in his work as something that is as truthful to human behavior as he can, as interesting as he can possibly be. I think the writer fails in his responsibility if he writes a boring work that nobody wants to read.

M.B.: Do you think the writer's job is more difficult today with society's visual reliance on film and television?

W.K.: I don't think the writer's job has changed. I think his audience is somewhat diminished, although you wouldn't think so looking at the best-seller list and seeing how many books are being sold today. It doesn't seem like we are in a state of decline, but television is now beginning to proliferate and I don't think that it gets better. I switch the television dial every night when I go to bed trying to find something that I want to watch and it's very difficult. Every once in awhile there's a good film. Every once in awhile you see Bill Moyers talking to somebody and making a great deal of sense, but that's a rare thing on television. Most of the time it's trendy music or sappy soap opera or ridiculous, and sometimes very entertaining, sitcoms and old movies that are sometimes great and sometimes unbearable.

I still think that the intelligent public, at least, is going to turn to the book. I can't believe they are ever going to be able to do without it, because you can't watch television in solitude and focus intelligently. I mean if the decline of our intelligence becomes so rampant that everybody stops writing books and reading books and just watches television we're going back to the Pleistocene Age.

M.B.: Has your work in film affected your writing?

W.K.: It hasn't affected the way that I write, that I know of. I certainly don't write novels for films because that's silly. If I want to write a film, I'll write a film. But it's given me access to certain worlds that I have not lived in before and it's good sport. I guess my name is better known because of *Ironweed* and the film made from it. I probably sold thousands of books that I would not have sold had the book not been made into a film, though it did extremely well independently of the film. I would never confuse the two genres. I know exactly what the difference is between them.

I would say that I have been influenced all my life by cinema and by television. I've grown up in the whole television age and I was born right on the cusp of the age of talkies. So everything that I absorbed from a very busy lifetime at the movies has influenced my work. And you can't help but be besieged by visuality, by the force of the film age, so my books, as a lot of people have noted, do have a very visual quality. We don't write like writers of the nineteenth century. We are far more visual than they were. They would go on for pages describing something. We don't have to.

M.B.: Do you have a writing routine that you follow?

W.K.: I just write every day. Sometimes I go away, but I take what I'm working on with me, to read and to rewrite. I realized a long time ago that concentration really makes a work work. I interrupted myself in 1983 writing *Quinn.* I got a call from Francis Ford Coppola to write *The Cotton Club* and it was a great deal of fun for six months. When I came home, I picked up *Quinn* again and to figure out where I was I had to start from scratch. You must stay with the words. You must keep it in your imagination, keep it alive, keep all of the nuances fresh. It's very difficult to write fiction and keep all of the threads together.

M.B.: What do you see as the greatest challenge facing writers today?

W.K.: The greatest challenge is getting published.

M.B.: I thought that after the difficulties you had getting *Ironweed* published that might be your answer.

W.K.: There are some good editors out there. But it is hard to find a good editor that is on your wavelength. People in the publishing business, like everywhere else, need to make money. That's the good housekeeping seal of publishing and it keeps publishers at work. I'm not saying that a book shouldn't make money. But there is a sense of responsibility toward the financial aspect of publishing, there is not a universal responsibility to rescuing the highly qualified, underfed writer.

I must say in another context that, in general, the unknown is a little better off than the writer who is trying to get his second or third novel published. Because again it goes back to the money. If you haven't been published you might be the next Jay McInerney or Scott Fitzgerald. But if you've written something, for instance, like *Billy Phelan,* and it hasn't made a whole lot of money, they will look at you with a warier eye.

In the old days a good writer would be able to build up a reputation just by being published as a normal function of distribution. Magazines were publishing everything that writers would write. The shelf life of books was much longer. It wasn't the same kind of business as it is today. Now everything is speeded up and it's hard to get the focus.

M.B.: Your editor Gerald Howard said that much of the sense of suffering in your books comes from your Irish Catholic background. Do you see yourself, in any sense, as an Irish-American writer?

W.K.: Yes of course. I couldn't be anything else. That's exactly what I am. I didn't know I was so Irish and I probably wasn't so Irish until I started to write. I have a friend, another Irishman, who is very suspicious of me for having become more Irish than I used to be. He doesn't understand it. I'm not sure that I do, except that I have accepted that I grew up in an Irish Catholic neighborhood, though I didn't really feel that Irish. I felt very American and I knew I had some Irish connections but I never asked about them. I wore a piece of green on my lapel on St. Patrick's Day and that was about it. Maybe you sang some Irish songs, "My Wild Irish Rose."

I'm an Albanian writer as well. I'm a product of this city. I'm a product of this state and the Western World. I was raised a Catholic. I know very little about being Presbyterian or being a Jew or being a Muslim. I know I could not write about those things. The things that shaped me are what I write about and I'm really not interested in being Irish or Catholic or Albanian, except that these forces, the religion, the place, the ethnic heritage, my profession as a newspaperman, my major in English, these things shape you. And I reflect those things. I reflect growing up as a child of the movies. I think that I am always looking around to discover what the world is doing to me and to my friends and to people I don't know, whom I value or find interesting to study—and people I invent. And I try to rediscover the forces that might have played on them. That's what this new book is all about. That's what *Quinn's Book* is all about. This new book is more direct in a certain way about a certain inheritance.

But I don't think of myself in a category. I don't think of myself as a hyphenated writer, the Irish-American. I think of myself as a writer who's using these materials of Irish American life to partly form an existence. I felt like an anonymous citizen of the world in my early short stories. I was a tourist when I was in Puerto Rico, just another Yankee in the subtropics trying to find out what to do with myself, how not to be bored. I think that the best kind of writing comes out of a sense of identity with a heritage and with a place, whether it's Dickens and Cockney London, or Melville and the sea, Joyce or O'Neill. I mean you don't think of any of these people as ethnic writers. It's not something any serious writer would aspire to, no more than he'd aspire to be a local colorist. It's a diminishing title for a writer. I wouldn't say it's demeaning, but it diminishes the ambition.

M.B.: The protagonists in your books are often outcasts of society—like Legs Diamond and Francis. Do you see them as a form of American hero?

W.K.: I wouldn't call Legs a hero. He certainly wasn't a hero, but he was a celebrity and that was fascinating to me. People did like him and people make gangsters heroes in way. I was in a restaurant in New York a few weeks ago and the owner told us that John Gotti, probably the most famous mafia man today, had eaten there recently. And he had sat with his back to the window; he was so sure of the FBI men following him that he wasn't nervous. That sort of flamboyant behavior, that was one of the things that made Legs Diamond the spectacular figure that he was. He was as much of a celebrity as a rock star, even more than a rock star. He was almost a superstar. *The New York Times* devoted page one and two to his obituary and *The Daily News* devoted miles and miles of their paper to him. His wife sold her memoirs to the tabloids twice and his mistress became a famous stripper, all using his name. And his legend goes on, I mean there's a version of his story on Broadway now. So that's not exactly focusing on a hero, that's an extreme figure. Extreme is always he word that I come back to. A man who will take life as far as it can go to survive. Billy Phelan perceives his own courage as inviolable and refuses to violate it even for the bosses of the time. Francis Phelan is an extremist for a totally different reason. He is a survivor. You can call him a hero but I would call him a kind of warrior figure. Billy is a warrior. Legs is a warrior. Quinn is a warrior. They all struggle and fight against themselves, if nothing else, against tides that are very strong against them, against wars in their own minds and in their own societies. So in a sense they are a form of not heroes but extreme figures who are willing to go to the limit.

M.B.: Often the families in your stories are fragmented. Do they represent the modern demise of the traditional family?

W.K.: The book I'm writing now is totally about family. It's a family that has stuck together so traditionally that it's created another whole set of problems for people, closeness for example. The strong influences one family member asserts over another.

I think the Phelan family has an integrity. Billy is there. Peggy is there. Danny Quinn is there. Annie is there. George Quinn is there. That's five. Francis went away, but Francis came home again. The Staats family came from the middle ages into Albany and carried the line forward. The Fitzgibbons are a line of entrepreneurs. . . . Family is just an excuse for proximity. Home is the place where you go because they can't throw you out, but that's not entirely true.

I think that when you look at my work you can't conclude anything specific about fragmentation, for instance, or extremism, or anything until I'm finished. When I'm dead and I'm not writing anymore then somebody can look at it and say, well he did this and he did that and he didn't do this. But now I'm still working on it. Let's see how it comes out.

M.B.: What did you mean by "good fiction singularizes life"?

W.K.: We're sort of used to sermons and generalities and bromides and things that put us into categories and tell us how we are like everybody else, which is not very true. Everybody is not like everybody else, not in our brains and in our psyches and in our habits and we should celebrate that difference and cultivate an attitude that will express that singularity.

Fiction seems to me to be better equipped to do this than anything else. Take film, since you asked the question about film. If you look at the movies one cop hero is very like another cop hero after awhile. The genre demands certain behavior. But in serious fiction, if you look at a character like Jason Compson in *The Sound and the Fury* or Ahab or Leopold Bloom or Gatsby, you see these characters are singular. They are not like anybody else. Bartleby is not like anybody else in the world. And they tell you something about how people become singular and how one's likely to move into a particular condition and discover that you are not like another. If you are Bartleby you have to die. If you're Bloom you have to smile. I mean look at Beckett. However gloomy it gets, there is always a joke right in the middle of the mud.

Singularity, that's what I mean. In a piece of writing the world can be created, but in film, in theater, and in poetry, there are serious limitations on the actuality. There are sets or the absence of sets, as in *Our Town*. There are the abstractions of set designs, or fanciful costumes, or masks, and you can certainly get a lot of good talk in an intelligent work of theater, but it takes the fiction writer to really represent the complete world and its singularity, in all elements of its singularity.

A work like *Ulysses* puts you suddenly into an entire universe. You get Molly and her lover and her singing and the dead child and the husband and the husband's full day and you're in that universe. What film has ever been able to do that. What theater piece can do that? Even if you're talking about Shakespeare, he's left it to the imagination to find out what Othello looks like. It's a totally different world from fiction. There may be a singularity to my work and there may not, but I could never have done it in any other medium.

The Art of Fiction CXI—
William Kennedy

Douglas R. Allen and Mona Simpson / 1988

Published in *Paris Review* 21 (Fall 1989): 35–59.
Reprinted by permission.

January 1983, the month of his fifty-sixth birthday, heralded the beginning of a marvelous era of fame and fortune in the life of William Kennedy. *Ironweed,* Kennedy's fourth novel, was published to widespread critical acclaim, and that same month the MacArthur Foundation awarded him a six-figure tax-free grant to use as he pleased. Two of his previous novels, *Legs* (1975) and *Billy Phelan's Greatest Game* (1978), were reissued in paperback, and later in 1983 Kennedy began a collaboration with Francis Ford Coppola on *The Cotton Club* screenplay.

Using part of his MacArthur grant, Kennedy established the Albany Writers Institute, which would bring internationally-known writers such as William Styron, Seamus Heaney, John Updike, and Toni Morrison to Kennedy's hometown for lectures and workshops. In December 1983 Kennedy published *O Albany!,* a book of lyric essays celebrating the real life of the city he had recreated as a mythic entity in his novels.

William Kennedy was on a Midas-like literary roll. In 1984 he won the Pulitzer Prize and the National Book Critics' Circle Award for *Ironweed;* and his first novel, *The Ink Truck* (1969), was reissued in both hardcover and paperback. Mario Cuomo declared that Albany had "found its Homer' in Kennedy, and he added the New York Governor's Arts Award to Kennedy's collection of honors. Kennedy sold the film rights to three novels, and signed contracts to write the screenplays (*Ironweed* became a film in 1987). Later in 1984 the New York legislature renamed the Albany Writers Institute the New York State Writers Institute and provided a $100,000 grant for it. In 1988 Kennedy published his most recent novel, *Quinn's Book.* Kennedy's novels had put Albany on the map, and he was becoming a highly-visible public man of letters.

The first interview session took place in July 1984 as Kennedy was finishing a magazine piece about working on the screenplay for *The Cotton Club.*

Kennedy talked for most of a Saturday afternoon at his home outside of Averill Park, a small community east of Albany and the Hudson River in a region of rolling hills where the landscape is sprinkled with picturesque lakes, meadows, and woods. A second interview was conducted in Spring 1988.

The Kennedys live in a handsome nineteenth-century farmhouse, a large white clapboard house with green trim and shutters, shaded and decorated on three sides by mature blue spruce, Norway spruce, and sugar maple trees. At the back of the house is a wooden deck, and across an expanse of lawn a swimming pool that was a sparkling invitation in the hot July sun on the day of the first interview session.

Kennedy, tall and fit, looking younger than his fifty-seven years, in spite of the fact that his Irish red hair showed signs of thinning on top, appeared at the front door wearing a red-and-white striped sport shirt with rolled-up sleeves, white cotton pants, and white dress shoes. Born and bred in the city, a well-traveled, cosmopolitan man, he gave the clear impression of being very much at home in the country.

After a short excursion outside in the midday heat, Kennedy suggested that we go to his air-conditioned writing studio, a spacious corner room on the second floor.

Shelves of nonfiction works lined one side of the upstairs hallway, and his studio was filled from floor to ceiling with books against three of the walls: fiction, poetry, plays, and one large section of books on films and film criticism. A large wooden desk took up most of the space between two windows that looked out on the spruce and maple trees in the yard. Bookcases at each end of the desk were filled with reference books. The top of a cedar chest on the green shag rug was covered by more piles of books and papers, and nearby were boxes of letters Kennedy had received from his readers.

Collages of memorabilia decorated the back of the door to the hallway and the wall behind the desk: a poster of Francis Phelan from the cover of *Ironweed;* announcements of public readings Kennedy had given; a poster announcement of a reading by Saul Bellow at the Writers Institute; award plaques, and an honorary doctorate of letters; and photographs from Kennedy's days as a newsman.

A straw hat with a black band hung from one of the curtain rods. It belonged to William Kennedy Sr., who wore it in the 1920s. Another link to family and the past was Kennedy's typewriter, set on a sturdy wooden leaf pulled out from the desk—a black L. C. Smith & Corona, 1934 vintage, that

belonged to his mother, Mary Kennedy. Although he now has a word processor for revisions, Kennedy still composes on this machine.

Kennedy sat at his desk in a wooden swivel chair that creaked slightly
when he leaned back. Choosing his words with precision, he was often pen-
sive with a serious, faraway look in his eyes as he talked of his life and his
work.

Interviewer: Can you explain the circumstances under which you got the
MacArthur Award?

William Kennedy: Well, in January I got a call from a man named Dr.
Hope, and he asked me, was I William Kennedy, the writer, and I said I was.
He said, Congratulations, you have just been awarded a MacArthur Fellowship, which will give you $264,000 tax-free over the next five years. I'd
gotten a Chinese fortune cookie that week which said, this is your lucky
week. I thought it had to do with the fact that I was getting reviewed in about
five different major places in the same week. I thought that was good enough,
but then I got the MacArthur. Quite a week!

Interviewer: Is there any particular achievement to which they give recognition?

Kennedy: They give it to you with no strings attached; they give it to all
sorts of people—scientists, historians, translators, poets. Their first award to
a writer that got widespread recognition was given to Robert Penn Warren.
They give it to you on the basis of what you've done, but more important, I
think, is their belief that you are going to do a lot more. It's an award given
with faith that the person is going to be productive. You don't have to do
anything for it; it just all of a sudden comes at you, like a health plan to
cradle and protect you.

Interviewer: Has the award changed your life?

Kennedy: The change is that I have more options now to do things that
have nothing to do with writing. Everybody wants me to become a fundraiser
or a public speaker or a teacher or go back to journalism or sit still and be
interviewed. I've also become a correspondent. I've got something like a
thousand letters, and the only thing I can do is try to answer some of them.
Some I'll never get to, but I keep trying. All this is very time-consuming.
The fact is that it's also very pleasant. I'm solvent, I can travel, I've been
able to rewire the house, dig a new well, install a new furnace, put in a pool.
Somebody accused me of going Hollywood in Averill Park, but that's not

accurate. I wanted a pool for twenty years. If I have a pool I'll swim in it. If I don't have a pool I won't swim. And I don't exercise, I don't do anything . . . I never walk. I tend to dance at parties, which is a good way of having a heart attack if your feet still think you're a nineteen-year-old jitterbug. The change has been very pleasant. People ask will I change the way I write, and I don't believe I will. The work is based on what I see in the world, what's around me and what I take home from that. It's a superficial response if you change your writing because of a temporary change in your personal condition.

Interviewer: Success came to you very late. *Ironweed* was turned down by thirteen publishing houses. How could a book which won the Pulitzer Prize be turned down by so many publishers?

Kennedy: Yes. Thirteen rejections. Remember that character in "Li'l Abner," Joe Btfsplk, who went around with a cloud over his head? Well, I was the Joe Btfsplk of modern literature for about two years. What happened was that I sold this book, then my editor left publishing; so that threw the ball game into extra innings. They gave me an editor in Georgia and I said, "I don't want an editor in Georgia; I want an editor in New York." They didn't like that. She was a very good editor, but she only came to New York every two months. Georgia is even more remote from the center of literary activity than Albany. She was living on a pecan farm, as I recall. So that got the publisher's nose out of joint. My agent was not very polite with them and finally we separated. In the meantime, my first editor came back to publishing and, finding that Joe Btfsplk cloud hanging over my head, was not terribly enthusiastic about taking me back. So I went over to Henry Robbins whom I had met at a cocktail party. Henry at that point was a very hot new York editor. He had just gone over to Dutton. Everybody was flocking to him. He was John Irving's editor. Joyce Carol Oates moved over there. Doris Grumbach moved in; so did John Gregory Dunne. It looked like Dutton was about to become the Scribner's of the new age. So anyway, at the cocktail party he said, "Can I see your book?" And I said, "Of course." I sent it to him and he wrote me back this wonderful letter saying that he loved the idea of adding me to their list. I picked up the paper a week later and he had just dropped dead in the subway on his way to work. So I then went over to another publisher where a former editor of mine had been; she was somewhat enthusiastic, thought we might be able to make it if there were some changes in the book. And then she was let go. I bounced about nine more times. Then fate intervened in the form of an assignment from *Esquire* to do an interview with Saul Bellow, who had been a teacher of mine for a semester, in San Juan. He had really encouraged me at a very early age to become a writer. So he took it upon himself—I didn't urge him, and I was very grateful to him for doing it—to write my former editor at Viking, saying that he didn't think it was proper for his former publisher to let a writer like Kennedy go begging. Two days later I got a call from Viking saying that they wanted to publish *Ironweed* and what did I think of the possibility of publishing *Legs* and *Billy Phelan* again at the same time.

Interviewer: It would seem that Bellow was the answer.

Kennedy: I think he's probably had several manuscripts sent to him since then. As have I.

Interviewer: During this there must have been an immense amount of frustration. Did that experience give you ideas for changes that can or should be made in the publishing industry to encourage the writing of first-rate serious fiction?

Kennedy: I don't know what to do to change the world that way, except to generate a running sense of shame in their attitudes toward their own behavior so that the next time they might pay more serious attention to the work at hand. So much of the publishing world is run on the basis of *market-place* success, and so when a book is rejected as a financial loser, it immediately has a cloud over it, especially if the writer is already established with one publishing house and this house chooses not to take his next novel. That carries a stigma; you're like a leper. You go from house to house, and they say, well, why didn't so-and-so publish it? They published your last book. So you live under that cloud until you find some editor who understands the book and is willing to take a chance on it. I don't know how to change human nature about this. I'm very pessimistic about it. I just see one good writer after another in deep trouble.

Interviewer: So the difficulty in getting books like *Ironweed* published is not necessarily due to the lack of good editors at the major publishing houses, but might be more closely tied to the prevailing corporate policy you're speaking of?

Kennedy: I think that there's a casualness about the way things are read. I think subject matter tends to play a large part. If you have a novel of intrigue or romance, with adultery or exotic locale, or a spy thriller, you probably won't have too much trouble getting published. If you have a major reputation, you're not going to have any problem getting published. But it's the writers who fall in the middle, who write serious books about subjects that are not the stuff of mass marketing, they have the problem—the so-called "mid-list" phenomenon. If the publishers don't think it's going to sell past a certain amount of copies, then they're not interested. And I would think that that was the case with *Ironweed.* People had decided it was a depressing book, set in the Depression, about a bum, a loser, a very downbeat subject. Who wants to read a book about bums? So they chose not to accept it. Yet it's not a downbeat book. It's a book about family, about redemption and perseverance, it's a book about love, faded violence, and any number of things. It's about the Irish, it's about the church.

So, again, I don't see how you're going to change the way editors think. They can't contravene the commercial element in their publishing house. They're as good as the books they bring in, and if those books don't make money, what good are the editors? Very sad.

Interviewer: All these years of being turned down with books and short stories. . . . I understand even *The Paris Review* turned down one story.

Kennedy: That's true. You did give me a nice rejection slip, although I must say it wasn't as nice as the one I got from *The Atlantic.* That one said, "You write with a facility that has held our attention." But my story had their coffee drippings on it, even so.

Interviewer: You started as a journalist in Albany. What was your favorite aspect of journalism? Why did it appeal to you?

Kennedy: It was the uncertainty of general assignment that was terrific: the police stories, the disaster stories, the politics, the squirrelly interviews with some guy who had just walked across the country from Montana wearing a taillight and the dopester who had a perfect system to beat the horses and wanted the world to know about it, but he was broke because he was unlucky. That sort of thing was fun, but Albany, I thought, was moribund. I had exhausted the city in a certain way—at that age—and so along came the possibility to go down to the tropics and work in San Juan. That seemed very exotic. I applied and got the job. I went down in April 1956 and started to work on a newspaper called *The Puerto Rico World Journal.* It had existed during the war years as a publication for soldiers and sailors who were stationed in Puerto Rico and for the American civilian component. It was a stepchild of the major Spanish language daily, *El Mundo.* It only lasted nine months, but it was a valuable experience. I love Puerto Rico. I had a great time socially, as a columnist, and I wound up being assistant managing editor when the city editor went to lunch one day and never came back. When the newspaper died, I got married. I met Dana just when the paper was on its last legs. Then I went over for an interview at *The Miami Herald* and got a job writing about Cuban exiles, Castro in the hills, the C.I.A., revolutionaries, political thieves. It was great stuff.

Interviewer: What, other than journalism, were you writing at the time?

Kennedy: Having failed miserably as a short-story writer, I decided it was time to go out and fail as a novelist. I started in Miami, and I realized that I couldn't do it full-time—the job was very time-consuming. I was writing good things for the paper, but I was bored, really. Some of the stories I was writing were not unlike what I had done at the *Times-Union*—a story on a cop giving a ticket to a little kid in a kiddie car, an escaped jaguar attacking a tomato plant in a woman's back yard. I stayed with the coverage for seven months and then decided that it was as deadly as everything else I was doing and I really had to get out. So I quit, went back to Puerto Rico and wrote a rotten novel. It went around to an agent or two and nobody liked it. So I put it on the shelf and it hasn't seen the daylight since.

Interviewer: What influence did Saul Bellow have on you?

Kennedy: I met Saul in Puerto Rico when he was teaching at the university at Rio Piedras. I was managing editor of another brand new daily paper, the *San Juan Star,* but was writing yet another novel before and after work. I sent it to Bellow and he accepted me in his class. It was an important development and I took his criticism very seriously. He would explain that my writing was "fatty"—I was saying everything twice and I had too many adjectives. He said it was also occasionally "clotty"—it was imprecision he was talking about, an effort to use a word that wasn't quite precise and so screwed up the clause or sentence. When he pointed that out to me, I would go back through the whole book and slash—it turned me into a real fiction editor of my own copy, and it later helped when *I* became a teacher. If I was ruthless with my own stuff, why shouldn't I be with everybody else's? Bellow also talked about being prodigal. He said that a writer shouldn't be parsimonious with his work, but "prodigal, like nature." He said just think of nature and how many billions of sperm are used when only one is needed for creating life. And that principle was, it seemed, at the heart of *Augie March,* a novel that exploded with language and ideas. I never became that kind of writer,

but I think the effusion, the principle was important. I was never afraid of
writing too much, never thought that just because you've written a sentence
it means something, or that it's a good sentence just because you've written
it. You know, I wrote *Legs* eight times, and it was taller than my son when
both he and the manuscript were six years old. I have a picture of them
together. One day Bellow was reading this section of a story where I had
gone back and rewritten the things he had suggested I change. He looked up
at me, and he said, "Hey, this is publishable!" Nobody had ever said that
about anything I had written before, so I went out and bought a bottle of
champagne and went back and had a party with my wife and some friends.
Having come that distance—twelve years of writing in the dark—then having
somebody of value suddenly say that, well it put me onto a different level of
existence as a writer. It verified the apprenticeship, moved me into journeyman status. And I kept writing.

    Interviewer: Because of your isolation and all the rejections, did you ever
think: This is not my profession. I should really be doing something else.

    Kennedy: No, I never thought that. As I used to say on Thursday after-
noons—when I was on my day off from the Albany *Times-Union* and waiting
for the nurse to descend and discovering that it was the muse's day off too—
you have to beat the bastards. I didn't even know who the bastards were, but
you have to beat somebody. You have to beat your own problematic imagination to discover what it is you're saying and how to say it and move forward
into the unknown. I always knew that (a) I wanted to be a writer and (b) if
you persist in doing something, that sooner or later you will achieve it. It's
just a matter of persistence—and a certain amount of talent. You can't do
anything without talent, but you can't do anything without persistence either.
Bellow and I once talked about that. We were talking in general about writing
and publishing and so one, and he said there's a certain amount of talent
that's necessary. All sorts of people are out there with no talent trying very
hard and nothing comes of it. You must have some kind of talent. But after
that, it's character. I said, "What do you mean by character?" And he smiled
at me, and never said anything. So I was left for the rest of my life to define
what he meant that night. What I concluded was that character is equivalent
to persistence. That if you just refuse to give up, the game's not over. You
know, I had had enormous success in everything I'd done in life, up until the
time I decided to be a writer. I was a good student; I was a good soldier. I
got a hole-in-one one day on the golf course. I bowled 299, just like Billy

Phelan. I was a very good newspaperman. Anything I wanted to do in journalism, it seemed to work; it just fell into place. So I didn't understand why I was so successful as a journalist and zilch as a novelist and short-story writer. It was just that time was working against me. You just have to learn. It's such a complicated craft . . . such a complicated thing to understand what you're trying to bring out of your imagination, your own life.

Interviewer: Did you find yourself getting better and better at it?

Kennedy: Well, I thought I was terrific when I wrote *The Ink Truck* and they published it—Jesus! But then I wrote *Legs* and everybody kept saying, "This is not good." People would turn it down; my own editor, who wanted to publish it, kept saying, "This is not working." I couldn't figure it out. It was six years of figuring and discovering. *Legs* was the novel where I really learned how to write a novel. And it takes you a long time to discover that, to probe whatever it is that you have in you. Where is your talent, where is your voice, where is your style? It was a complicated and sometimes painful struggle. To have an editor say to you, "We think you should turn this into a *biography* of Legs Diamond"—well, I immediately left that bind and went off on my own. And that was the night I sat down and decided to write *Legs* one more time, and that was the one that worked.

Interviewer: What was the solution?

Kennedy: I had been trying to do the book in a multiplicity of ways. I began thinking I would write it as a film-in-process, because the gangster had been such a charismatic presence in movies; I wanted to make a literary artifact in which the film would be a significant element. That became a silly gimmick. I tried to make it a surrealistic novel. I tried to pattern it totally on the *Tibetan Book of the Dead*; those chapters were pretty wild. The process of elimination left me with the Henry Jamesian wisdom that I really needed a point of view on this. I tried to write it from inside Diamond and it didn't work and I tried to write from outside Diamond with a chorus of voices and it didn't work. And then I discovered that if I used the lawyer who was in the book from the beginning as this intelligent presence who could look at Diamond and intersect with him at every level of his life, then I would be able to have a perspective on what was going on inside the man. So I did that and it made all the difference. It also made a difference that I spent three months just talking to myself, trying to figure out every character and defining the plot from scratch, narrowing it down. I had five years' worth of paper at that time but that three months' worth of work made all the difference. Then the book began to define itself. That's when you really understand craft.

Interviewer: It is a technical problem.

Kennedy: Absolutely. That's what I was up against. I had so much research, so much knowledge about this man, so many possible directions I could go in. I had done a massive amount of research because I wanted to discover what his life was really like. It turned out to be very complicated. He had been a celebrity quite apart from anything I had imagined of any gangster. I knew about the notoriety of Al Capone and I had heard of Legs Diamond, but it wasn't until I really began to go after him that I saw how much he had occupied the front pages of the newspapers of the country and the world. He was notorious, front-page stories about him every day, for weeks at a time. As a fugitive crossing the Atlantic on an ocean liner he was the cynosure of international news coverage. I knew he was a son of a bitch but even a life like his is worthy of attention in fiction. If you fix seriously on the transition from one life form to another, from defensible street life to the indefensible, where somebody begins to be a willfully cruel human being, that's worth doing. I wanted to understand the man but also the age, and I did not want to offer up another novel that would be historically inaccurate. So many books and films about Diamond and his kind were travesties. And so I got hooked on research, couldn't get out from under the library's microfilm machine until I finally realized I was doing myself a great disservice; because your imagination can't absorb all that new material and synthesize it easily. If you're trying to transform the material, which is what fiction must do or else it remains journalism, or biography, then you have to let your imagination have a little rest. So I quit. I could have done another six months of research on Diamond, but I gave up. That's when I sat down, slowly absorbed all that I'd collected, and invented Diamond—a brand new Legs Diamond—from scratch. Authentic but new.

Interviewer: Would he recognize himself?

Kennedy: Oh yes, he already has. After I finished the book and it was about to be published, my wife had a dream: Legs Diamond came up to our front door and knocked on the door. Then he got down on the lawn, laid back and rolled around and kicked his legs in the air. He said to Dana, "Bill got it just right."

Interviewer: What a relief! Do you get letters from people who are historians of the twenties who say, "No, no, you didn't get that right?"

Kennedy: Every once in a while, somebody writes me and says I didn't get the death of Legs Diamond right, but I never defined who killed him. That's still a mystery.

Interviewer: How important is a sense of place in your fiction? How did Puerto Rico and Albany affect your fiction?

Kennedy: The Puerto Rico short stories I wrote seemed to have no resonance, I suppose because I lacked a full historical sense of the place. They represented what Eudora Welty once called "the Isle of Capri novel," the transient story that could be set in Paris or Honolulu, all events taking place in a villa or a resort. The shallowness is evident; soap opera, really. I was leaving out the density of life in a given place and I came to know it. I kept reading Faulkner's *The Sound and the Fury* over and over, trying to understand how he'd done it. It was extraordinary to see how he knew so much about a group of people and at the same time reflected an entire cosmos, and with such remarkable language and invention. I wanted to understand any place I wrote about in the same way; and I believe that book more than any other led me to the sense of place in a novel. I started to write about Albany when I was still in San Juan and I realized how little I knew even my own home town. When I came back to Albany to live I immersed myself in its history and I still can't get enough of the place. Some people have said that *Ironweed* could have been set anywhere because it has a universality about it; and that's nice to hear. But it couldn't have taken place in Capri, or Honolulu; not every town has a skid row and a mission, or trolley strikes with the heavy violence that made Francis Phelan what he was. Even being Irish Catholic—it's not the same even in Ireland as it is in Albany.

Interviewer: How would you assess your development as a stylist?

Kennedy: Somewhere back in the late sixties a friend of mine named Gene McGarr—we were sitting in The Lion's Head in Greenwich Village one afternoon—said to me, "You know, Irishmen are people who sit around trying to say things good." That is the purest expression of style I've ever come across. I remember being enormously impressed by Damon Runyon's style when I was a kid because it was so unique. It just leaped out at you and said, "Look at me! I'm a style!" And Hemingway had a style. These people were egregiously stylish. Then I read Graham Greene and I couldn't find a style. I thought, why doesn't this man have a style? I liked his stories enormously, and his novels, but what was his style? Of course he has an extraordinary style in telling a story, great economy and intelligence. Obviously these were adolescent attitudes toward style, valuing ways of being singular. I admired journalists who had style, Red Smith and Mencken. You wouldn't mistake their writing, you'd know it right away. What I set out to do very early on, in college, was to mold a style; and then I realized it was an artificial effort. I was either imitating Red Smith or Hemingway, or Runyon, or whomever, and I gave up on it. I realized that was death. Every time I'd reread it, I'd say that's not you, that's somebody else. As I went on in journalism I was always trying to say something in a way that was neither clichéd nor banal, that was funny if possible, or dramatic if possible. I began to expand my language: sentences grew more complicated, the words became more arcane. I used the word "eclectic" once in a news story and it came out "electric." It was a willful strain at being artsy, so I gave that up too. And as soon as I gave up, I wrote the only thing that I could write, which was whatever came to my head in the most natural possible way. And I evolved into whatever it is I've become. If I have a style, I don't know how to evaluate it. I wouldn't know what to say about my style. I think *The Ink Truck* is an ambitious book in language. I think certain parts of *Legs* are also; but Marcus is still telling that story in a fairly offhanded way, using the vernacular in large measure. *Billy Phelan* goes from being inside Martin Daugherty's mind, which is a far more educated mind, to Billy Phelan's, and the narration is really only in service of representing those two minds. This was very different from what I came to in *Ironweed,* where I set out at the beginning to use the best language at my disposal. I thought my third person voice was me at first, but the more I wrote, the more I realized that the third person voice was this ineffable level of Francis Phelan's life, a level he would never get to consciously, but which was there somehow. And that became the style of the telling of the story; and the language became as good as I could make it whenever I felt it was time for those flights of rhetoric up from the sidewalk, out of the gutter. Francis moves in and out of those flights sometimes in the same sentence. A word will change the whole attitude toward what he's thinking, or talking about, or just intuiting silently. I think that as soon as you abandon your overt efforts at style, that's where you begin to find your own voice. Then it becomes a matter of editing out what doesn't belong—a subordinate clause that says, "That's Kafka," or "That's Melville," whoever it might be. If you don't get rid of that, every time you reread that sentence you think: petty larceny.

Interviewer: The first chapter of *Ironweed* sets the tone for the rest of the book by showing us Francis Phelan through the eyes of the dead, and through his own encounters in memory with the ghosts from his past, with many shifts back and forth in time. The first chapter has a literary magic about it that persists throughout the book and makes the book work in a unique way— but I wonder if you encountered any editorial resistance to the narrative technique when you took *Ironweed* to publishers.

Kennedy: Considerable. There was one editor who said it was not credible to write this kind of a story and put those kinds of thoughts into Francis Phelan's mind, because no bum thinks that way. That's so abjectly ignorant of human behavior that it really needs no comment except that that man should not be allowed anywhere near a manuscript. Congress should enact a law prohibiting that man from being an editor. I also sent the first few chapters to *The New Yorker* and an editor over there said it was a conventional story about an Irish drunk an they'd had enough of that sort of thing in the past, and they wished me well and thought it was quite well done, and so on. That seemed very wrong-headed. It's hardly a conventional story about an Irish drunk when he's talking to the dead, when he's on an odyssey of such dimensions as Francis is on. I'd never read a book like it, and it seems to me that that's a comment I hear again and again. But again, you have to put up with editors who don't know what they're reading. One editor said there were too many bums in the book and I should get rid of some. And a friend of mine said, "I understand, I love this chapter, but there's an awful lot of negative things in it, there's vomit and a lot of death and violence and there's a lot of sadness, you know, and it's such a downbeat chapter that editors won't want to buy it. Maybe you should alter it to get the editors past the first chapter." Well, there was no way I could take his advice; I had written the book, and it was either going to stand or fall on what it was. I also felt that there was no real merit in the advice, although it was an astute observation about the way some editors are incapable of judging serious literature seriously. There were also people who just said, "I don't like it." Somebody said, "I could never sell it." Somebody else said, "It's a wonderful book, nobody's ever written anything better about this subject than you have, but I can't add another book to my list that won't make any money." These were more mundane, these were money considerations, but I think that other, more pretentious rejections had the same basis; they just didn't believe a book about bums was ever going to make it in the marketplace, but they didn't dare say so out loud. It's not a book about bums, you know, but that's the way it was perceived. I got a letter from Pat Moynihan after I won the Pulitzer and a story had come out on the AP wire, describing *Ironweed* as a book about a baseball player who turns out to be a murderer. Moynihan quoted that back to me in the letter, and he said, "Perhaps you will have a better understanding of what we poor politicians are up against."

Interviewer: The most prominent characters in your novels are seekers after a truth or meaning or experience beyond the repetitive patterns of daily life. Do you find your own world view changes as a result of creating these characters and moving them through a series of life experiences?

Kennedy: I think that my world view changes as I write the book. It's a discovery. The only thing that's really interesting to me is when I surprise myself. It's boring to write things when you know exactly what's going to happen. That's why language was so important to me in journalism. It was the only way you could heighten the drama, or make it funny, or surprising. In *Legs* I was endlessly fascinated to learn how we look at gangsters. I discovered what I thought about mysticism and coincidence when I wrote *Billy*. I feel that *Ironweed* gave me a chance to think about a world most people find worthless. Actually, anybody who doesn't have an idea about what it is to be homeless, or on the road, or lost and without a family, really hasn't thought very much at all. Even though I'd written about this, the small details of that life weren't instantly available to my imagination until I began to think seriously about what it means to sleep in the weeds on a winter night, then wake up frozen to the sidewalk. Such an education becomes part of your ongoing frame of reference in the universe. And if you don't develop Alzheimer's disease or a wet brain, you might go on to write better books. I think that some writers, after an early peaking, go into decline. Fitzgerald seems to me a good example of that. He was writing an interesting book at the end of his life, *The Last Tycoon,* but I don't think it would have been up to his achievement in *Gatsby* or *Tender Is The Night.* But if you don't die, and you're able to sustain your seriousness, I don't think there's any rule that you can't supersede your own early work. I remember an essay by Thomas Mann about Theodor Fontane, the prolific German novelist who believed he was all done somewhere around the age of thirty-nine. But he lived to be a very old man, and published his masterpiece, *Effi Briest,* at age seventy-six. I believe in the capacity of the imagination to mature and I am fond of insisting that I'm not in decline, that the next book is going to be better than the last. It may or may not be, but I have no doubt I know more about how to write a novel, more about what it means to be alive, than I ever have. Whether another dimension of my being has faded, and will refuse to fire my brain into some galvanic achievement, I can't say. We may know more about this when the next book is published.

Interviewer: Did your work in journalism hinder you in writing novels, or was it primarily helpful?

Kennedy: It was both. It was very difficult to overcome the fact that I was a journalist for a long time. It had to do with the way I looked at material—my feeling that the world was there to be reported upon. Even when I was inventing in those early books—I'm not talking about the ones that were published, I mean the early ones I wrote that weren't published, and all the early stories—I tended to believe that experience alone would save me, that I'd encounter life and therefore be able to report more clearly on it. But the journalist must report on life objectively, and the novelist must reinvent life utterly, and the world has to come up from below instead of down from the top as a journalist receives it. The feeling of insufficient experience was strong for a long time. But experience alone will produce only commonplace novels. The real work is a blend of imagination and language. On the other hand, journalism serves you extraordinarily well because it forces you into situations you would not normally encounter. It thrusts you into spectacles, disasters, high crimes and high art. It forces you to behave in ways that you would not normally behave: being objective in the face of a lying politician, or a movie goddess, or some celebrity figure whose work you've valued all your life, such as Satchmo when I interviewed him. I partly educated myself in writing by interviewing writers. When I came back to live up here from Puerto Rico in 1963, after seven years away, I left most of my literary friends behind in San Juan. I reentered the society here as a freelance and part-time journalist, trying to write novels, and the first thing I did was seek out people like John Cheever, Bernard Malamud, James Baldwin, and Arthur Miller for interviews. I could speak with these men about what was most important to me—literature. That kind of cachet that you have as a journalist is very valuable. Also, journalism forces you into an ethical stance through objectivity. You're forced into understanding that the world is not as you would like it to be. Yet you certainly cannot report on it your way, unless you become some sort of advocate for a cause. Even when you disagree with a cause you have to give it its due, and that presents you with a chance to understand complexities of human behavior that might otherwise take you a long time to come to. The other thing is that you use the language every day, and one of the pleasures of journalism to me was always being able to see the thing in print the

next day and have somebody say, "Hey, that was a good story!" Daily journalism to me was writing as fast as you could, still trying to be some sort of
interpreter and entertainer as well as objective reporter. And I was always,
from very early on, imbued with the kind of journalism that flowered in the
twenties and thirties and forties. People like Mencken, Don Marquis, West-
brook Pegler—I'm not speaking of Pegler's hate-ridden politics, just his ability to turn a sentence—or Red Smith, or so many of the reporters at the
Herald-Tribune in the forties and fifties, a remarkable newspaper. Some people have this kind of monolithic feeling toward their art and rightfully so. I
really consider myself a novelist preeminently but I came out of journalism
and I would never in any way try to disown it the way Hemingway did. I
think he was wrong-headed from the beginning about the destructive quality
of journalism—it was a kind of snobbery; he had elevated himself above it.
But what about Stephen Crane, James Agee, and García Márquez? What
about Michael Herr and his Vietnam book, *Dispatches?* What a piece of work
that is.

Interviewer: Do you have any advice for young writers, a way of starting,
or a way of looking at one's work as it matures?

Kennedy: I would think that he or she should discover language and discover the world, a sense of place, and not try to base his or her work only on
personal experience. Personal experience as a young person is very limited.
We have the great line from Faulkner that the problems of children are not
worth writing about. This applies to adolescence and early sexhood as well.
It's not that children in trouble are not great subjects, but what you need is a
world and a way of approaching the world. If you have these two things,
everything is interesting. It's not what you say, it's the way that you say it.
It's a sense of the person's existence, and not the person's experience. It's
the matrix translated into language. It's the sense of response, as opposed to
problem. So much great literature exists on that level of response, the essential element of some great moderns. Leopold and Molly Bloom respond to
their worlds with the most remarkable language of thought. Nabokov's language is everything. Take Cheever's language away and the work dribbles off
into absurdity; yet with those golden sentences he's the most durable of
writers.

Interviewer: Is sex something that's easy to write about in a book? Why
do writers have so much difficulty with it?

Kennedy: I think writers should research sex in the same way they research historical characters. It's not difficult to write about. What is difficult to write about is the actual pornographic element of sex. That ceases to be interesting. What you need to do is find the surrounding elements, the emotional content of the sexual encounters. Yet another struggle of the genitals is hardly worth writing about. It's done on every street-corner, fifty-five times a magazine. So, you know that's not the point. On the contrary, it's when you discover a character like Kiki Roberts who is Legs Diamond's girlfriend and you look at her, and discover this incredible beauty, obviously a great sex object for Diamond, who endangered his life many times for her. And she, reciprocating constantly. She was a fugitive from justice with him. When you look at that woman, you can begin to imagine what it was about her that led Diamond to behave that way. So that was quite a pleasant thing for me, to re-imagine Kiki Roberts.

Interviewer: Do characters have a way of taking off on their own?

Kennedy: I recall Nabakov looked on his characters as his galley slaves. But they do have a way of asserting themselves. Hemingway's line was that everything changes as it moves; and that that is what makes the movement that makes the story. Once you let a character speak or act you now know that he acts this way and not another. You dwell on why this is so and you move forward to the next page. This is my method. I'm not interested in formulating a plot to which characters are added like ribbons on a prize cow. The character is the key and when he does something which is new, something you didn't know about or expect, then the story percolates. If I knew, at the beginning, how the book was going to end, I would probably never finish. I knew that Legs Diamond was going to die at the end of the book, so I killed him on page one.

Interviewer: You said before that you don't write novels to make money. Why do you write novels?

Kennedy: I remember in 1957 I was reading in *Time* magazine about Jack Kerouac's success with *On the Road.* I felt I wasn't saying what I wanted to say in journalism, wasn't saying it in the short stories I'd been writing either. I had no compelling vision of anything, yet I knew the only way I would ever get it would be to give my imagination the time and space to spread out, to look at things in the round. I also felt that not only did I want to write one novel, I wanted to write a series of novels that would interrelate. I didn't know how, but this is a very old feeling with me. I came across a note the other day that I wrote to myself about "the big Albany novel." This was way back, I can't even remember when—long before I wrote *Legs,* even before *The Ink Truck.* It had to be in the middle sixties. It was a consequence of my early confrontation with the history of Albany when I did a series of articles on the city's neighborhoods in 1963 and 1964. I began to see how long and significant a history we had had, and as I moved along as a part-timer at the *Times-Union,* writing about blacks and civil rights and radicals, I began to see the broad dimension of the city, the interrelation of the ethnic groups. The politics were just incredible—Boss Machine politics, the most successful in the history of the country in terms of longevity. And I realized I could never tell it all in one book.

Interviewer: Is this enormous sort of Yoknapatawpha County in your mind? Do the characters emerge as you think about them? You give the picture of being able to dip into this extraordinary civilization.

Kennedy: Every time out it's different, but one of the staples is the sense that I have a column of time to work with; for example a political novel that could move from about 1918 to maybe 1930; and in there is a focal point on a character, probably the political boss. But that's not always enough, having character. I once wrote a novel's worth of notes about three characters and I couldn't write the first sentence of the book. It was all dead in the water. There has to be a coalescence of influences that ignite and become viable as a story.

Interviewer: What do you think the ignition thing is? It's rather frightening that you work on these things and do not know whether it's going to come together. How do you know?

Kennedy: You don't. It's an act of faith.

Interviewer: *Ironweed, Billy Phelan* and *Legs* were reviewed and marketed as a trilogy of Albany novels.

Kennedy: Trilogy was never my word and I don't want it to be the word. Cycle is my word. It started with *The Ink Truck,* and continues with *Quinn's Book,* the newest novel. I called it a cycle because I don't know when I'm going to stop. As long as I write books, it seems I have enough variety of intention, both in subject matter and in approach to the material, that I'm not going to be bored by my opportunities. People say, "Why don't you write about someplace else?" Well, I don't think that there's anyplace any more interesting to write about. I don't *have* to go anyplace else. The more I stay here, the more interesting the cycle becomes. If I'm able to convey a society in transition or a society in embryo, that's worth doing. In one way I'm really trying to write history. But history is only a tool to ground me in telling a story about what it means to be alive.

Interviewer: What is the feeling when you're done with a book?

Kennedy: I remember the day I finished *Ironweed.* I came down and I said, "I'm finished." My wife was there and one of my good friends; they had read most of the book along the way and they sat down and read the ending. Somehow they didn't respond the way I wanted them to respond. I was thinking of an abstract reader who would say what every writer wants you to say to him: "This is the best thing I ever read in my life." I knew something was wrong, though I didn't know what; I knew the elements of the ending should be powerful. I thought about it and their lack of proper response. After dinner I went back upstairs and rewrote the ending, adding a page and a half. I brought that down and then they said, "This is the best thing I've ever read in my life."

Very Bountiful Bones: An Interview with William Kennedy

Tom Smith / 1992

Published in *Weber Studies: An Interdisciplinary Humanities Journal*
10.1 (Winter 1993): 21–44.
Reprinted by permission.

William Kennedy was born in Albany, New York, on January 16, 1928, where he was educated by the Christian Brothers and graduated from Siena College in 1949. After a two-year stint in the U.S. Army in the U.S.A. and Germany (1950–52), working on army newspapers, Kennedy became a reporter in Albany, and later in Miami, Florida, and Puerto Rico, where he became the founding managing editor of the *San Juan Star,* the English daily, in 1959. His journalistic assignments included sports, politics, literature, and especially film criticism which led him to co-author the film *The Cotton Club* with director Francis Ford Coppola in 1984. He also wrote the screenplay for his own novel *Ironweed,* filmed in 1987 in Albany under the direction of Hector Babenco. In 1961 Kennedy gave up journalism to write serious fiction and has since taught creative writing at Cornell University (1982–83) and the University at Albany, SUNY, where he is currently Professor of English.

After Kennedy was awarded a MacArthur Foundation fellowship in 1983, he founded and directed the New York State Writers Institute at the University of Albany. His awards include the Pulitzer Prize for *Ironweed* and the New York Governor's Arts Award, both in 1984. Kennedy lives with his wife, Dana, a former professional dancer, in Averill Park, near Albany. They have two daughters, Dana and Katherine, and a son, Brendan.

Written after *The Ink Truck* (1969), Kennedy's acclaimed "Albany Cycle" of novels includes *Legs* (1975), *Billy Phelan's Greatest Game* (1978), *Ironweed* (1983), *Quinn's Book* (1988), and *Very Old Bones* (1992). His non-fiction works include *O Albany!* (1984), and *Riding the Yellow Trolley Car,* a collection of essays, memoirs, reviews, and reportage, scheduled for publication in 1993. With his son Brendan he has co-authored two children's books, *Charlie Malarkey and the Belly Button Machine* (1986) and *Charlie Malarkey and the Singing Moose* (forthcoming).

I interviewed my good friend William Kennedy on a cool night in Albany at the time of the publication of *Very Old Bones* in the spring of 1992. Our unrehearsed, spontaneous conversation (one of many) took place while we sat before a crackling fire in the much-used party room of Kennedy's home in Averill Park, NY, a short distance from

his native, mythic Albany. Kennedy's world-class pool table stood in
the background with the spirit of Billy Phelan hovering close by.

Smith: Bill, *Very Old Bones* is your sixth novel, the fifth novel in what's
called The Albany Cycle by this time. Now that *Very Old Bones* is launched
to the world, do you look upon it as a kind of fulfillment or perhaps even a
culmination of one mighty torrent of your fiction, the whole saga of the
Phelans and the Quinns of Albany and all the things that get embraced in
those families? Is there something, perhaps not finality, but is there some
kind of fulfillment or culmination that *Very Old Bones* represents?

Kennedy: There's a completion in a certain sense that at the end of *Bones,*
Orson is speculating on the future and he says, "We're not long for this
house." You know, how long can Peter, his father, live, and then I'll be out
of here, God knows what's going to happen to me, and so on. And that really
brings to an end that particular family coherence that began for me back in
1959, which was when I created the Phelans for the first time. That first book
was *The Angels and the Sparrows* and *Bones* is an extension of it. Certain
elements were already present there, certain plot lines, and characters. Francis
was there, Molly was there under a different name, Sarah was there, and the
parents were there under different guises. That family cohesion was there
from the beginning, and it seemed to me a strength on which I drew as I
created all these various Phelans, and also the spinoffs from them, the
Quinns, and Billy's life, and Francis's outlaw life and so on. George Quinn's
life is still to be told, as is Danny Quinn's, but those first Phelans were a
nucleus around which I could invent freely, and with great variety, the kind
of life I had seen and observed but hadn't ever penetrated very seriously in
any other way except through fiction. Even personally—not knowing the profound insides of my family. I never got that close to them. We were always a
close family but to talk about history or ancestors or what was the influence
of your mother or grandmother, etc., etc. I didn't have that, and certainly I
never could write about it in journalism or essays of any sort, or biographies
or autobiography. Autobiography is unthinkable except as a casual thing in
O Albany! But this way, this continuity of family, was a way of looking at
something important, and in *Bones,* I came to an ancestral influence that
seemed to be at the heart of a lot of things I knew about people of this kind.

Smith: Now you're talking about the Malachi episode back in the nineteenth century, the prehistory of the Phelans of Colonie Street.

Kennedy: Right, yes. You know there are episodes in history in Ireland that are parallel to the Malachi story and there's also a certain element that is ongoing in Irish history—the relationship with the church, and the superstitions, and the profound ignorant behavior of some people; and I saw how it could have affected subsequent lives. That was central to me in the culmination of this book.

Smith: I want to go back after a while to some of those ancestral roots, both in the novel and also the whole cycle, but when *Very Old Bones* ends, I mean in the final page in 1958, there are still Phelans and Quinns alive, so we can't talk about absolute finality, which is not to say that you are going to write a sequel to it tomorrow. But not only is Billy Phelan still alive, but the principal narrator and focal character of *Very Old Bones,* a new character in the cycle, Orson Purcell, Peter Phelan's bastard son, is still very much alive, too. Now is there some significance that this whatever it is, fulfilling or culminating novel, is told mostly by a bastard son of the Phelans?

Kennedy: That's an evolutionary event. I started to tell it through Daniel Quinn who, in a certain sense, being the son of George Quinn and Peg, was somewhat akin to myself. And I could not make that work. I felt that that was artificial. I was full of constraint. I find it very difficult to invent out of my own personal life. But when I was able to find parallel figures in my own acquaintances who could be coalesced into a single character and who would behave quite differently from me, have experiences quite different from my own, then I was able to see a narrator and hear a narrator and believe a narrator. Until then I couldn't. I didn't believe it. Whenever I was going to use a parallel to my own life, as Daniel Quinn, if I tried to invent outside of my own experience, and if I reached too far, I would say, "That can't happen. I would never do that. Danny Quinn would never do that." But of course, Danny Quinn very well might do such a thing and it's a fallacy that autobiographical fiction is really commonplace, for it isn't really. I think there must be an awful lot of writers like me. I don't believe Hemingway was like his prototypes, his principal characters, like Jake Barneses. I think that he may have been closer to them than I am to mine, but he had to invent, he had to find a way to leap out of his own skin. And that's in a certain way what I did when I found Orson. Orson was able to go crazy and be outlandish and have experiences that were really very, very far afield of my own. His World War II experiences, his whole experience with the Nazis in Germany, was very much different from what I was ever involved in. But, I knew about people

who had comparable experience, and I was able to fuse all that. The principle
I suppose is that you can't lie, and the lie is the contravention of your own
self and your own capacity. And that contravention would be a lie; whereas
if you *invent* this wild man, then anything is possible and it's not a lie anymore.

   Smith: Well, you've actually anticipated and really gone a long way
toward answering my next question on the strategy, the literary strategy of
having a bastard and a mad man tell this enormously complicated chronicle
of *Very Old Bones;* and I suppose with the equal emphasis on the bastard and
the madman—the kind of liberating aspect and the different kind of vision
that the Phelan and the Quinn saga would get from someone who was a
bastard and someone who goes crazy right in the middle of the novel, as a
matter of fact.

   Kennedy: Well, Orson was capable of it and, because he was a bastard he
had far more interest (than Quinn) in this family that he chose to acquire.
And so instead of alienating himself from it because of his bastardy, he chose,
perhaps involuntarily, but maybe it wasn't so involuntary, to go crazy in New
York and know that the chances were he'd wind up in Albany, being cared
for by his aunts and uncles and so on. And so maybe that drive to madness
was to find an honorable way to move into the family's life and then chronicle
it, and chronicle his own life as well. *Quinn's Book* was comparable to *Bones*
in the sense that Quinn was looking back from an advanced age to his childhood and young manhood, whereas Orson is looking, not only at himself, but
at everybody around him, trying to comprehend, and put into some profound
family focus, what really was the underpinning behavior of this peculiar family. And he discovers Malachi, although it's too easy to explain it away with
just Malachi. But you also have Malachi's influence on a woman as strong-
minded as the mother of this family, Kathryn Phelan, a matriarch of great,
great strength and will. And however wrong-headed she became in the subsequent years, the foundation of her beliefs, and the beliefs she imposed on this
family were rigorously moral and comprehensible. It's just that as time
moved along, they became corrupting. They didn't change with the times,
and it is this inflexibility that we see in the church today—in terms of abor-
tion, birth control, celibacy of priests and so on. The disintegration of the
church is before us all the time because of these things. That wasn't really
why I was writing—not to have a parallel to the church—but just to know
that these strong-willed people who are influenced by these incredibly power-

ful historical events, are moral in themselves too. You know, they are not villainous people.

Smith: I want to get back to that soon about the whole way that Irish-American Catholicism is part of this mighty torrent of your work, as I put it before, but I still want to talk a little bit about the character of Orson in terms of that tradition. Where did that character come from—quite apart from the literary strategy of having the bastard and the madman tell his story which you talked about? In the mythology of the Phelans and the Quinns as you gestated them over the years, from 1959 on, was the character Orson Purcell lurking somewhere? Where did that character really come from?

Kennedy: When I started to write this book I had him as a cousin who was considered, as George Quinn calls him, a floo-doo, whatever that means. He was crazy in some way. I had him behaving in a very negative way, burglarizing the family home after it's closed down, stealing things he felt he either should have or could profit from. I had him stealing one of his father's paintings that was in the house.

Smith: Yes, Peter Phelan, his father, is Francis's younger brother and the artist who creates the Malachi suite, which is very much a part of *Very Old Bones*.

Kennedy: That version of Orson existed in several early drafts when Danny Quinn was telling the story. But then I began to have this trouble trying to create Quinn, because he didn't have the experience Orson had. Orson was wilder. Orson was known as a madman, and he looked to be a likely candidate for a narrator, a very smart guy who was a navel-gazer of a kind, but who also had a sense of history and had this profound interest in the family. It didn't seem profound at first glance, but as time went on he became more interesting to me; and I rejected the idea of him being this second-rate cousin who's really a cheap burglar and winds up in a kind of scandalous moment at the end of the book with a woman and the police. It was a terrible ending for Orson, even though it was the kind of life he was living. So I chose not to go in that direction, for as Orson began to talk, he made sense. He came to see Billy Phelan, talked to Billy, heard Billy confess things to him; and then he began to confess himself, for he trusted Billy in a way he had never before trusted anybody. So he tells Billy his story about Germany, and his cheating at cards, and his magicianship, and so on. I felt Orson had evolved into a much more interesting character than the sleazeball, lost, crazy-headed, sex-crazed cousin he was originally.

Smith: It's very significant that, in addition to being a bastard and madman, he's also a magician. Magic as practiced, and as metaphor, figures very prominently in your work in the Albany Cycle, certainly in *Ironweed* and *Billy Phelan* and *Quinn's Book,* and very much so, in many ways, in *Very Old Bones.* And I'm thinking of Orson, his talent as a magician and also well the whole phenomenon of the dark world of witchcraft and things like that, that go back in the Malachi episode in the 19th Century, that wonderful dramatic blasphemy that's part of that episode. Is this some kind of full circle?

Kennedy: I would think so. I think that magic has always been central to the Irish, from he Celts forward, the belief in the mythic life of people and birds and creatures, on through to the miracles of the church, and the witchcraft trials. And magic is the basis for the church, the whole foundation of the life of Christ—all those miracles—walking on the water, and the loaves and the fishes multiplied, water into wine—these wonderful, magical concepts that have galvanized the imagination of the entire world for two millenniums, and which have, as their foundation, the infusion into the minds of the children this belief that magic is possible, and miracles are real. You must believe in the Trinity, which you can't even explain. It's an anomaly, but don't try to fight it, just believe it. That was definitely in my makeup, and also I had a magician's kit, and I read *Mandrake the Magician* when I was a kid, and I always wanted to be able to fool people, but never got the hang of it. Then later I got to know about card thieves, which is magic of another order.

Smith: There's a kind of paradox in the Irish tradition that I think is crystallized in your novels, and particularly *Very Old Bones,* perhaps as dramatically as anywhere. On the one hand, this is how James Joyce referred to the Irish, the most priest-led race in Europe, and, by extension, the world, and tremendously under the sway of the imperatives of the church, the theology of the church, the strictures of the church. On the one hand, there are the imperatives, the theology, the strictures of the church and the official mysteries of Catholicism, while on the other hand, there is the great tradition of pagan magic. You put those things together very dramatically in the history of this family. And I wonder if that paradox is something you felt all along as you were gestating not only the grand design of the Phelan-Quinn-myth, but also maybe your own consciousness?

Kennedy: Well, I don't know about my own consciousness but I can see that the idea of putting the church and magic together is not anything except historical perception. The church put it together. When you read the *Malleus Maleficarum—The Hammer of Witches,* a book that was quite widely accepted by Popes and hierarchy of the church, and affected a great many lives, you can see that here was a belief that there were such things as witches, those pagan figures who worshiped Satan, yes, but God knows what else they worshiped. They were viewed as heretical, out to destroy the civilized world as the church tried to represent it, out to overthrow the priests, out to emasculate men, out to denigrate women. Everything evil that you could do to a society was being done by these witches, and the church ganged up on them, found a way to put them away, put witchcraft away to burn them, destroy them, crucify them, whatever they needed to do to maintain a grip on this utterly false front of legitimate miracle.

Smith: Wasn't there always a tension, an ironic discrepancy, between the miracles of the Church and that other kind of renegade "magic"?

Kennedy: Magic was everywhere in my life, legitimized and not. And both forms were absolutely fascinating. I discovered that these pagan rituals from the Middle Ages were still being carried out right up until the late 19th Century in Ireland, and probably in this country as well, so I just moved it all, in *Very Old Bones,* as I do with everything, to Albany. If it can happen there, it can happen here.

Smith: Time-present in *Very Old Bones* is 1958 and much of the action takes place in the 1953 to 1958 frame with significant episodes from earlier times. Is 1958 simply a very plausible, strategic date as far as the ages and the experiences of people in that particular family? Or, do you think that that is a kind of culminating time or at least symbolically so for that whole era?

Kennedy: Well, it was the year the Albany Senators baseball team went out of business.

Smith: Well, that's very significant.

Kennedy: it was there when these Phelans were coming into their, what is it, senectitude, is there such a word—*De senectute*—and they were just dying. Orson just happens to be privy to the final illumination of the line through his father, who is about to die almost any minute, but who has, through this great force of will, completed this suite of paintings, the Malachi suite, which has brought into focus all of the anomalies that he's been monitoring for so many years, that he was witness to when Francis came home but couldn't understand then; and, as he points out, Francis went to his grave not knowing why his sister and mother wouldn't let him come home. Francis probably assumed it was the bitterness over Katrina and such things, but without understanding what underpinned those things, and what was so profound in their motivation. I felt that at some point, in an arbitrary year, something had to happen. There's a certain logic that dictates how far you can go in time, and I think it had to follow on the heels of the Korean War, if I was going to use that experience with Orson where he goes apeshit in Germany, and then his marriage falls apart. How does it ever come back together? And, if it does, under what circumstances? If Giselle does have a career, then she has to have time for a career. So five years is not unreasonable for her to extend herself into the world of photography and then think, well maybe there is something else in life. And so her return is possible. Also, Molly's getting old, very old, Tommy's dead, Sarah's dead, the house is going to go up for sale pretty soon, Peter's going to die. Molly would just as soon live in Saratoga, especially if Orson doesn't stay in the house. So all of these things are cumulative, and you just finally decide on time logistically, such as, where is Billy? When did Broadway close down? That was a contributing factor, for Broadway was still around but fading very fast in 1958. I remember when I came back in 1963 it was practically gone. So it was on the wane in '58. I may have hastened its waning a little bit in the book, but, more or less, that was what was happening. It was vanishing.

Smith: In other words, the historical particularities of Albany, the real Albany, Albany history, intersect with the fictive trajectory of these characters and the family. But is there some, you know, even more external vision that you have in 1958, or the end of the 1950s, as really the historical and mythic end of a way of life, or of a mentality that those generations, particularly of Phelans and Quinns, seem to express; that perhaps you'd write a whole different kind of cycle of novels about the next, and the next generations that would go through the '60s and '70s and '80s?

Kennedy: Yes, that's true. I have thought about a novel in the 1960s that would have theological, ecclesiastical conflict and I'm not sure I'll ever write it, but I might. The church, after Vatican II—those were extraordinary times for Catholics, and for most of the Irish and so I know this is hindsight now. And perhaps that was a contributing factor to *Very Old Bones,* knowing I couldn't come into the 1960s without acknowledging the hippie movement, and the open church, and the guitar-playing friars, and the folkies singing at mass, and mass turning into English, and Pope John XXIII, and everything that went with that, which was quite that opposite of the church in the time of Pius XII, his predecessor. And so in *Very Old Bones,* it is the time of Pius XII. He lived well beyond his years, in some kind of collusion with the Nazis, and on into our time of great liberation and demarcation. So that undoubtedly contributed. I'm not denying that. These things are conscious as you write. You know these historical periods. You know how far you can go, when you have to restrain yourself from getting into situations that you don't want to explain, that do not relate to the story at hand.

Smith: But you grew up in the historical period before Vatican II, and went to school in the 1930s and the 1940s, raised in a conventional working-class, middle-class family of Irish Catholics, went to a solidly-Catholic Christian Brothers Academy in Albany, and then to Siena College, long before there was any revolution in Catholic higher education.

Kennedy: They were Franciscans at Siena.

Smith: The Franciscans, right. Now, when you think of your particular environment at that time, and I'm talking about your education in the Henry Adams sense, what was the loss and gain of this? The Phelans and the Quinns were really haunted by a kind of morality, and a kind of logic of both belief and sin and punishment. I'm talking about things that might be free-floating, like the anti-intellectualism, the kind of goad to piety that we see in so many of the Phelan women particularly, that self-denial and also sexual repression, that had all kinds of consequences. Then there were, as you said before, mysteries and maybe the structure. What was the loss and gain of going through a very parochial education during the '30s and '40s?

Kennedy: Well, I think the gain is the acquisition of mythology, and of a theology that grounds you in every way, prepares you for any number of encounters with the rest of the world that does not happen to coincide with your belief. But if you understand Catholicism, it's not a big leap to Buddhism. If you're a believer in the communion of saints you're not uncomfortable with the Greek gods. They make a great deal of sense to you and you just put them, as Joseph Campbell did, into a wonderful fusion of human psyche, how it came to be. I feel that my education was restricted because of the emphasis on religion. I felt that they overdid it in high school and college with the philosophy, with the restricted philosophy of Catholic theologians and Catholic philosophers, and with the formalized imposition of religious dogma, even when you were a senior or junior in college; and it became really silly by that time. But it's not easy to shed those beliefs and those imposed attitudes that you've gotten in your head since you were in grammar school. From first grade on they sent us over to the nuns, and three times a week I was getting religious instructions. So from the time I was six years old until—you know that's fifteen years—until I graduated from college, there was nothing but the imposed Catholic religion; and it took me a while to shed it and respect it. I respected it originally out of fear, but eventually out of appreciation. I came to understand the difference between the meaning of the church and its individual priests. I couldn't separate those in childhood. And as I grew older, the negative elements of it, the fear of sin, fear of hell, fear of damnation, this ridiculous purgatory, and limbo—where you went after death if you were not baptized, for nobody who was not baptized could enter the kingdom of heaven—these things I swore I was not going to impose on my children, for however much I admired the church, I did not want my kids to grow up with this medieval idea of the afterlife, and so I haven't. If they come to any kind of crisis concerning the afterlife it'll be of their own making, their own discoveries. They didn't have it shoved down their throat. If they have any guilt it'll be genuine guilt. They'll have to have done something to earn it, and not be plagued by the gratuitous guilt that's imposed on you, like original sin. I had an argument in Puerto Rico one night about everybody being guilty, and I really think I argued that that was the truth. I think I was somehow still reflecting my catechism at an advanced age; I must have been 26 or 27. Whatever guilt we have it's certainly not earned under those circumstances. It's a delusion that's imposed on you.

Smith: I wonder if that overdeveloped sense of guilt that involves formidable moral structures and moral imperatives is something that really does inform your novels? There's no doctrinaire aspect of it, but what people do really matters. I mean, they are haunted people, but on the other hand there is that sense that we are responsible, and we have to live with our consciences. I just wonder if that's part of this loss and gain.

Kennedy: Yes, I think when Francis comes home and we see him in his great conflict of loyalty to the family, and abandonment of family, and guilt over dropping the child, and the guilt over running away, he knows there's something here that really is important. There is a moral imperative that has been driving him all these years so that he keeps coming back to Albany; and yet he never can go home. And we see in *Very Old Bones* that he comes home to his mother's funeral and he's ready to, maybe, confront his wife, but he never does. Four years go by before he meets his son Billy Phelan, who bails him out of jail and then gives him the signal that it's time. And the drive to go home is still there, this internal machinery that has been imposing guilt on him for how long, and he says "without my guilt I have nothing," and he does go home and he assuages that guilt. It's his purgatory, that's what the book is based in, *his* purgatorio, and Dante's. And the whole feeling I had when I was writing it is that he has this kind of escalating series of encounters that parallel some of the language in Dante, which was a moral construction that helped me look at Francis's escalation into a time of paradise, his liberation from that guilt, his feeling that he had at last entered into a kind of paradise where he was able to forget, which is what happens when he crosses the rivers into paradise out of purgatory. He encounters two rivers at the end and he does begin to forget. He forgets the marks on Helen's soul, and he forgets the way Gerald looked in the grave, and he's at ease with himself in a certain way. A good many people thought that was because he had died. But he had not. He had just, in a certain sense, begun to live with himself.

Smith: I remember Humphrey Bogart once said, "I don't trust anybody that doesn't drink." I've modified that to mean, "I don't trust unfallen people," and that's what maybe this is all about, that whether it's Francis with his guilt, or everybody, all of us, we are all fallen people, and that sense of guilt, if it doesn't kill us, gives us a kinship with humanity. And I think that that's what is so powerful in your books and why the Albany Cycle is "moral" in a non-doctrinaire and non-pietistic way.

Kennedy: I suppose that it's a triumph for the church in a certain way. Even when you get out of it you don't get out of it.

Smith: When you were going through your own religious education, now this is in the late 1940s when you were at Siena College, what were you allowed to read as far as the sanctioned literature that had any impact, and then at the same time what was your underground literary life when you were a college student? Or had that not congealed yet?

Kennedy: No, it hadn't. It just was beginning to congeal as I was getting out of school and getting to know something about Hemingway and Faulkner. I had really a simplistic childhood education. In college they taught us Keats and Byron and *Beowulf* and Shakespeare, classic works, but I never got a modern writer. I never got a Hemingway story. I never got a Joyce story. Yeats was in the text, but we never got to Yeats.

Smith: Well, Joyce of course, at that time, was very much a heretical writer, and Yeats was a Protestant, even though they were these great Irish giants.

Kennedy: They somehow found their way in to our literature book, but they weren't taught—not to me. And there was also a Hemingway story in the text—"The Undefeated," but we never got to it. So modern literature was a foreign country to me.

Smith: During the decade of the 1950s—which, as we were saying, is also the decade of most of the action of *Very Old Bones,* in Albany, but after you finished Siena—you became a newspaperman, not in Albany at first but in Glens Falls. Then you were a journalist in the Army, back to Albany and then on to Puerto Rico. You had really quite an education, after college, in the newspaper business and just about every aspect of journalism, isn't that right? How did that work as part of your education as a writer?

Kennedy: Well, just to correct the chronology, what happened was that I came out of college and went to work as a sports writer, went in for two years of writing Army sports, back for three and a half years to the *Times-Union* as a general-assignment reporter and all sorts of things, including being weekend city editor, and then to Puerto Rico as a reporter/columnist, and I wound up as assistant managing editor. And all that happened in Puerto Rico in nine months. Then I went to the *Miami Herald* for about eight months and I made the decision there to quit journalism, went back to San Juan and free-lanced for a couple of years, became the *Time-Life* stringer, *The New York Times* tourism stringer, the *Vision* Magazine stringer and so on.

Smith: What years were these?

Kennedy: In 1956 I went to San Juan for the first time, then to Miami in '57, and back to San Juan later in '57 until 1963. In the summer of 1959 we started *The San Juan Star,* an English language daily in the bilingual community, and it's still going, and it's now owned by Scripps-Howard. Then it was owned by Gardner Cowles of *Look* Magazine, and I was the managing editor. Bill Dorvillier, who is still alive up in Woodstock, New Hampshire, was the editor, and Andy Viglucci, who is now the editor, was city editor; and the three of us really put the paper together with some businessmen who handled the business end of it. I had a good time for two years and then I quit, which was my swan song as a full-time journalist. I realized that after those years as managing editor, which is as high as I ever aspired, I wanted to return to fiction. The editor's job was an offer I couldn't refuse—starting a newspaper from scratch and helping it grow in two years to 20,000 circulation, and be very influential. The editor won a Pulitzer Prize that first year for our editorial campaign against the church.

Smith: How appropriate and prophetic.

Kennedy: But I felt that that was as far as I wanted to go, and that if I didn't get out soon I'd get to the point of no return.

Smith: Now, while you were managing editor of *The San Juan Star* for two years—that would have been 1959–61—during that particular period you had a momentous and significant encounter with your future as a fiction writer. That's when Saul Bellow came to Puerto Rico and you connected with him. You want to talk a little bit about what the nature of that significance was?

Kennedy: Well, I was working full-time as managing editor and, in our first year, I think it was 1960, Saul came down. We ran his picture in the paper and the story with it said he was accepting applications for a fiction-writing course he was going to teach. So, I said OK, I'll give it a whirl, and I submitted the novel that I was working on and he accepted me. And he also accepted a couple of my friends. And we all wound up seeing him individually at the faculty club. You went over and spent an hour shooting the breeze with him, and he would have read your chapter or your story, or maybe he'd read it then and have it fresh in his mind, and then you talked about it as long as was necessary. He was highly critical of the first things I showed him, but he had accepted me, and he felt that the chapters were substantial, even so, and were on the way to being something. He gave me this criticism, and it was enormously helpful, for when I gave him a revised version two weeks later, he said, this is terrific, this is publishable. And that was the first serious encounter I had with anyone in the literary world who understood what was really publishable. A lot of my friends were aspiring writers with literary educations but they did not know what the publishing world was, didn't know the dimensions of the critical apparatus of that world, or how it would view such a thing as this book. But Bellow did. Well, he was wrong, it turned out. That book, when I finished it, didn't get published. But it almost did and it got me an agent who tried for a couple of years to sell it and failed.

Smith: Now what specifically, what piece of fiction was it?

Kennedy: This book was *The Angels and the Sparrows.*

Smith: Which, as we said sometime ago, was really the first version of the creation of the Phelan family.

Kennedy: I hadn't written anything like that before, and it's where I really began to feel that I was working out of some kind of strength. I had never felt that when I was writing short stories about North Albany in the old days at the *Times-Union* because I was such a beginner. And I never felt it in what I wrote about Puerto Rico from 1956 to 1960. None of those stories seemed to engage what was deepest in me, and what seemed to be worth reading. But this book did, and a lot of people, not only my friends, realized that this was good and probably publishable. But it wasn't, ultimately, and I remember Belle Sideman, who was the wife of the circulation director of *Look* Magazine, and who was an editor at Random House—she read the book, whose title at that point was, I think, *One by One.* And she said this is very good, but it's not going to get published. And the reason is that every time you read another chapter you know that that person's dead, or is going to die, or is useless, or forget about it. So it was a mistaken exercise in the construction of a novel. It wasn't a novel. It was a series of episodes, as is *Very Old Bones,* but in *Bones,* they're all integrated. *The Angels* just brushed against one another in each one of their stories, an amateur effort with a certain primitive power in the writing.

Smith: Now, these characters, were they called Phelan?
Kennedy: Yes, they were.

Smith: Which characters really survived, obviously transformed as your writing evolved, but which characters from that first, unpublished novel, really survived in the form that we know them in the Albany Cycle?
Kennedy: Well, Francis was there, but he wasn't married, and so he wasn't really Francis yet. Peter was totally different. Peter was bright but weak. Molly was there, but I think she was called Mary, which is Molly's real name—Molly is just a diminutive of Mary. Sarah was there, only I called her Sate and I think that was short for Satan. There's an allusion to that in *Bones* where she wants to be called Sate because her mother was called Kate. She wanted to be everything that her mother was. In *Bones* she's Sarah. Tommy was there, the moron. The father was very different, but the father is dead in *Very Old Bones,* long since. He dies in 1895, in a train accident. The mother, Kathryn, is more or less the same, but much more complex in *Bones.* The china closet episode was there.

Smith: Is that right?
Kennedy: Yes, but for totally different reasons. Molly's pregnancy, the

taking of her husband's corpse, were both there. Molly's was a far more clandestine marriage than in *Bones.*

Smith: But the fact that that cast of characters was there in association with each other and with also some of these major themes that, granted, were much transformed in both style and form; but I think that's quite remarkable. Now, when Bellow read this, did he encourage you to become a serious novelist and get out of journalism, at least full time, as soon as you possibly could?

Kennedy: Well, the impetus to get out was there from the beginning, and if I had never met Bellow I would have eventually left journalism; and I would also have published, because I had that drive. Nobody was going to stop that. I was going to become a novelist. There was no way out of that. It might have taken me another ten years. But it took me years as it was. I mean we are talking about 1960. I didn't sell a book until eight years later. Whatever my encounter with Bellow was, it was not instant access to fame and glory and money. When I sold *The Ink Truck* in 1968 I made $3,500. That was hardly big money, but for me it was a mountain of gold. I didn't care. I would have accepted $500 just to get the book published and confirm that I was a writer. Because that was a very isolated and excruciating decade for me.

Smith: That's the 1960s you're talking about?

Kennedy: Yes, the '60s. I mean it was also a great decade. My children were just beginning to grow up, and I was free to write, and I was also free to starve, and I was working at the *Times-Union* and having a great time covering the Civil Rights Movement and slum lords and becoming a movie critic, all these things with a very low level of income, so inadequate that I used to go out of the house in the morning with a dime in my pocket, a dime to make a phone call in case of an emergency—so I could call and get money from somebody else.

Smith: This was after you had returned to Albany and you were working?

Kennedy: I was working part-time for the *Times-Union,* working for $100 a week. I came back in the summer of 1963.

Smith: But, before you did, and we'll get back to that particular period and what came out of that, what really came out of that connection with Bellow? Was it mostly a symbolic or inspirational encounter, or did he actually have an editorial impact on you manuscript?

Kennedy: He didn't have an overview. He never read the whole book, for it wasn't finished then. He read maybe four of five sections of it. Some of the sections he'd tell me, These are good, I don't have any complaints; and another one he'd tell that the writing was fatty, clotty, and he corrected my sentences. You know he said, you're saying everything twice. That sort of criticism was very important. He also said something I never forgot, which was the idea that you should be prodigal. He said, just think about it, the billions of sperm that are expended in any given act of sex, but it only needs one to make a life. So, he said, be prodigal. Write as much as you need, to get what you want, and throw the rest away.

Smith: Many, many people have, in one way or another, noted the tremendous vitalism in your fiction. Were you aware that in Bellow's fiction at this time, and I'm thinking particularly of the two novels that he had written prior to when you encountered him in 1960, *The Adventures of Augie March* and *Henderson the Rain King*—that in both novels there's a kind of almost heroic vitalism about the characters, and they also have the prose that goes with it. Was that something you noted at the time and is it something that you feel somehow evolved in your own fiction?

Kennedy: Well, I had read *Augie March* partially, I think, before I met him, and I was reading *Henderson* when I was studying with him. I had been reading it before that. I loved *Henderson* and I liked *Augie* a lot. I had a harder time with *Augie* only because of the extent to which he went in developing characters. These were not necessarily story-related expansions of the characters. They were character expansions for their own sake, it seemed to me, and then the story would resume. My experience with *Henderson* was that it was one man moving through this exotic world; and it was always his consciousness. Everything was an impulse forward, no matter how many digressions there were. He was always central to the story. And in that sense I thought it was a better novel than *Augie March.* Yet there is so much in *Augie* that is terrific. What *Henderson* did was make me feel that I was a rank amateur, that I would never get anywhere with that kind of novel—and I still can't aspire to that sort of novel. Bellow has a mind that is far more learned and far more interested in ideas than mine could ever be. My world is the world of event, and speculation, and language, but certainly not the expatiation of ideas or philosophical attitudes.

Smith: Many of your characters seem to be the embodiment of a kind of life-force—including Francis Phelan. Bill, I'd like to talk particularly about

the making of *Ironweed.* We've talked in the past about the evolution of the
Phelan and the Quinn families going back to *The Angels and the Sparrows.*
But I'd like to talk about how the individual characters crystallized in certain
novels. Now, for example, you said that Billy Phelan was inspired by your
uncle Pete McDonald. And of course he is one of the centers of consciousness
of *Billy Phelan's Greatest Game.* How about the Francis Phelan of *Ironweed?* How long did that character evolve in the context of that novel? I
mean, who is Francis? Where did he come from? I know you said when you
were doing *Angels and Sparrows* Francis was there, but in the making of
Ironweed, the novel, how did he come about?

Kennedy: I wrote the first Francis in Puerto Rico, and he was a young
guy, thirtyish maybe, who was already drunk, and who had left home and
was sort of a bum on the road. He finds out his mother's dead and he comes
home, and he's a bad and nasty drunk. He comes into a saloon and they give
him some "hellos" and he's nasty even to his old friends. Then he goes out
and he gets *really* drunk and winds up at the mission. He comes out of the
mission and goes to confession. He is not interested in the preacher at the
mission to confess—but he's impelled to go back and respond in some way
to his own past, his own peccadillos, whatever they were. That confession
was a cliché, but Francis did have an original vitality in that book, which I
liked. And so when I did *Billy,* I reached back and lifted Francis out. In the
meantime, I had done some reporting on winos in Albany and there was this
guy I came across and I called him Buddy. I called him that in a series of
articles that I wrote about the wino life. Buddy was a very articulate, funny
fellow, a desperately-defeated guy at the bottom of the world getting drunk
every night, a real wino, but with this very engaging intelligence. There was
something that caught my attention in that idea—that here is this incredible
intelligence in a human being at the bottom of the world, and you know he
was almost hallucinating sometimes when we'd talk—he'd be rambling. And
that idea pervaded my creation of Francis—the idea that here was a man at
the bottom of the world, and yet he is still witty, resilient in a way, ready to
get up tomorrow and start over, but not in any way that moved toward personal redemption or success in any form whatever. The opposite really. He
was driving obviously towards self-destruction. At the same time he was
riding on a rainbow of hallucinatory, boozy arcs. Rising up, peaking, going
down, depressed, drunk, getting up in the morning, rising up again. That was
a remarkable thing, and it struck me, when I began to write it, that that's
probably the way Francis lived. He gets up out of an old field full of weeds,

snow in his ears, and he walks towards the bridge to commit suicide because he doesn't want to stand another night like this, but he can't kill himself. He turns around and he goes on and lives his life. I suspect that I had this feeling that Francis also had a drive toward redemption. Where that comes from, I don't know, but I suspect that that was the way I felt about the man who belonged in this particular story, for that's what the story was about. It wasn't a tragedy of disillusion and dying alone. Even Helen's disillusion and dying alone isn't a tragic thing in itself because she's somehow justified, and at peace with death, through her own thought. That's the way I felt about her anyway.

Smith: Now, when you started to write it, and we're talking about the genesis of the novel *Ironweed,* you had completed *Billy Phelan's Greatest Game,* and Francis had made a brief but significant appearance in that novel. When did this crystallize? You've created many unforgettable characters in your novels, but Francis Phelan is one of the gigantic, memorable, fallen characters in contemporary fiction, maybe twentieth century fiction. Readers all over the world seem to be bale to empathize and identify with this character who is a drunk, a renegade, a runner, a killer—one could go on—and yet, he's a character of enormous moral complexity, which is why he is this gigantic character. Where did all that moral complexity come from in your development of Francis Phelan?

Kennedy: I'm not sure. It comes out of me, obviously. The moral complexity of Francis is somehow my idea of what a man would be, given this incredible matrix of psychological, psychic, physical suffering and, at the same time, he would still be a man of moral means, a man who had a populist, quasi-heroic—almost—streak in him from childhood, who was a daredevil. It's like juxtaposing the daredevil element of a life with the worst that can happen to that daredevil, and then seeing what comes of it. I mean the physical, psychic, and moral odds against him are staggering. He must strive constantly to stay alive physically, psychically, psychologically, sexually, professionally as a baseball player, and emotionally as a family member. He's always challenged at every level you could imagine a man being challenged at, and he survives.

Smith: And, of course, Francis appears again, and finally, unforgettably in *Very Old Bones.* How about the title, *Very Old Bones,* for this very complex, elaborate, brooding and yet ebullient novel about these Albany families? When did you know that that was your title?

Kennedy: I had it as a working title for a long time and I called it *Old Bones.* I didn't like that much. So I added "very."

Smith: That was my next question. Why *Very Old Bones?*

Kennedy: Well, the story of Malachi, and the dredging up of that skeleton in the family closet, so to speak. I felt that that was one element of bones. There were other bones. There were the mastodon bones and . . .

Smith: Very ancient relics.

Kennedy: . . . also Billy's broken leg and Tommy's chipped backbone, and Peter's arthritic hips, and the corpse of the infant in the cellar; and there is that final skeleton dance in the last chapter. But this was a book about ancestry, and its influence on the contemporary family. I felt that was an apt title—to think of those old bones moldering in some pauper cemetery somewhere in Albany and still exercising an influence three generations later. Not only that—these old bones being a product also of much older bones. The antecedents of the pernicious attitudes of Malachi are absolutely central to what he becomes in his own time, and what he does to affect the lives of those who come after him.

Smith: There's a wonderful sentence right at the end of the book which I wonder if you could elaborate on in terms of this multiple meaning, multiple resonance for the title. This is Orson, who at the tag-end of *Very Old Bones* says, "We are, after all, a collective, a unified psyche that so desperately wants not to be plural. I am one with the universe, each of the Phelans say, but I am one. It's a problem we have."

Kennedy: It's the idea of the Phelans being what they were; and what they have become in Orson's mind. He sees the collective behavior that distinguishes the Phelans from other families. He knows they're not so different from other families, and he has been able to perceive the similarities—the weirdness in their lives, the religious zealotry that has warped so many of them, the fear of life that existed in them, the clandestine life of Molly. Not that that is so unusual, but when Orson looks at it all together, he sees this behavior and considers it a collective. He says, "we want to be plural." They're all striving for their individual destinies, but they seem afflicted, somehow, by this code that they don't even know exists, but had been promulgated before they were born, and has worked its way into the consciousness of their parents, their grandparents, and their ancestors of untraceable distance—and it has made them what they are—"You made me what I am today, I hope you're satisfied."

Smith: And all the while that you have been writing this great cycle of novels about individual character and collective fate, you have also been writing journalism, nonfiction, movies—including movies of your own novels. But the main focus is on your fiction, is it not?

Kennedy: The only thing that makes me tick is my novels. If I were doing only journalism and movie scripts, I would be a very unhappy person because I would not feel like a serious citizen of the world. I don't think I'm as serious as I can be in journalism, and I'm certainly not in the movies. Movies are great fun and journalism is wonderful, but all these are composite operations that have to deal with approval by other people, even approval of yourself to deal with the other people. You have to really wonder how movies ever get made, once you get into the movie business, because it is so ridiculous as a life pursuit. I would never do that and I'm counseling my son Brendan not to do it either. But it's fun.

Smith: OK. All these composite activities, or changes of pace, which are fun and rewarding in various ways, and stimulating in various ways, do you worry at this point that they'll undercut your energy or your focus to go on and on and write novels, write serious novels which obviously come from the depths of your imagination?

Kennedy: I don't think that they will undercut it. If I thought they would, I would stop doing them. I think of them as a source of diversion and money. You do make money when you write novels but that's not really why you write novels. You can think of any number of things to do over a four-year period that would make you more money than you get writing a novel. But I'm always writing novels. I'm accumulating novels now. I'm going back and discovering what I had in my notebooks, five, ten, fifteen, twenty years ago and exercising the imagination on that old stuff which is—I don't know really what it is. The more I discover, the more I wonder what it means.

Smith: Well, I was going to ask you. I have heard serious novelists say that they were worried at some point that they would exhaust their material. If you lived to be 150, do you think that you would exhaust your material for what we now call the Albany Cycle of novels?

Kennedy: I don't know. I think that I have an awful lot of books in my head. But they're not all equal. All pigs are not created equal. Some are more equal than others, and those are the ones that leap forward and get written. Some of them have too much water in their blood at this stage, but usually that's a product of insufficient thinking, insufficient imposition of the imagination on the material, because you never like the book when you start it. If I lived to be 150, which is not that far away, it's only 86 years, I have maybe five books right at this moment that I could begin to focus on. There are always five out there somehow. Because the more I go, the more I learn about these various moments in history, and then more and more people demand attention. I mean, Quinn of *Quinn's Book* is an incomplete character. Whatever happened to him? Well, I'm going to have to figure that out sooner or later. Whatever happened to Maud? Where did George Quinn come from? Where did Danny Quinn come from? Six novels. I forgot about Puerto Rico. Somewhere I've got to do Puerto Rico, but I don't know how, and I'll probably be as transient about it as I was in the treatment of Germany.

Smith: Well, more and more I've thought that there is something Balzacian about you, that you're a kind of nineteenth century novelist in the twentieth century, and I'm not alluding to *Quinn's Book,* but in the sense that the more you create, the more is there. That both you and I think your attentive readers wonder about, yes, what indeed happens to Maud and Quinn at the end of *Quinn's Book,* and then you could go on and on. So it really is inexhaustible in the way it was for the great nineteenth century novelists.

Kennedy: I hope so, because that's really all I want to do. I have this world at my fingertips, really. It's as far away as the library and a shelf of Albany books, and a decision to enter a particular column of time that seems significant for me. I have a political novel about Dan O'Connell, the old Albany political boss and all of that crowd. I have a novel about the '60s somewhere. I have a fragment of a Puerto Rican novel. I have the conclusion of Quinn. I have a novel about the making of the play *The Flaming Corsage* and the beginning of movie-making in this country, the silent movie period.

Smith: And those six novels will generate six more?

Kennedy: Maybe. I hope so. And one of the things I'd love to do is go back and do a novel about the colonization, and the old Dutchmen that were around here.

Smith: Seventeenth century.

Kennedy: Really early seventeenth century, a wilderness novel maybe. I haven't figured that one out yet. That's really problematic and seems a long way away. There's also a very good Revolutionary War novel here with a lot of the principal figures of the Revolution being present.

Smith: That's a great omission in serious contemporary letters. We need a good Revolutionary War novel. Do you have a Watergate novel, a War of 1812 novel?

Kennedy: No, not yet. But there is a great history in the Revolution and there are two great characters. Three. There seems to be high drama there. I'm not sure I want to take it on at this stage. It might be something I'll save for a later time, when I get older. In my nineties, maybe.

Smith: There is a sense that your fiction seems to gravitate towards hope, towards deliverance, towards an ultimate redemption even. I think of the great endings of your novels—the ending of *Billy Phelan's Greatest Game,* Billy's deliverance back into the world again, back into the only cosmos in town. I think of the ending of *Ironweed*—Francis Empyrean, both his spiritual and emotional home, he has a vision of it at the very tag-end of *Ironweed.* And I think of that wonderfully satisfying, maybe the ultimate happy ending, the union of Quinn and Maud (at least for the time being) in *Quinn's Book,* and then of course that magnificent, mythic lunch on the 26th of July 1958, which ends *Very Old Bones.* Yet, on the other hand, Joshua, the run-away slave in *Quinn's Book* says what I think is maybe the quintessential, or one of the quintessential, Kennedy lines, "If you lose, it's fate, if you win, it's a trick." And what I'd like to ask you, two things, is there a contradiction there and what are the odds?

Kennedy: Well, I don't think there's a contradiction. I think what's inherent in that is that both things are eminently possible, both visions are eminently possible. "If you lose, it's fate. If you win, it's a trick." And Francis is trying to obviate that at the end of his life. I mean, he's won in certain ways. He's won psychologically and psychically by getting away, and he's won also by having gone home and found redemption. But he's also killed somebody else unpremeditatedly, and he's on the run, and so he really is nowhere again. That's hardly a totally happy ending. It's a psychically happy ending for Francis because he really has redeemed himself in a way that's very significant and very clear to his soul. He's a man who has arrived at a certain form of peace, found a way to live in the world without trying to kill himself constantly out of guilt and self-hate. But his fate is that he's again alone on the road. Billy Phelan, well, Billy is redeemed for the moment but, as you know, he doesn't go along with everything, and it looks like his victories were maybe just a trick. Or maybe just fate? Either one, it doesn't matter. He's still wondering where the hell he is in the world. I never feel that these endings are the ending of life. It's not a finale to a film or anything like that . . . and they lived happily ever after. It's a moment in which these characters become defined up to this point.

Smith: Sort of interim reports.

Kennedy: For instance, Orson and Giselle. What's going to happen there? They're going to remarry and have a child, but where is the future? I have no idea. I don't know where Maud and Quinn are. I don't know where Billy Phelan's going to go from here, but he's still alive in 1958. He's only 51 years old.

Smith: That's young.

Kennedy: You bet.

Smith: Well, in other words, there is no contradiction between those apparent "deliverances" or genuine redemptions, and Joshua's observation, "If you lose, it's fate. If you win, it's a trick."

Kennedy: Well, it's especially poignant to hear that coming from a black man, because the ways of the trickster are how so many balcks felt that they survived. That's why they loved the trickster figure in slave literature or *spoken* literature—the idea that you are always tricking the white man. The other side of that is that you're black and you're going to be a slave forever, and die a slave. That's what's happened to so many people. And it's still a terrible life for so many black people today.

Smith: And we are still working with those odds. You're still working with those odds for all those characters past, present and future. You're a novelist with a highly developed historical and social imagination. As we approach the millennium, are the odds nine-to-five or six-to-five, as you conjured with in a recent non-fiction piece of yours—will we make it?

Kennedy: Damon Runyon's idea was, I used to think, that "all life is nine-to-five against." Peter Maas corrected me on this and said the line was that "all life is six-to-five against, just enough to keep you interested." I'm interested, but I'll go with the nine.

Smith: Well, that's about as optimistic as one can get, I think, for the moment. So this is not our last conversation between now and the end of the century. But maybe we ought to end it on that.

Kennedy: Nine-to-five.

William Kennedy: An Interview by Don Williams

Don Williams / 1994

Published in *Poets & Writers* 22 (March/April 1994): 42–49.
Reprinted with permission of the publisher, Poets and Writers, Inc., 72
Spring Street, New York, NY 10012

A fortune cookie tumbled from a platter in a Chinese restaurant in January
1983 and came to rest in front of William Kennedy. The slip of paper tucked
inside read, "This will be your lucky week." The next day the MacArthur
Foundation awarded Kennedy a $256,000 grant. Before the week was out he
had burst into prominence on the literary landscape, for what was also the
week that Viking published *Ironweed* and reissued his novels *Legs* and *Billy
Phelan's Greatest Game,* to excellent reviews.

Kennedy smiles.

"That was one of the great weeks of history," he says in the brisk, mid-
register cadences of a born optimist. "It ended on my birthday, January six-
teenth."

Kennedy's thinning reddish hair, assertive nose, and white arc of teeth
were soon appearing on magazine covers across the country. Critics recognized the Albany trilogy as a literary tour de force. With the addition of
Quinn's Book (Viking) in 1986 and *Very Old Bones* (Viking) in 1992, the
trilogy has become a five-volume epic, with no end in sight.

A decade after becoming famous, Kennedy's smile still engages. At sixty-
four, his hair has gone gray, and he walks with a slight stiffness in his right
leg due to recent hip surgery.

Still, he walks as briskly as he talks, past the fountains and hanging green-
ery in the atrium of the Hyatt Regency in Knoxville, Tennessee, where he is
in town to give a reading from his growing treasure of books.

"Can we see James Agee's old neighborhood?" Kennedy asks, invoking
Knoxville's own Pulitzer-winning native son of Irish descent. "Agee was an
early influence on me," he adds as we sit in the motel restaurant and order
coffee.

Agee, the author of *A Death in the Family* and *Let Us Now Praise Famous*

Men, was one of those tragic, misplaced writers who could never go home again. Unlike Agee, Kennedy found his way home gracefully at age thirty-four, when he moved back to Albany, New York, in 1963 following a long odyssey.

Kennedy had been savoring the expatriate life in Puerto Rico, an exotic and romantic setting for a young journalist, especially a would-be novelist who was also in love.

The object of his affections was Dana Segarra, a dancer from Puerto Rico, who performed under the name Dana Sosa in such shows as *The Pajama Game* and *Me and Juliet.* The Broadway musical *New Faces,* in which she had been performing, had recently closed, and she was visiting her family in Puerto Rico when Kennedy met her at a party on December 27, 1956. They were married thirty-four days later and soon set up housekeeping in Dana's homeland.

Kennedy has described Puerto Rico as "a Spanish-language community full of hostility and reverence for the United States, with all sorts of politics, and left- and right-wing beach bums to write about." He wrote about them often from 1956 to 1963, freelancing between jobs at the *World Journal* in San Juan, the *Miami Herald,* and the *San Juan Star,* of which he was the first managing editor. Writing in the mornings and late at night, he attempted short stories and novels, but he could never make the island world come alive.

"I didn't know the Spanish language as well as I wanted, and so could never possess the literature of the complex world of Hispanic and Latin scholars . . . the Puerto Rican reality."

There were days when he would abandon his fiction to sit and turn desultorily through old picture books of Albany. At night, before he fell exhausted into sleep, he sometimes saw the city whole—a corrupted and blessed microcosm complete with history, customs, and idioms, and with hundreds of stories to tell.

Eventually, he found he could write about the psychology of almost anybody in Albany—"whether it was a baseball player or a politician or an artist or a drunk or a spinster or a clandestinely married woman"—far better than he could anyone in Puerto Rico. He found himself growing homesick for the scruffy, bustling city he had spurned in his youth.

In the early 1960s Kennedy tried to shape his vignettes about Albany into a novel. That manuscript would never be published, yet all of his fiction owes something to that work, which he called *The Angels and the Sparrows.*

"It created the Phelan family," says Kennedy. "It created Francis. He was a young man on the way to becoming a bum. I liked him a lot."

So did readers two decades later, when Kennedy made Francis the protagonist of *Ironweed.* Francis Phelan has become Kennedy's most enduring charter, and perhaps America's most famous derelict. Played by Jack Nicholson in the movie adaptation, for which Kennedy also wrote the screenplay, Francis is hard luck personified.

When Kennedy sat down to write *Ironweed,* the manuscript came in a rush that lasted six or seven months.

"It was all of a piece," he says. "The language, everything, was there." The book was poignant enough to earn Kennedy the Pulitzer Prize in 1984.

To fully appreciate Kennedy's approach to writing, you have to understand his relationship to Albany.

"Growing up, I loved Albany in a certain way," he says, "then I began to loathe it. I left it because I thought of it as provincial, corrupt, moribund, run by old men who were narrow-backed hypocrites. Then I realized, hey, that's all very interesting stuff.

"North Albany had everything," he recalls. "It had wild country, a creek, an old apple orchard, a swamp, rolling hills. There were a few people who had money and they all went to the same church. Eddie Carey was our landlord. He lived at the top of the hill and was involved with the politicians. He was a very nice man who made his fortune through city contracts. He built all the houses that we lived in. For three or four blocks, he built every house.

"Political bosses bought the elections every year. They stole millions. There was a ridiculous story about a Jeep. I think it cost the city twenty-eight thousand dollars to rent the Jeep from a contractor now and again. It would have only cost eight hundred to buy it." He laughs. "That was just a way of funneling money back from the city and the country to the city bosses."

Gangsters, gamblers, and derelicts haunted Albany at night, and Kennedy followed newspaper accounts of their comings and goings, but it would be years before he saw their dramatic possibilities. More fascinating were the heroes and villains Kennedy saw projected on the giant screens in Albany movie houses such as the Strand or the aptly named Palace.

"Probably nobody ever remembers the actor Lee Tracy anymore," he says, "but in the Thirties he always played this wisecracking Irish reporter with a fedora, and he's always in the city room." Kennedy liked his style.

By the time he graduated from Christian Brothers Academy, a military high school, Kennedy was set on being a newspaperman, and when he registered at Albany's Siena College in 1945, the first thing he did was look up Matt Conlin, the Franciscan priest who was in charge of the paper. Conlin was a generous, outgoing man, and he gave Kennedy what he still considers one of his great lessons in writing.

"I had a composition in which I used language that was all out of proportion to its context. I was writing about a rainstorm and I called it 'an infinitesimal cataclysm,' which is a contradiction in terms, isn't it?"

He laughs, shakes sweetener into a second cup of coffee.

"I felt bad, but I never did that again. I learned how to write straight. I wound up as the editor. All through college I was mad for being a newspaperman, absolutely out of my skin for becoming a columnist like Damon Runyon. I never wanted to be Walter Winchell, but I wanted that feeling of being at the center of things."

With that goal in mind, he took the best job he could find after college: assistant sports editor at the *Glens Falls Post-Star.* When the Korean War started, Kennedy joined the army, spent some time in Fort Benning, Georgia, then was sent to Europe in the first wave of Americans to go back there since World War II. Military life didn't slow his journalism career; he was assigned to his division's newspaper.

He admired the great war reporters, especially Ernie Pyle, but Kennedy was never sent to the front. Without a war to cover, he began sending a humor column home to the *Post-Star* called "This New Army."

The army, meanwhile, assigned him to cover the 1952 Olympic Games in Helsinki for military publications. One day he sat down to file a story, and there was Red Smith, the legendary columnist for the *New York Herald Tribune,* sitting in front of him, and Kennedy felt very important just to be near him. Never forgetting his journalistic roots, Kennedy scoffs at the notion that journalists can't also write great fiction.

"Of course they can," he says, "otherwise how do you account for García Márquez, Ernest Hemingway, Theodore Dreiser, John O'Hara, Stephen Crane. There's a drive, I think, when you want to be a writer, that, if you've got that in you, nothing is going to stop it. Newspapers, wars, anything else is going to be a temporary interruption to your otherwise illustrious future as a novelist."

Two such interruptions followed his service in the military. The first was when he took a job working on the city desk at the Albany *Times-Union*. The second was when he moved to Puerto Rico, little realizing he was leaving behind the raw ore from which he would forge his best work.

When Kennedy returned from Puerto Rico to Albany in 1963, his journalism complemented his fiction in unexpected ways. He came home to tend his father, who had pneumonia but refused to see a doctor. Kennedy loved being home again, and he knew instinctively that his success or failure as a novelist depended on his being there. He took another job at the *Times-Union*, this time as a feature writer.

Almost immediately, he was assigned to write a series of articles on the origin of Albany's neighborhoods. He spent four months doing it and gained an intimate knowledge of the city's myths, heroes, ethnic texture, and history. He was out of the office so much that the paper's editor thought he had left town, but he came up with twenty-six articles that were published in early 1964.

A strike at the newspaper inspired Kennedy's first novel: a rollicking, surrealistic effort called *The Ink Truck,* published by Dial in 1969. Kennedy's love affair with Albany blossomed with *Legs* (Coward-McCann, 1975), his second book and the first of the trilogy. Crafting that novel, he says, taught him more about writing fiction than anything he has ever done.

"I wrote that book eight times, and it didn't start working until the seventh draft."

Ironically, part of Kennedy's problem was the great wealth of material available to him.

"I had this authentic American figure, Jack 'Legs' Diamond, the most widely known gangster on the East Coast, as my subject. People were always giving me tips—here's a guy who drove booze for him, here's a sheriff who arrested him, here's a girl who used to sing for him in a saloon. I would go out and interview and discover another whole facet of his life, his times, his character.

"There were memoirs by cops, by show people, and so on who couldn't even get his name right. The things I like best about these stories were the lies, because I knew that people liked exaggerating in order to aggrandize themselves and put themselves in that privileged historic position. Everybody wants to be close to the myth, the legend."

At last Kennedy had heard enough.

"I came to the conclusion that if I didn't stop doing research I would never finish the book." He typed furiously, voluminously. He found he was writing about a self-conscious legend, and tried to climb inside his subject's head.

"Diamond came to believe he was misunderstood, but he was a genuine killer and thief of a major order. He graduated from thievery to murder."

And in describing that change in Diamond, Kennedy taught himself to distill vitality from faded newspaper clippings, to brew mythology from biographical data, to turn anecdote into drama.

Such were the things he learned how to do, and in mastering them, Kennedy graduated from journalist to novelist.

Others took note of Kennedy's work, and by the mid-Seventies he was getting teaching jobs, first at SUNY Albany, and later at Cornell.

The next book came easier. *Billy Phelan's Greatest Game* (Viking, 1978) is a fast-moving tale told in the third-person. It spills forth from two points of view. One is that of an urbane newspaper columnist who writes about Albany's underground, but who is equally at home in the city's theaters and drawing rooms. The other is that of a professional game player—pool hustler, card shark, bowler, and dice man who breaks the rules of a corrupt system and becomes an outcast in his own hometown.

The theme of a native son at odds with his community is continued in *Ironweed,* but if Kennedy himself ever felt like an outcast in Albany, those days are long gone. He strengthened his attachments to the city by using part of his MacArthur Foundation award to initiate the New York State Writers Institute in Albany, where authors such as Saul Bellow and Toni Morrison have lectured and given readings.

With the recent publication, by Viking, of *Riding the Yellow Trolley Car,* Kennedy's career has come full circle. He is excited by the book, which contains profiles, reviews, and essays distilled from his newspaper and magazine writings. Still, he has savored the freedom from journalistic deadlines of the past two decades.

"Journalism is a killing profession, in the sense that you use the language all day," he says. "It's hard for a newspaper writer to sustain an imaginative position on anything, because he has to clear his head every day for the new story, the new interview, the new disaster. Also, knowing that it's very ephemeral—tomorrow they wrap fish in it—is counterproductive for an imaginative writer, unless you find a way of overcoming it."

Kennedy's method was to take voluminous notes on his next novel's subject matter and to keep rereading the notes, even while working on other projects. He still tends to overresearch. He has accumulated so much material for a work-in-progress that it threatens to become two novels.

"The new work includes the decades from the 1890s until the 1930s. It includes the rise of the Irish to control the Democratic party, the advent of Al Smith, FDR, the period that laid the groundwork for the rise of John Kennedy.

"I don't know the dynamics of the book, or books, yet. I might be my own narrator this time and have multiple points of view. That won't come until I'm ready to write.

"Reading a note I made to myself twenty years ago may dictate the theme or give a character's function. When all that fits together, which is very slowly, then a book takes shape. After a while you have a natural flow of events that defines your characters. Your plot evolves slowly.

"Somebody called plot 'the faintly contemptible vessel that carries the story.' It's never the reason for the book."

As Kennedy talks, Dana Segarra Kennedy quietly sits down beside him. With graying hair, she is pretty, dark and petite, possessed of musical laughter. The couple have a son who lives at home and two grown daughters who come and go at the Kennedys' Albany residence.

With their child-rearing days mostly behind them, the Kennedys often travel together to see the country. Today they want to see Knoxville, so I pretend to lead, but mostly I follow through the streets of the Old City. A recently revived portion of Knoxville, the Old City thrived before Prohibition, then picked up again after Prohibition ended, only to become a slum in the middle of the century. A long list of notables, including Cab Calloway and outlaw Harvey Logan (aka Kid Curry), partied and brawled here.

Kennedy listens intently to stories of corruption, Southern Style, as he drinks red wine in Patrick O'Sullivan's Restaurant, a former saloon in which Buffalo Bill and some Indians, it is said, created a disturbance in 1897 when they got drunk and fired their guns.

Kennedy revels in such tales. He understands time and loss and legend. He knows that very old bones reside here. The bones of a city, a time, and a writer who did for Knoxville what Kennedy did for Albany—turned it into myth by delineating its particulars, real and imagined.

Kennedy reads from *A Death in the Family* as we walk through the remnants of James Agee's old neighborhood, and the sky takes on the hues of wine. The luck of the Irish breaks the spell. William Kennedy bends down and picks something up from the dust in the sidewalk.

"Look, I found a penny—heads up." He rubs it with his thumb to get a look at the date, then puts it in his shirt pocket.

He smiles.

"You can't spend it, you know, if you want your luck to hold."

A Conversation with William Kennedy

Rudy Nelson / 1994

Published in *Image: A Journal of the Arts & Religion* 8 (Winter 1994–95): 63–75.
Reprinted by permission.

William Kennedy vaulted into national prominence in 1983 with the publication of the Pulitzer Prize-winning novel *Ironweed* (later made into a feature film with Meryl Streep and Jack Nicholson) and the award of a MacArthur Foundation grant. His cycle of novels set in Albany, New York—now numbering five and counting—comprise *Legs, Billy Phelan's Greatest Game, Ironweed, Quinn's Book,* and *Very Old Bones.* These novels have created for his home town an almost mythic quality clearly implied in the title of his non-fiction book *O Albany! Improbable City of Political Wizards, Fearless Ethnics, Spectacular Aristocrats, Splendid Nobodies and Underrated Scoundrels.* Kennedy was interviewed by Rudy Nelson, a friend and fellow professor in the English department of the State University of New York at Albany.

Image: In one of your earlier interviews, you made a statement something like this: "I don't need Buddhism or Zoroastrianism. I've got Sacred Heart Church in North Albany. Can you elaborate a bit on that?

William Kennedy: I don't know where Zoroastrianism came from—probably a college history course—but the way I was educated in high school and college was immersion in religion. I lived in the North End and Sacred Heart Church was the bulwark of all the spiritual guidance I was getting. It stayed with me—and it always will. I consider it a strength, although I've long since ceased to give allegiance to the Church in any formal or ritualistic way. But I value my religious education as I value so many of the priests I've known through the years. I value the way it became a substructure for my life. It was a way or engaging the world, confronting moral dilemmas. It was a broad education in human behavior and I'm very grateful for that. I had to learn probably half of the Baltimore Catechism, the Ten Commandments and their explanations, the virtues of faith, hope, and charity as defined by the Church. And all this can have high validity, whether you're a Catholic or a

Zoroastrian. So many people in my life and in my books have grounded their moral behavior in these imposed tenets of the Faith; and when they transgress, it is often against those same tenets.

Image: Your use of Catholicism in your fiction—as institution and as system of belief—is significantly different from the way other Roman Catholic writers have used it. For example, Flannery O'Connor, J.F. Powers, Walker Percy, Ron Hansen. Will you comment on the ways Roman Catholicism enters into your fiction?

WK: I wouldn't know how to compare myself with those people. I admire them all, but I haven't read any of them extensively enough to be sure. It's a question I've asked myself in the book I'm writing now, which takes place at the turn of the century: How does religion come into play in this particular relationship I'm writing about? I probably won't answer the question, but it's something that I don't leave out. It's like politics. In *Very Old Bones* there isn't much political overtness, but politics underpin the behavior of the characters. In *Bones,* Tommy has a job in the city water works, and it's obviously a political appointment. He dies there—he falls into a filtration pool and drowns. The politicians gave him his job and the politicians pay for his funeral. It's a given, even though it's not explicitly stated. That kind of politics was a part of my family's life—and my life for many years. Religion enters my novels in a similar way. Religion is more overt, has highly visible significance in *Very Old Bones,* and it probably will in the novel I'm thinking about now. I may write about a priest. So religion is something I can't be without. It's gotten into my imagination and my language. It's true enough what they say about the Church. If they get you young enough they've got you forever.

Image: Which reminds me of a comment Marcus Gorman, the narrator, makes in *Legs*—referring to himself, his father, and the criminal Jack Diamond: "Products all of the ecclesiastical Irish sweat glands, obeisant before the void, trying to discover something."

WK: The Church was on your back when you were a working man. Edward Daugherty's father, Emmett, a significant character in my novel in progress (he's also in *Ironweed*), actually did help build the Sacred Heart Church that still stands. That church rose on the shoulders of the faithful, paid for with their pennies, nickels, and the sweat off their backs. But I suppose in that "sweat glands" phrase I also meant that those men were believers, but quizzical ones, instructed by the clergy that they were living on the rim of hell's fiery caverns. And if this didn't cheer them, it at least made them sweat.

Though they couldn't see anything except the void we all see, they kept believing, after a fashion, and they kept working and sweating through daily life and the life of the soul, anxious, at least at Sunday Mass, to get away from that hellish rim and onto the road to the cool pastures of heaven.

Image: In *Billy Phelan's Greatest Game,* Edward Daugherty's son Martin takes a rather anticlerical position. Isn't his own son about to enter the priesthood?

WK: Yes, he's about to be come a Franciscan.

Image: Martin doesn't like that very much.

WK: Well, no, he feels it's a loss to the family. He feels he's losing his son, for he doesn't believe in the Church the way his son does. He's seen the extremes of people who enter the religious life and are lost to the family forever, and that's not what he wants for his son, or himself. It's a very selfish attitude on the part of Martin, but what he's trying to do is get his son to strike some kind of balance between the real world and the sacred. The balance of the sacred and the profane, I suppose, in the same sense that Martin believes he himself has balanced his life. Martin has a mystical streak, a visionary quality that is little understood by himself, but he knows that he has it, and it impels him to reverence before the unknown. And yet he's a very mundane citizen of the world—even a profane one, I'm constrained to say.

Image: What you say about Martin in *Billy Phelan* is that "despite his infidel ways, the remnants of tattered faith still had power over his mind."

WK: Yes, that tattered faith is what I'm trying to talk about in people I know who grew up Catholic, then fell away and yet retained some kind of association with the faith they didn't believe in. You revere God, if there is a God, but you don't really believe there is. It's mystical atheism. You believe there's something, but it's not necessarily God as any religion would have its God.

Image: In a way, Martin represents a sort of middle ground, doesn't he, between religion's often arrogant assumption that it has all the answers and has God in its hip pocket and, at the opposite extreme, the equally arrogant assumption of reductionist naturalism that there is no transcendent reality. Martin senses the pull in both directions and is somewhere between those extremes.

WK: You meet a lot of people in life with a religious calling, and you hear them espouse what they consider the manifest proof of the existence of God. They preach as if they are in unarguable possession of supreme truths, but you know they haven't got a metaphysical bone in their accumulated bodies. Also you find people like Martin Daugherty, truly a spiritual figure, who knows that a great deal of religion is what the Irish would call blarney, and knows also that something exists that's far more powerful than the fanciful theology offered up to him as inviolable truth. This thing that Martin knows is a mystical vision he has; and it is absolutely inexplicable, well beyond the naturalistic state he inhabits every day. He *knows* there is a surreal dimension to his life but he doesn't create a religion out of it, nor does he try to impose it on others. It exists side-by-side with his palpably real knowledge of the universe.

Image: Francis Phelan is a different kind of character, of course, from Martin Daugherty, and yet there's some pretty profound religious significance to Francis's life as you portray it in *Ironweed*. Although it would surely be stretching a point to call him a saint—he wouldn't stand for it, for one thing—he is far from irredeemable. In fact, it seems clear that by the end of the novel he has experienced a redemption of sorts and even makes gestures of grace in his chosen way of life. He gives his last bit of food to a man with hungry children in the hobo jungle, and says offhandedly, "Got some stuff here I can't use."

WK: Well, that's true. *Ironweed* was meant as a book of redemption. It didn't start out as one. I was not sure how it should end when I began it, but I became sure by the time I finished the first chapter set in the cemetery. That's where Francis communes with the dead and speaks with his son Gerald who died when he was thirteen days old. This miraculous creature in the grave mystically imposes on Francis the obligation to perform acts of expiation for abandoning the family, and tells him, "When these final acts are complete, you will stop trying to die because of me." By then I knew Francis was on his way to redemption. Thereafter he slowly becomes aware of what he has been consciously and unconsciously avoiding—going back home and confronting the worst that he's done in life: abandoning his wife and two children for twenty-two years in order to flee his shame for dropping Gerald and causing his death. And so the book became an odyssey. In some measure, language and certain events from Dante's *Purgatorio* are woven into Francis's experience, particularly in the psychic realm, the ineffable, unconscious element of his life and thought. He could never speak it, but in time did intuit it; and it was in those segments that I used the most exalted, most Dantesque language I could muster, as a reflection of Francis's soul rising from purgatorial depths toward absolution for his grave sin, and then on to ultimate redemption. This language was not accessible to Francis—or to me either, until I started to write it. I then tapped into some unconscious flow of language, images, and ideas that I didn't know were part of my imagination. And the writing then became a calculated effort to arrive at what is deepest in any human being. When the book was going around and around, some editors argued that bums didn't think this way.

Image: Which is curious. There's certainly a venerable tradition of writing that way in American literature. Faulkner often did it. But I'm sure there were some editors who didn't approve even when *he* did it.

WK: Any editor who would say such a thing to a writer should be exiled to mathematics.

Image: The action of *Ironweed* appropriately takes place on All Saints' Day. I think it's a fascinating commentary on the creative process that you didn't choose that time frame specifically for *Ironweed,* that you were already locked into it by the action in the earlier novel *Billy Phelan's Greatest Game.*

WK: The thing that's comic about this is that *Billy Phelan* was purposefully set close to election time. I wanted it to be a gubernatorial year so Governor Thomas E. Dewey could be attacking the Democratic machine—as he actually had in 1938—and I would be able to reveal the machine in all its machinations and incredible power. So I had to set the action not on election day itself but during the primary campaign. This is when Francis comes home to register to vote, and he registers twenty-one times, at $5 per, and earns $105. Well, the story is played out, the kidnapping takes place, Francis is arrested for the multiple registrations, and Billy saves him. Such things take time, and so the story came to the end of the month; and there it was— Halloween, then All Saints' Day and All Souls' Day—those three very holy days in the Christian calendar. This brought back a world I had studied in the Catechism, with the nuns in fifth and sixth grade, and the Christian Brothers in high school. The memories came back of All Saints' Day, a holy day of obligation, and All Hallows' Eve, and All Souls' Day when the dead walk abroad and you pray for all the suffering souls in purgatory. It fit perfectly with the odyssey Francis was on, his purgatorial venture; and I find it comic that I was led to all that by Albany politics. The irony is that Albany politicians were always very close with the Church in my younger days. The priest and the bishop and the political boss were close friends and allies in defeating the scurrilous Protestant Republicans who tried to take City Hall away from them.

Image: Let's stick with *Billy Phelan's Greatest Game* for a bit here. The father-son motif in that book seems to have an almost archetypal quality to it, what with the various pairs of fathers and sons. Primarily, of course, it's Francis and Billy, but also Martin and Peter Daugherty (and Martin and *his* father), Patsy and Charlie McCall . . .

WK: Patsy is Charlie's uncle. Bindy's his father. But yes, Patsy's a surrogate father. He's also the patriarchal figure of the community.

Image: Then there's also Jake Berman and Morrie. This father-son motif is nothing if not religious in its significance, but it escalates to a new level and an even greater resonance because of the references throughout the novel to the Abraham-Isaac story. Do you want to discuss your use of that biblical allusion?

WK: I don't recall the origin. I suspect that I was reading the Old Testament and some Hebrew scholars. I had a number of conversations with a Jewish colleague, an academic who was writing a philosophical treatise. I think that was a period in which Abraham came very much into my consciousness. I used to go around asking people, "What do you think about Abraham and Isaac?" And I'd get this weird look. My conclusion was that Martin Daugherty would conclude that Abraham was a prototypical fascist, because of the way he behaved toward his son. My own son was about three or four years old at the time, and the concept of sacrificing him for some higher power was unthinkable. I'd sacrifice myself before I would touch him in any hurtful way. That archetypal faith of Abraham was something very foreign to me and foreign to what Martin was thinking. I'm not Martin, I didn't have the experiences Martin had, but I knew how he would think in many situations, and that was one of them.

Image: Martin thinks: "All sons are Isaac, all fathers are Abrahams, and all Isaacs become Abrahams if they work at it long enough."

WK: That's the way it turns out sometimes. There's also a line in the book that says we're all in a conspiracy against the next man. I woke up one night with that as a headline I had seen in a dream. I didn't know what it meant but I decided I would use it. It becomes clear in the context of Martin's thinking in *Billy Phelan's Greatest Game.* Martin is feeling hostile toward his own son, trying to deny him his vocation—and he perceives this hostility in himself. The quest for balance is not a quest for total liberation of the child. In the same way, his own father was a very difficult mentor for him as a writer. Martin takes a walk in the park with his father at one point, and his father makes light of his writing and tells him his novel is a joke. His father says that he should write about something more serious. Jake Berman has taken the same attitude toward his son Morrie, one of the kidnappers. Martin sees the cycle of change—that as you become older, as your son becomes more antithetical to what you are, you move into the Abraham role—in a metaphorical way if nothing else.

Image: Still on the father-son theme. There's a significant rhetorical echo in *Billy Phelan* that will take us a step farther. Referring to Francis and Billy, Martin says: "For I know how it is to live in the inescapable presence of the absence of the father." Then, only a few pages later, he makes a comment on what he wants for his own son, who, as you say, is headed for the priesthood: "Balance: that was what he wanted to induce in Peter. Be reverent also in the presence of the absence of God." Which seems to indicate, doesn't it, that all this talk about earthly fathers is somehow connected with the heavenly father?

WK: Well, it certainly is in that context, because of what Martin is trying to infuse into his son: Have a little reverence for somebody like me, he's saying, for whom God is not as present as he is to you. The statement does have an intended meaning at a theological level. There was always that tendency in the Catholic Church toward condemnation of the pagans, the infidels, anyone not of the Christian faith. It's too bad about you, you're going to be damned. Even as a child, that didn't make any sense to me. And yet it was a tenet of the Church for so many years. Even though they've softened their position on that in recent years, I suspect there are a good many in the hierarchy who still believe it.

Image: On this concept of the absence of God, which is certainly a part of Martin's approach to life, the novelist Sue Miller (who I know is a friend of yours) has made a comment about her own work—specifically with reference to her upbringing in the Protestant church: "Fictionally, I've chosen to place myself outside that world. And my intent has been to examine via my characters a life lived without the conviction of faith, and yet with a strong awareness of its loss."

WK: Yes, we're talking about the same thing, aren't we. You bemoan the loss of faith because it was so comforting in its own way. You could have this solidity of belief that everything was organized and the only way you could miss going to heaven would be if you got unlucky and died before you got to confession on Saturday. The Church was the font of wisdom and absolution. No matter how bad things got, you could go and see your priest and talk about it and he'd tell you, "Okay, just say a couple of Our Fathers and a couple of Hail Marys, go home and you'll be all right in the morning." If that's faith at all, it's a very childish faith. You grow into something a good deal more problematic.

Image: Let's take a different angle, and this may move us along to two more recent novels: *Quinn's Book* and *Very Old Bones*. It seems to me that perhaps the most important and far-reaching religious dimension in your work has to do with the sacredness of the novelist's calling. You treat this in the 1990 Hopwood Lecture—somewhat tongue-in-cheek but no less seriously—when you play off the Catechism's answers to the question "How do we sin against the faith?" Here's the paragraph that introduces that section: "But it is in the virtue of faith that the writer grounds himself (or herself) in the true religious experience of literature: and faith was defined early on for me as a firm belief in the revealed truths—truths of God as religion would have it; truths of the writing life, as I would have it."

WK: Is that where I went on to talk about the necessity of learning how to write and having to read everything that was worthwhile, knowing the canon of literature from the Greeks on down to the lyrics of the Beatles?

Image: Yes. And another way of sinning against the faith, as you quoted from the Catechism, is "By not performing those acts of faith, which we are commanded to perform." Or as you would have it: "This means you should write even on Christmas and your birthday, and forswear forever the excuse that you never have enough time."

WK: Well, that *was* comic, but it was typical of my going back to those forms of thinking that I learned early on. I was talking about what it means to be a writer. I don't want to exalt writing above other callings, but I felt that way about it: there can be a sacredness to it—"the priest departs, the divine literatus arrives." The feeling I have of the calling is that some writers have done sacred things; the fact that the writing world values them so highly, and the fact that I had valued them so highly, gave a private sacredness to certain texts and certain writers whom I read as if they were producing holy writ. I feel that still, but I also know, as a printer once told me, that the guys working in the marble quarries up in Granville have a tough time of it too, and their work is not to be diminished by any hyperbolic exaltation of a mere writer.

What I remember thinking is that I couldn't call myself a writer—even though I had written twenty or thirty short stories and a couple novels—because nobody had published me. The idea was that until you were anointed into the priesthood of literature you weren't really a writer. And public acceptance was the only way you were anointed. But then many people do anoint themselves and one day decide, as I also did, as so many writers have to do, that you want to be a writer—the same as deciding you want to be a priest or a brain surgeon—and you work your way toward it. One day you get your degree and you can cut people's heads open; or you can open their imaginations if you're a writer. There must be a lot of unknown texts. There certainly have been writers whose work has died with them in the grave—"born to bloom unseen"—and what are we going to do about those? I don't know. I don't think there's anything we can do.

Image: You say there were certain texts by certain writers that you read as if they were holy writ. Who were a few of those writers?

WK: I would say certain works of James Joyce and William Faulkner have this quality for me, and many poems of Yeats, the prose of John Cheever and Saul Bellow, work by Nathanael West and, when I was younger, much of *Winesburg* by Sherwood Anderson and the short stories of Ernest Hemingway. Chekhov and Tolstoy and *The Stranger* by Camus, and *One Hundred Years of Solitude* by Gabriel García Márquez are a few of the books that have wonderfully impressed me, but more for their story than for their language. I've read all the latter group in translation, all the former in my own language, and the difference is that I go back to the works in my own language and linger over the sentences, which are their essential glory. A particularly felicitous English translation of poetry, of Dante, say, will have the same impact on me. The holy writ of literature, for me, resides not in story but in the artistry of the word.

Image: This summer I read *Riding the Yellow Trolley Car,* the collection of your journalistic writings that goes back to the earliest days of your writing career. What impressed me was your long disciplined apprenticeship—in the artistry of the word—which counters the mistaken notion that you came out of nowhere in 1983 with the publication of *Ironweed* and your reception of the MacArthur grant.

WK: Well, writing can be a world that you enter very casually and then stay in forever. You think you can probably master this craft with your left hand and a little time—that's the way I thought about it at first—but the farther I went, the more difficult I perceived it was. I failed with the short story, decided I should go on and fail with the novel; I did, and I learned a lot. I became this figure who didn't know how to arrive, always on the quest. And even though I've subsequently been published, this is not in any way a culmination. I don't think I've arrived. I'm still trying to write things that have been nagging at me since childhood. Seventeen years I've worked on the novel I'm writing now. I started it in 1977. These things are part of a lifetime's engagement, a lifetime's belief that this is a valid way to spend your life. I suppose there's a spiritual quality to that sort of commitment.

Image: In almost every one of your novels I find one or more characters who, to some extent at least, embody this role of the artist. There's Martin Daugherty as journalist-narrator of *Billy Phelan's Greatest Game,* Orson as the memoirist of *Very Old Bones,* Daniel Quinn as the emerging young writer of *Quinn's Book,* and especially Peter Phelan as the painter in *Very Old Bones.* We'll need to get to Peter, who I think is of crucial importance in the context of this discussion, but let's talk about Quinn first. I had a very different impression of this book in my rereading of it this summer. When the novel first came out, I read it as *Quinn's Book* (as distinguished from Francis's book and Billy's book). This time I read it as *Quinn's Book*—the main thrust of the novel being the making of a writer, a true writer. I see some of William Kennedy in what's going on in the development of Quinn as a writer.

WK: Yes, I suppose there's something of me in every one of those characters you mentioned. Quinn is specifically an effort to reeducate myself in what I've lived through, by casting a comparably aspiring mind back into the nineteenth century to see how it would have negotiated the early stages of Irish-American life, especially those teeming years when the Irish were here in such great numbers, were so loathed by nativists, and were themselves in many ways a hateful people. Look at what they did to the blacks in the Civil War period. The Irish eventually transcended that—as I did (though I don't remember ever feeling violent antipathy toward anybody). But I knew it was in the genes somewhere, as was the aspiration to journalism and then to writing of a different order. And that's what I chose to track in the life of Daniel Quinn. In the course of doing that, I suppose I imposed some of my own knowledge of artistic progress on his trials and tribulations, on what he learned and lost and found valuable.

Image: The thing that he seems eventually to find which makes him a true writer, as he understands the process he's been going through, includes the concept of mystery. The word mystery is used often throughout the text in reference to Quinn becoming a writer—and it almost seems to take on a metaphysical quality. Quinn says, for example, "I knew that what was wrong with my life and work was that I was so busy accumulating and organizing facts and experience that I had failed to perceive that only in the contemplation of mystery was revelation possible."

WK: The importance of mystery in art first came home to me in reading an essay about or by Luis Buñuel, the great Spanish filmmaker. At some point in his life he said that mystery is the basic element of all works of art. That seemed like a pretty heavy statement to make. I now live with it under glass on my desk.

Image: I noticed it in one of the scenes in the PBS documentary "William Kennedy's Albany." I was going to ask you about that.

WK: That's exactly it, and if you look closely at that little piece of paper you'll see that it's full of holes. Those are thumbtack holes where it was pinned to the wall for twenty years. Finally I put it under glass because it was beginning to disintegrate. I thought that was a very interesting thing to say about anything artistic. And of course Buñuel's work is full of mystery. He was one of the original surrealists. I knew this, I suppose, when I was writing my first novel, *The Ink Truck*. I had been very involved with the surrealistic works of Salvador Dali, Max Ernst, René Magritte and many of those in the surrealist school of the twenties, and those pictures were hauntingly interesting. I can look at them again and again and always draw some new reaction out of myself—unlike the pure aesthetic response to color or shape in abstract painting. The surrealists touched something much deeper in me when I looked at their work, deeper than most other artists did. And their strong point was obviously the belief that there is something mysterious in everyday life that is, for a time, incomprehensible. In Buñuel's movies, like *Viridiana* and *The Exterminating Angel,* you have these mysterious events taking place in everyday life—for example, people who are locked in a room and can't leave. Why? Why can't they leave the room? Why is it locked?

And so I began to examine everything I was writing. In my journalistic upbringing I was looking for crystallization, thinking that if I could get at the crystalline center of a moment I would reach some kind of wonderful truth. I'd really get to "the way it was," as Hemingway used to tell us to do. Now if I get to that crystalline moment, I know there's a lot left to be discovered. And that should be implicit in everything you write—that you are never bottoming out, that this isn't the definitive statement on this particular person, this particular incident, or even this particular line of dialogue. Just look at the way you read the title of my book in two ways. That second way—I don't think I had thought of it in that way. It was just an offhand way to label that book when I was writing it. I didn't have a title for it. This is a book about Quinn—Quinn's Book. Like a slug on a newspaper story, that you put at the top of every page. I felt that I would find another title, but the farther I went, the more I saw that Quinn was actually writing this book. He was looking back at his own life, and this was the very book of that life.

Image: And the first words of your book become the first words of the book he's writing about Magdalena, his fiancée's larger-than-life mentor.

WK: Right. There's also a great deal of mystery in Quinn's life. He can't explain any number of things—the way I can't either—yet that very mystery is what I'm trying to achieve. Mystery is important in creating fiction. In creating anything.

Image: There's a little four-line poem by Emily Dickinson that doesn't often get anthologized: "Lad of Athens, faithful be / To Thyself, / And Mystery— / All the rest is Perjury—"

WK: That's a fascinating statement, isn't it. She's saying that if you believe anything is less than mysterious, you're a liar.

Image: Paul Tillich has said that the shock of being—the awareness at some deep level of the Mystery at the heart of all there is—is the matrix out of which proceed both religion and art. Wouldn't it follow, then, that any serious attempt to explore and understand the mystery of being—in literature or music or drama or the visual arts—is fundamentally religious? It doesn't have to deal with dogma or religious institutions, or speak the language of piety.

WK: I wouldn't argue with that. We're all trying to go back to some kind of first cause in whatever we create, some kind of origin of this human being we're writing about—or in the case of the novel I'm writing now, this situation involving six human beings. The characters are infinitely complicated and will never know each other's secret motives—and may never know their own—and yet you're trying to explore and define them as well as you can in order to understand the nature of the complexity. And maybe you'll arrive at some kind of illumination. That in itself, the illumination of the mystery that pervades these lives, is the beginning of something. And beginnings are holy events more often than not: births, marriages, self-anointings by writers.

Image: You're making these comments with regard to the novel you're working on right now. I wonder if in your most recent novel, *Very Old Bones,* that same kind of process was involved. *Very Old Bones* seems to me a tying up of many loose ends we've confronted in earlier accounts of the Phelan family—a digging down to the roots of various family tragedies and troubles, and finally a healing of some of the destructive forces that have been at work. And the agent of the healing process is Peter, the artist, by way of his se-quence of paintings called "The Malachi Suite." The healing comes, first, by painting scenes of this horrible legacy and, second, by planning the family luncheon at the book's climax. I can't help but wonder: What Peter attempts to do as a painter, Kennedy tries to do as a novelist. Does this ring a bell or is it off the mark?

WK: Well, I am trying to write about these people I know in the same way Peter was painting pictures of the people he knew—or, in some cases, knew only marginally or by osmosis through his mother. He couldn't have known his insane uncle Malachi. He was in his mother's womb at the time of Liz-zie's murder. And he was born into the livid aftermath of that horror a few weeks later. Then, for some reason (is it mystical or is it just because he intellectually arrived at the moment of confrontation with old newspaper ac-counts of that story?) Peter decided to illuminate these events for his siblings and for himself—to see what it meant after he was able to paint it. I think that's the kind of impulse writers and painters experience: trying to convey some sense of learned or intuited experience that will be valuable to some-body, even if it's only to the artist himself, or herself, at the outset—which is almost enough. The interpretation of the mystery, the revelations that Peter brought to that horrible set of events, were to me not the final resolution of what really took place. It was impossible to really know what took place, because you could never know what was in the mind of Malachi. You could only know what Malachi did and said. What was it that impelled him to become this madman who burned his wife as a witch in their own home, in their own bed? That's a madness that's very hard for any artist to explain.

Image: That madness in the Phelan family history underscores the fact that your fictional universe is clearly a fallen world (to use a theological term), filled with disappointment, despair, violence, corruption. But Daniel

Quinn makes this statement: "In writing about what was worst in this world, an unconscionable pang of pleasure dogged my every line."

WK: It's a funny thing about writers—that's what happens. You create a great murder scene . . . it's like watching a horror movie. But the murder is not what is thrilling about it. It's the perception that you were able to execute it and tell something that was truly important. That's the motivation, I believe, and these important acts of madmen or arch-criminals, *isolatos* or derelicts like Francis, or exiles like Billy Phelan, are really the extremes that illuminate the ordinary. The high drama of imagined worlds becomes a Rosetta Stone—the key that unlocks the very real mysteries and complexities of our daily lives; and so fiction at its best has extraordinary significance for all of us. The indecision of Hamlet, the cruelties of Lear's daughters, or the mad jealousy of Othello—all of these powerful things—the evil nature of Iago— are not easily penetrated; and yet they are milestones in human history. To have these things to help us live from minute to minute, to help us know that others have lived here this way—this seems to me the most valuable kind of work we can do.

That Albany State of Mind

Dan Cryer / 1996

Published in *Newsday* 28 May 1996: B4–B5. Newsday, Inc., Copyright 1996. Reprinted by permission.

I came to see [Albany] as an inexhaustible context for the stories I planned to write, as abundant in mythical qualities as it was in political ambition . . . as various as the American psyche itself.

—William Kennedy in *O Albany!*

William Kennedy, Albany-born and bred, is pointing out the sights of his favorite city. Though the 68-year-old writer has served as unofficial tour guide and raconteur extraordinaire for countless visitors, there's no hiding his enthusiasm.

From the stately to the monstrous, from the legendary to the humble, virtually every building in view calls up a story, an odd character, a tantalizing fact that endows it with meaning. Almost anything here could ignite the imagination of the author of *Ironweed, Legs,* the just-published *The Flaming Corsage* (Viking) and other acclaimed novels set in the state's capital city.

H.H. Richardson, one of the most illustrious architects of 19th-Century America, Kennedy explains, designed this building: Albany's beautiful City Hall. And contributed to the design of the most imposing of all: the State Capitol.

Kennedy eases his Jaguar down Dove Street toward a handsome rowhouse. "This is where Legs Diamond was shot and killed," he says, referring to the Prohibition-era gangster and bon vivant transformed in his imagination into the central figure of *Legs*. The novelist, who has a nice feel for symbolic gesture, bought the building and once used a room there as a quiet haven for writing.

He swings back toward the South Mall, the massive concrete office complex built in the 1960s to house much of the state bureaucracy. "Fascist architecture," *Time* magazine's critic sneered when it was completed.

"I've gotten used to it," Kennedy allows. The mall's monumental size dominates the skyline, overshadowing the more dignified 19th-Century buildings nearby. Yet the writer says the project "saved the city" by stimulating a gentrification that spared downtown from an otherwise inevitable decline.

But North Albany is where Kennedy's heart lies. The neighborhood has the look of an aging uncle whose dreams are threadbare but whose pint-sized front yard is as tidy as ever. It remains the working-class bastion it was when he was growing up there in the '30s and '40s, the only child of a secretary and a gambler-turned-deputy sheriff. But in the decades since, the area's ethnic identity has shifted from solidly Irish to African-American, Hispanic and Vietnamese.

We pause on North Pearl Street before one of the three modest clapboard houses that were once home to Kennedy. A bronze plaque on the front porch proclaims that William Kennedy, winner of the Pulitzer Prize in 1984 for *Ironweed,* lived here.

Outside stand three Hispanic youths. They are told that the man posing for a photographer is the man mentioned on the plaque. "Was he in the movie?" one asks about the screen version of *Ironweed,* starring Jack Nicholson and Meryl Streep. "I started the book," another one offers.

Until now, many books and a few movies have occupied Kennedy's artistic life. But the writer's first play, *Grand View,* is about to be produced at Albany's Capital Repertory Theater, and the fledgling playwright admits to being anxious. On a single day, reports the play's director, Margaret Mancinelli-Cahill, he faxed her 70 pages of script changes. (Michele Solomon, who gave the play a decidedly mixed review in the Albany *Times-Union,* noted that the author still refers to the play as a work-in-progress.)

Kennedy's new novel, *The Flaming Corsage,* is receiving nothing but praise. Many critics regard it as his most accomplished book since *Ironweed.* Set in Albany from the 1880s to 1912, the book follows the ill-fated marriage of Episcopalian society woman Katrina Taylor and Edward Daugherty, who rises from working-class Irish-Catholic beginnings to become a famous (and scandalous) playwright.

It's hardly coincidence that Kennedy's first play is emerging at the same time as *Corsage.* He originally conceived the novel as a play-within-a-novel. But in the middle of this ambitious project he realized that he really didn't know how to write a play, much less achieve the cumbersome task of stuffing it inside a novel. Eventually he did teach himself how to write for the stage, and the result is *Grand View.*

"I've learned a lot about playwriting and I feel up to the challenge—at least to figure out what can really be done in the theater," Kennedy says.

"I'm just beginning to understand so much of it, and I really like it. Not that I'm going to change professions or anything. I'm not going to stop writing novels. . . .

"The novel," he contends, "is the supreme form as far as I am concerned. You can do anything in the novel." As an example, he cites Francis Phelan's interior monologues in *Ironweed.*

"It's like the ineffable element in all our lives, that we know things that we can never express—dream elements, spiritual elements that confound us. You can't find the language, the access to the secret code that will unlock the door." But the gifted novelist can.

Before Kennedy could earn his keep as such a novelist, he spent nearly three decades as a journalist. Given that he grew up in a household that devoured most of the newspapers produced in the cities of Albany and New York, becoming a newspaperman was a natural progression. At Siena College, he started writing for the student paper before classes had even begun.

Kennedy has covered sports, crime and politics. He has been a movie critic, a travel writer and a columnist. His career has taken him from the *Times-Union* to the short-lived *Puerto Rico World Journal,* from the *Miami Herald* to the *San Juan Star* and back again to Albany.

"It was magical to be a newspaperman and also to be a writer," Kennedy says. "I wrote a column everywhere I went. I always wanted to be a Don Marquis, Damon Runyon or Heywood Broun, one of those [syndicated columnist] guys. I thought I would become a writer who would work for newspapers and on the side turn out a short story now and again. For a dollar a word, like Runyon."

During the '50s in Puerto Rico, where he met his future wife, dancer Dana Sosa, Kennedy struggled to write a novel. But the distance between writing for a newspaper and writing fiction was far greater than he had imagined:

"That's a journalist's syndrome," Kennedy explains, "that you can go out and report on the world and come back and turn it into literature. I used to think that's what Hemingway did . . . I really wanted the world that I was reporting on to be the raw material for my life as a writer. But it took me a while to see how to use it. And what you have to do is just absorb it and then let it become part of your memory and your imagination and then evoke it when it's necessary."

That problem aside, Kennedy had to lay claim to a subject. Although the Puerto Rican culture around him was fascinating, he found that he couldn't bring it to life in fiction. Much to his own surprise, he decided to look home-ward.

"I didn't like the city very much in those days," he admits. "It struck me as an old man's town. It was run by people my father's age, and it wasn't a very exciting place to live, for me as a young man. And, on the contrary, Puerto Rico was so vibrant, so full of life."

From the vantage point of Puerto Rico, Kennedy plunged into a novel about Albany. Titled "The Angels and the Sparrows," the book was his initial exploration of the Phelans. Thus were born Francis of *Ironweed,* and his son, Billy, of *Billy Phelan's Greatest Game.*

Although that first book was too amateurish for publication, writing it gave rise to a revelation: Albany had become the true lodestone of his imagination.

"A lot of writers wish they had what I have," he realized. "They don't have any roots. The society has become so transient. People move so easily now—from one coast to the other, wherever the job market is, or wherever your whim takes you.

"I'm very happy that I have a set of roots that yield a literary crop. I have endless things to write about here. I've got three novels right now in my head and another play.

"Albany is only a springboard. I'm very interested in the essential details of the city whenever I write about it. But I'm also totally open to changing that detail whenever it is necessary. I am not a sociologist. I'm not a historian. I'm a novelist, and I can do anything I want with it."

Kennedy cities, for example, The Angels of the Sepulchre, a brooding marble figure sitting atop a 19th-Century tombstone that we visit at Albany Rural Cemetery north of the city.

"I wanted to use that statue someplace in the work. I didn't know where. I'd known about it for years and years. And I knew exactly how it got to be where it was and who the people are who were buried underneath it, and so on."

In *The Flaming Corsage,* Kennedy makes good use of the monument. A virginal but sexually curious Katrina Taylor seduces Edward Daugherty at its foot.

"You can't tell what's going to trigger you," the author continues. "But the triggering is the most important thing. That's the starting point. You start with the real world, and you have a character somewhere moving in that world and then it's the intersection of history with that character that catapults you into the creation of the novel."

Critics used to speak of *Legs, Billy Phelan's Greatest Game,* and *Ironweed* as the Albany Trilogy. Of course, that was before Kennedy had published yet more Albany novels. With the addition of *Quinn's Book, Very Old Bones* and *The Flaming Corsage,* the unofficial designation of his work became the Albany Cycle. And that's not even counting *The Ink Truck,* the writer's first published novel, back in 1969.

What does link the books of that so-called trilogy is their setting in the 1930s. This is the ever-fertile stomping ground of Kennedy's youth.

And what an Albany it was! For today's bureaucrats, substitute Dan O'Connell's Democratic machine. For professors at the State University at Albany, substitute numerous "accountants" like the author's father.

"The machine allowed all kinds of illegal things to happen [because] the machine would get its cut. We never thought of it as illegal. Everybody played the numbers. They'd post them in the grocery store.

"It was wide open. There were twenty-four-hour bars, a red light district, card games that went all night. Saloons were allowed to operate after hours because they took Hedrick's beer, which was Dan O'Connell's beer."

Since writing the '30s "trilogy," Kennedy has roamed backward and forward in time. And there seems no end to the cycle in sight. The novelist has plans for books set in the 1930s, the '40s and the '50s. He has no interest, however, in writing a novel about the Albany of today.

"A completed world appeals to me," he says. "It's manageable. It's not as chaotic. And I have this feeling that, as soon as I embark on that kind of project, that I'm being a journalist in pursuit of the moment. It's like eating raw turkey. I don't think I like raw turkey sandwiches."

Despite his age, Kennedy seems unusually energetic and vigorous. The only apparent sign of aging is a slight deafness in his right ear.

Does he worry that he'll run out of time, that the books still in his head may not make it to the publisher?

"That's something I don't bother with," he replies. "That's the breaks. I'll tell as many of them as I can."

Meanwhile, there are the glowing reviews of *Corsage* to savor: "It's a nice development to think that I'm not being kicked in the head for imitating myself or anything like that. Hemingway got that at a late hour. And then he wrote *The Old Man and the Sea.*

Kennedy Stakes Out Novelistic Turf in Revered "Albany Cycle"

Robert Friedman / 1996

Published in *The San Juan Star* 2 June 1996: 2, 7.
Reprinted by permission.

"Almost everybody asks me when I'm going to write about something else," said author William Kennedy. " 'How come you're not writing about contemporary times; when are you going to write about Newt Gingrich?' "

Probably never. Certainly never, if current events do not impinge upon the city of Albany, or if certain Albany people do not venture out into the contemporary world.

We're talking fiction here, of course. Although the highly acclaimed author of the Albany Cycle—a growing body of work that so far includes six novels and one play—has staked out novelistic turf that is becoming as revered in literary circles as Faulkner's Yoknapatawpha county, still he gets vibrations of "a smoldering resentment that I write about the past, and about Albany. They [presumably friends and foes alike] think I'm a Johnny One-Note."

Kennedy considered: Maybe he should write a novel about Puerto Rico, or Cuba. He is very fond of both lands and would enjoy writing about them. He got his Puerto Rico experience as the first managing editor of the *San Juan Star* in the early 1960s. His wife, Dana Sosa, is from Ponce. He makes frequent trips to the island.

The Cuban revolution became a part of his consciousness during his pre-Castro years in Miami.

"I knew the revolutionaries before they went on the boats. I saw their success and saw how Cuba under the revolution turned into an anachronistic empire."

He met Castro during a trip to Cuba some years ago with Colombian novelist Gabriel García Márquez.

He sipped a glass of Cabernet Sauvignon in his luxury hotel suite during an interview as he considered the possibilities. "I could do it as a guy from Albany who goes into Cuba. . . ."

Still, "even if I write about Cuba it would be part of the cycle. Why would I want to write about anything else?"

Why indeed? Critics agree that that middle-sized American city has become under Kennedy's hand a timeless nexus to gritty urban living everywhere. In its quirky particulars, Kennedy's Albany has become as universal as Joyce's Dublin or Nelson Algren's Chicago.

Kennedy said he is not obsessed with his hometown. He is *possessed* by it. "I possess Albany, it possesses me."

The 68-year-old author noted that, despite his "archival rummaging" through old newspapers, which has led to a colorful, pulsating portrait of the upstate New York city, he is not a historian.

"I try to present the time and events fairly accurately," he said, but added he "wouldn't even blink" to move major events out of sequence, as he has done, to make the reader see what is, after all, the Albany of his mind.

He sets his books in the past—*Very Old Bones,* book five in the cycle, had the most "contemporary" setting (1958), while *Quinn's Book,* number four, begins in 1849—because "I want to see a period that's completed, at least in my own mind, before I write about it."

He elucidated: "I don't want cucumbers. I want old kosher dill pickles."

The books in the cycle switch back and forth in time as characters—mostly Irish-American, mostly troubled, mostly compassionate in failure, always vibrantly alive and deeply human—appear and reappear in all their multidimensions throughout the works.

While each book in the Albany Cycle does stand on its own, at the same time, the sum of the cycle is greater than its parts. Kennedy's vision deepens through consistency and accumulation; you read one, then two, then three of the Albany books and you realize that Kennedy is delving into conflicted hearts and portraying human foibles on as grand a scale as any American writer today.

His latest novel, *The Flaming Corsage,* which Kennedy was plugging in the nation's capital, transports the reader back to turn-of-the-century Albany.

The book switches back and forth in time between 1884 and 1912 as we follow the life of Edward Daugherty, an Irish-American playwright who rises from the Albany bog to prominence in the wider world.

Central to the novel is Daugherty's relationship with Katrina Taylor, of the Dutch-English aristocracy. Katrina becomes Edward's great love, his wife and, eventually, his spiritual nemesis, contributing to his downfall. Her fascination with death plays against his fervor for life, both real and imagined.

The novel is an intriguing mystery, a highly entertaining melodrama and, finally, a poignant tragedy. The book opens with the so-called "love nest killings," when a husband enters a Manhattan hotel suite occupied by his wife and another couple, pulls out a revolver, kills his wife, wounds the man and commits suicide.

Who did what to whom and why unfolds in just over 200 pages chock full of other happenings—a horrifying hotel fire, violent fights, questionable rapes, scandal, suicide attempts, other deaths. It is the age of lingering melodrama and that form spills into the lives of the time.

All these highly dramatic events lead to the fall of Edward Daugherty, who is brought down by that which compelled him to rise: ambition to break the social and artistic boundaries of his day.

The reader will find many of Kennedy's main concerns and themes in *The Flaming Corsage*—the travails of Irish-Americans, the importance of imagination, the immutability at the core of character, the inevitability of human loss.

Mention should be made of the barroom scenes, where—as in all Kennedy's novels—sardonically humorous one-liners and swift epiphanies of character roll off the pages. Kennedy has written some of the great barroom scenes in American literature. Only Nelson Algren comes to mind as a rival.

So, is there a grand design to the cycle? Was it constructed first in outline and is he now filling in the pieces?

Not at all. The cycle, in fact, "grew from the inside out—an organic growth, like a plant, like a tree, like a wheat field. One book begets the other."

There always was, however, "the concept of doing related stories," inspired not only by Joyce and Faulkner, but also by J.D. Salinger, who wrote about the Glass family, and by Sherwood Anderson, whose protagonist George Willard wanders through the interrelated stories in *Winesburg, Ohio.*

"I always loved to read about a family of people who you knew, but not completely. They invade your imagination."

Around the time he was reading about Seymour and Franny Glass, Kennedy was creating in an unpublished novel his own family: the Phelans, whose members play such a large part in his published works.

Francis Phelan is the protagonist in *Ironweed,* Kennedy's most honored book (Pulitzer Prize, National Book Critics Circle Award), and Francis' son, Billy, is the man in the middle of a political kidnapping in *Billy Phelan's Greatest Game,* arguably the cycle's best book, certainly its most entertaining.

In an introduction to the soon-to-be-published "An Albany Trio," which includes reissues of the first three books of the cycle (*Legs,* about the Albany gangster Legs Diamond, *Billy Phelan* and *Ironweed*), Kennedy decided that one Daniel Quinn, a peripheral character in *Very Old Bones* and the grandson-namesake of the protagonist of *Quinn's Book,* would be his surrogate. Quinn would be the author behind the entire cycle.

That wasn't planned from the beginning either. "I decided that Quinn was the writer [of the cycle] when I wrote the introduction last February," Kennedy said.

He acknowledged that the appearance of the new-found author in the introduction opens up "new possibilities."

Daniel Quinn in Puerto Rico or Cuba?

The possibilities of cycles, said the author, are endless.

William Kennedy: Past, Passing, and to Come

Martin Preib / 1996

Published in *The Boston Book Review* June/July 1996: 30–31.
Reprinted by permission.

The Flaming Corsage is above all about rising up—Edward Daugherty's rising up from the world of a "mudhole mick from the North End" to marry the aristocratic and beautiful Katrina Taylor, his rising up from proletariat playwright to fully matured, fully celebrated artist. The consequences of that rising up, of course, are mixed.

Martin Preib recently spoke with William Kennedy about this latest installment in his now six-volume Albany cycle.

MP: Was it Katrina or Edward who drew you more to this book?

WK: Well, it was the marriage, really, so it was both of them. But Edward was the problem. In the beginning he was ill defined. As I went, I could see that he would have a career that would make sense to me. I could handle his connection to the Albany aristocracy, the plutocracy. I felt I knew more history now. I knew more about the life of a woman like Katrina. I read and had been in the houses enough, and read enough about the history of such families, and I suppose the imagination was also working at its own speed for whatever it was I was trying to figure out, and what way this was going to be told.

I finally got ready and started to ask serious questions. That's the way it usually proceeds.

MP: Would you call the novel a mystery?

WK: I knew there was an unknown element. Working it out was very complicated and it took me a long time. I always knew there were going to be these killings that were a mystery to me, because—I didn't know who did it. I didn't know who was shot, I didn't know who would do the shooting. I knew it wasn't Edward. I knew he was in some way going to be victimized by this. But how it was going to happen I didn't know. The mystery developed gradually over the years. I kept designing those events with various characters, and finally when I got Maginn, that finally made it make sense to me.

MP: How long was it until he came into the novel?

WK: Recently. I started the book in 1976. I would say he didn't come in [until] about '92 or something like that. I thought there was always going to be a journalistic buddy of Edward's . . . I always had that character somewhere in my head, but he was always [a] much more benign character. As things developed, I thought that Maginn was a serious prospect.

MP: Did you have any journalists in mind when you created him?

WK: I knew people who have had high promise, talent and all that kind of thing, and it comes to nothing. There's a line out of Yeats's "To a Friend Whose Work Has Come to Nothing." Something happens in their lives. They're sort of destined to never succeed or finish anything, or never believe in themselves, or believe that the game is played in a different way than it really is. I mean success is not the goal here, and Maginn thinks it is, and he envies what happens to Edward.

Edward does what he wants to do, and what he has to do. He writes the disaster of his life, *The Flaming Corsage*. It's killed but it isn't. He'll achieve some kind of status eventually from that. That work is better than anyone knows when it first comes out, which is very often the way it is. Just think of Melville and Moby Dick.

MP: I kind of felt that Edward never really found the voice he was looking for.

WK: I think Edward finds a voice that he doesn't know he has. I think that he had written a piece of literature for the stage that will survive despite the contemporary criticism, and the negative aspects of it.

I even think of what happened to *The Playboy of the Western World*. How it was vilified when it appeared in Ireland. Yeats was a great defender of it. People didn't even have to see the play—they just got revved up by the priests and the Grundys who were just killing on general principle. It's like what's going on with this moronic censorship of *Catcher in the Rye*.

MP: In this novel you went so far back, all the way to the 1600s. That whole speech to Edward's future in-laws when he goes all the way back to Cromwell. Did you feel the need to go way back with the history for this novel?

WK: I had to. I had to familiarize myself with Cromwell's letters, and read books on the history. It took me a long time to decide on how to write it. I had been thinking about the Cromwell thing since 1973. I wanted to write it somewhat journalistically. I always felt that Cromwell was an extremely important statement to make, somewhere in one of my books. It seemed apt now.

I was able to project myself backward into the 19th century because I knew the old people when I was young. I remember them very well.

MP: There is also personal history in the cycle. Edward has a son, Martin, who is the protagonist of your earlier novel, *Billy Phelan's Greatest Game.* In that book isn't Martin still living under the burden of not having become a great writer himself, embarrassed that he is still writing for the Albany paper?

WK: Yes, definitely, Martin's still living under that burden. I haven't quite figured him out yet. I think maybe I might use Martin in the next book, which may be set in 1931. I'm not sure yet. He's sort of given it up, but I'm not sure yet what happens to Martin. He's definitely living in the shadow of his father. His son, Pete, does become a priest. Maybe I'll have a novel about him.

MP: Are you working on another novel now?

WK: Yeah, I'm working on two. I'm working on that one about Peter Daugherty, and another on this other story that's too vague to talk about.

I'm in no rush to go back and flesh out these characters. If they demand it then they'll get there. Martin may fit into the society that I'm writing about, and he may just have a significant role. I have a suspicion that he'll be important. He'll be present, but I don't know how important.

MP: Only your first novel, *The Ink Truck,* takes place in the present. All the Albany novels are in the past. Did you ever try and write about the Phelans and Daughertys in the present?

WK: I've never done it. I might become a writer who moves into the contemporary instant, and writes for an unknown tomorrow. It's always a completed world that I enter, not to recapitulate them for their own sake, but to inhabit them, as I said in *Prelude in a Saloon,* to inhabit them as a free agent. All those characters in history have to be free agents. I almost had Diamond doing things that would have contravened history when I wrote that book. That was a surreal gangster novel for that time.

This kind of analysis of method is hard. I want to be careful, because I can

sound like an idiot talking in circles about what I'm doing. It's all very
coherent when I'm doing it, but to try and recapitulate all the motivations
that carry me into a given time or given place, with a given character, I don't
know them all. I'm not able to articulate everything that shoves me into this
character or direction. I have to live with them before I even decide whether
I'm even going to stay with them.

I have a book I'm writing now, or starting to write—it's not gelled yet. I
have a couple of very strong characters and several very fascinating plot
lines, but nothing has happened to me yet that says "This is the book you're
going to write." It may or may not be the one, I don't know. I have a feeling
it's going to be a while before I know that because I can't even get near it at
this stage, with the play and the publication of the new book and all the
things that are happening at the writers' institute.

MP: I sometimes wonder if you thought the present is not really worth
writing about.

WK: Well I don't think that's true that our times are not worth writing
about. I think there are a lot of fascinating things happening now, or in the
now time of always. What fascinates me is where the families come from,
how they develop and how they rise and fall, and somewhere in those families, one of these characters is going to jump out at you, and point his finger
at you and say, "I'm it. Do me." It always happens and it has something to
do with time. You can see the condition under which the character lives and
dies or succeeds, or falls. You can see it in the round. To write about present
time, to me, would be kind of an autobiographical, or else purely journalistic
venture.

MP: The mystery just wouldn't be there?

WK: Well there's always the mystery about tomorrow. That's always
there. I just think I have a pluperfect imagination. It's already "had."

MP: The same sense of breaking through you described with *Ironweed*—
did that continue with all the Phelan and Daugherty novels?

WK: That was true. There was a kind of synthesis that was not quite
possible before.

MP: I wanted to ask you about *Legs*. You said you wrote *Legs* from seven
different points of view.

WK: I wrote about eight drafts and from multiple points of view.

MP: Was it by far the hardest book to write?

WK: It was up until that point.

MP: There must have come a point when you were writing *Legs* when you doubted whether you could pull it off.

WK: Oh yeah, there was. I mean I kept hitting these stone walls, and then I picked myself up and started over.

I remember once when I delivered a manuscript that I thought was quite extraordinary, and my editor hated it. He loved the novel in the beginning and he loved a lot of things as it went along. But finally I kept writing and writing and writing and delivering these new drafts. Ultimately he rejected the whole novel and I went elsewhere, and so did he.

That was hard to take because here was somebody who really loved the book, and I felt that the book was getting worse.

But I didn't think it really was. I think he was ultimately too impatient, or too anxious to have a demonstrably commercial piece of work, however literary it might be. It eventually was successful. It went into a second printing before we published in paper. It was published in England and various countries.

It was an absence of faith that I was going to be able to pull it off. I must say that I had a great many crises of faith in those days. It was six years in the writing, that book. I really learned how to write a novel and how not to write a novel.

MP: How did you deal with the crisis?

WK: The only way I've ever dealt with a crisis, which is to wake up in the morning and go back to work, because ultimately if you don't believe in yourself and that you're going to be able to solve the problem, whatever it is, you won't believe in anything.

That's the way I was in that period. I mean I don't believe in very much, and my faith in myself was reduced to a minus quantity. I felt very, very diminished as a writer, as an imaginative person, as a judge of what was good and not so good. But the only thing I could do if I didn't want to abandon the project and go into something else—and I didn't know what else I could go into—the only thing I could do was to continue to believe that I knew more about my own work than anybody else, and that I would be able to figure it out. I always had faith that given enough time I could figure it out. And so I rode out the trauma.

It really didn't take that long to get over it. I knew I was going to go back to work, and I'd go back to work and start over.

At one point I really did come to that crisis. I spent all day thinking I'm going to decide today. "Do I abandon . . . or do I start over?" It was almost a given from the outset that I was not going to abandon it, although I spent a whole day trying to figure out why I should go on and how I should go on.

MP: That scene from *Very Old Bones* when Orson gets the rejection from the editor right before he has the breakdown with Giselle. Is that at all autobiographical?

WK: There was an element of autobiography there. I knew an editor who was a little bit like that guy, and spoke a little like that, and I had some of those feelings, but I didn't have the breakdown Orson had.

MP: I didn't mean the breakdown so much. I thought you really captured what it must be like for a writer to have created something like Orson did, and then to be rejected.

WK: It's very often that that's the condition of a writer. I've seen writers collapse in tears when you just say something negative about something they've written. It's very comic to watch it. They can't handle it. They can't handle a negative statement about the work. They believe so totally that it's perfect, that it's inviolable and invaluable, and it isn't. And how do you tell them? I mean you try to tell them nicely.

The chances are that it's probably up for grabs really, a flip of the coin whether it's really good or whether it isn't. At some stage of the work, it can always be improved. Maybe you're the only one who can improve it. Some people can recognize it immediately.

MP: I read in your interview with Gabriel García Márquez that he has a few friends that are his guides. Is that true with you as well?

WK: I've had a few friends that have done that through the years. Very often there are a few friends who read things and their reaction is enough to let me know, really.

MP: Do you send copies and ask what do you think?

WK: Oh yeah, my editor now, and my agent, a good friend who died two years ago. Yeah, I have a couple of old pals who I show things to under certain circumstances. I hear what they have to say. Like I said, I value their reaction. There's some kind of reaction you're going to get sooner or later with a good reader anyway. Very often, this is post facto. It's written, I send it off to my editor, and then that's it. He decides on the basis of that.

Fire, Bones, Weeds, and Women: A Conversation with William Kennedy

Neila C. Seshachari / 1996

Reprinted by permission of Neila C. Seshachari

William Kennedy has just published his sixth novel, *The Flaming Corsage* (Viking 1996), in The Albany Cycle. Journalist, novelist, and screenwriter, he is also emerging as a playwright. His first produced play, *Grand View,* premiered in Albany in May 1996, breaking all local records. He is best known for *Ironweed* (Viking 1983), which won him both the National Book Critics Circle Award in 1983 and the Pulitzer Prize in 1984, and for which he wrote the screenplay when it was made into a movie with Meryl Streep and Jack Nicholson in stellar roles. *The Ink Truck* (1969), *Legs* (1975), *Billy Phelan's Greatest Game* (1978), *Quinn's Book* (1988) and *Very Old Bones* (1992) complete his current cycle of novels, which have elevated New York State's capital, Albany, to a mythic status. Kennedy's nonfiction collection of essays, *O Albany! Improbable City of Political Wizards, Fearless Ethnics, Spectacular Aristocrats, Splendid Nobodies and Underrated Scoundrels* (1983) has contributed equally to Albany's imagined and factual splendor. His latest nonfiction, *Riding the Yellow Trolley Car* (1992), gathers essays and articles spanning four decades, most of which he wrote when he was a journalist or freelancer.

I interviewed William Kennedy on Friday, 13 December 1996, at his sprawling, memorabilia-studded home in Averill Park just outside Albany and partook of the Kennedy family's well-known hospitality and Dana Kennedy's legendary cuisine. Kennedy came to receive me at the airport a day earlier and, before dropping me back at the airport, gave me his famous tour of Albany, including the Dove Street rowhouse where gangster Jack "Legs" Diamond was murdered in December 1931 and which Kennedy now owns.

For all his reputation as an outgoing, party-person, William Kennedy is a workaholic. After giving me a four-hour interview interrupted frequently by professional calls, he closeted himself in his office for the rest of the day, writing. When he came down for dinner, to which a number of his friends had been invited, he told me that he had just hit upon a different narrative strategy for the novel he is working on.

Seshachari: Tell me about the play, *Grand View,* your latest literary venture.

Kennedy: The play is my first produced play. It's the second play I have written.

Seshachari: What's the name of the other play?

Kennedy: At this point, it's called "The Sparrows," and it's taken from my novel *Very Old Bones.*

Seshachari: Is *Grand View* from your fiction too?

Kennedy: No, it's based in authentic political history in the Albany of the 1940s. Governor Thomas E. Dewey was running for President against Frank-lin Roosevelt, and was trying to break the Albany political machine to en-hance his image as a political white knight. The machine was run by Dan O'Connell, who controlled the city from 1921 until he died in 1977. I've written about Dan at length in *O Albany!* and I reinvented him in fiction as Patsy McCall in *Billy Phelan's Greatest Game,* and again in *Grand View.* The play's focus is the climax of the two-year war between Patsy and an unnamed Governor on Labor Day, 1944, just before the Presidential cam-paign begins. I've totally invented the private lives of the people, but there's an underlying accuracy to the political warfare.

Seshachari: How was the play received?

Kennedy: It broke all records at Capital Repertory Theater, and was ex-tended a week—boffo business in Albany. I was pleased.

Seshachari: Will it have a run off Broadway?

Kennedy: Maybe, but I'm new at this. I've rewritten it once since the production, and will do more before it's ever produced again. It's still a work in progress.

Seshachari: "Dinner at the Phelans," the one-act play that we published in *Weber Studies* [the journal I edit] in 1993—didn't you write that for some New York actors?

Kennedy: I wrote that play for two reasons. One for you, because I owed you a piece of fiction, and I didn't have any, and also for Norman Mailer, who was trying to raise funds for the Actors Studio. He solicited plays from established novelists to present as a series of staged readings. That series didn't happen, but I did send him my one-acter. He and Frank Corsaro, then the Studio's artistic director, liked it and asked me to turn it into a full-length play, which I did. This is the play I call "The Sparrows." At this point, it's too novelistic, but it's got some strong characters, and I'm convinced there's something substantial there for the theater.

Seshachari: Your novels are very dramatic too. Some segments in them could very well be dramatized.

Kennedy: That may be because of my respect for playwrights like O'Neill and Synge and Pirandello, who at times have meant as much to me as the novelists who shaped me as a writer. But theatre isn't the reason I'm a writer. I'm a novelist first, and always. I've got two novels going at the moment, and I'm not sure which is going to take me by the throat.

Seshachari: Have you written two novels simultaneously before?

Kennedy: No, and I don't advise it, but can't avoid it. I started what I thought was a novella, and I fused it with a novel, then separated them again. But that's this week. Next week may be different. I've written two projects at a time in the past but never two novels. It's too much to ask of one mind.

Seshachari: Your novel, *The Flaming Corsage,* concerns five characters who undergo major sexual and marital crises in their lives. Was the entire group the protagonist in your mind?

Kennedy: When I first created these people in *Billy Phelan's Greatest Game,* I knew Edward Daugherty and his wife, Katrina, were major figures; also Melissa Spencer, an actress. I had the so-called "love nest killings" taking place in a New York hotel room, but who were the people in that room? Were there two? Three? Four? The problem was finding out who was who, then structuring the story to get them into that room.

Seshachari: Maginn never appeared in any of previous your novels; am I right?

Kennedy: Right. He's new in this book. I always had a second newspaperman, an editor or a cultural writer for an Albany paper, who would be a colleague of Edward. This turned into Maginn, and he became a dark figure as the story went along.

Seshachari: *The Flaming Corsage,* more than any other of your novels, is nonchronological, nonlinear, quasi-mystical, though it's not quite noncohesive. In a 1969 interview, you cite Borges and say the future novel is likely to be nonchronological, noncohesive, and nonlinear. Did you have that in mind when you wrote *Corsage?*

Kennedy: I certainly wasn't talking in general about the future of the novel, and if I was, I was talking through my hat. I hope I was talking about the kind of novel that I wanted to write. I'd just published *The Ink Truck,* a nonlinear story that goes in and out of fantasy and reality.

Seshachari: *The Ink Truck* is a delightful book.

Kennedy: Thank you. I had great fun writing it. It was my resistance to literary naturalism as it had come down from the 1930s. I felt a novel should be doing something other than mundane realism, something other than what the [movie] camera could do so well. I wanted complexities and strangeness that would lift me out of the predictable forms I'd been working in, forms that bored me, and that didn't seem to reflect the surreal dimension of life as I knew it. Borges was one of my heroes then.

Seshachari: When Bailey goes on a hunger strike toward the end of *The Ink Truck,* I thought this novel was taking off in a new direction, specifically in the Gandhian dimension.

Kennedy: Gandhi was there, but so was Terrence MacSwiney, Lord Mayor of Cork, who went on a hunger strike for 74 days during the Irish troubles with England, and died a martyr. The world was watching, and Sinn Fein became more renowned than ever. MacSwiney made a famous remark before he began his strike: "It is not those who can inflict the most, but those that can suffer the most who will conquer." He was one of the visions Bailey has when he goes back in time in the depths of the library. Hunger was a theme of mine. Franz Kafka's "The Hunger Artist" was also speaking to me as a writer: the starving artist who lived for his hunger, and earned the world's indifference. I was a hunger striker and nobody gave a goddamn. I felt Kafka was pure wisdom.

Seshachari: You have said every good writer transforms one's chosen art form a micromillimeter or two. How do you explore new ways of investigating human experience in your novels?

Kennedy: I don't think you can consciously will a change in the art form. Everything's been done. If you achieve change it's an accident of history, a consequence of absorbing the masters and then shedding their influences, being mature enough to trust your intuitions, and your own language and then finding ways of putting together the improbable elements of your imagination. The fusion of improbables often, at least, *seems* to be new.

Seshachari: *Corsage* starts with the love-nest murders, then follows a murder mystery's perfect format—a suspenseful, intriguing double killing, followed by clues strewn throughout the narrative, and then the denouement. Did you plan this use of the trappings of murder mystery?

Kennedy: I didn't plan a mystery. I once tried one, but it turned into a comedy and I abandoned it. I started *Corsage* with the killings which I didn't understand, so mystery was a given. I didn't know whether someone was stabbed or shot or thrown out a window, but I knew there was tragedy in that room, and I had to solve it.

Seshachari: Was the love-nest killing the central image that triggered the whole novel?

Kennedy: It was central to Edward's life, and it started him writing what became his great play. But the marriage of Edward and Katrina was also central—dual stories—and that became the novel's structure. I opened with that love nest violence, but then had to keep the suspense as to how it came to be. I told the marriage story in chronological fragments, then did the same with the crime—the bull on the porch joke, the confession of Cully Watson, and so on. As you move forward, the marriage story fuses with the history of the crime, then it's one common thrust to the end. I'd read scores of mysteries and detective novels as a child, but I don't think I've read one in forty years.

Seshachari: You said in a couple of interviews you were attracted to Katrina, you wanted to explore her. Did you ever think of making her the only protagonist of *Corsage*?

Kennedy: I started with her marriage, and also with the disaster that prompted the play, *The Flaming Corsage,* that gave the book its title. I was intrigued by Edward's involvement in the love nest, which costs him dearly. He becomes like Job: he loses his wife, his reputation, his play fails, his house burns down. How does a man survive that? I was interested in personal disaster, and knew he would come out of it, to some degree; but I had to find out what resilience existed in him after his afflictions. I couldn't separate him from Katrina. I was in her thrall, and had already written about her at length in *Ironweed* and again in *Very Old Bones;* and she's briefly in *Billy Phelan.* But in the *Corsage* I did give her room to expand. Now we know where she came from and how she thought. I think she's my most complex female creation. I think Helen Archer in *Ironweed* is also a strong woman.

Seshachari: Let's talk about narrative technique. Edward Daugherty says in *Corsage,* "When the matter is ready the form will come." Do you believe that about your own writing as well? Which comes first, the matter or the form?

Kennedy: The matter is always first. How could form exist without substance? How could a building exist without a design? How many floors? Staircases? How do you get from here to there in it? What is its function?

Seshachari: Does that mean you have the whole plot in mind?

Kennedy: I never know everything there is to know. If I know too much I get bored. I have to invent constantly to keep myself interested, to find out what in this material is new to me, and worth doing.

Seshachari: Even in human relationships you invent new things, like Giselle in *Bones* being attracted to her aging father-in-law, Peter; it's a different kind of attraction that gives an unusual flavor to the ordinary.

Kennedy: Isn't that the way with human relationships? You suddenly discover what you'd taken for granted: another side to that person, and maybe it's dark, or quite wonderful—a surprise.

Seshachari: Some of your novels predict events in future novels. These seem to be floating in air. How do you keep them in tow? Keep tying loose ends as you find them? Is this cycle in Bill Kennedy's head, already formed? Is there room for more invention?

Kennedy: Always. A character separates himself from the crowd—the crowd in history, the crowd in my mind—and says to me: "I'm your next subject. Pay attention to me." I have that with a character now, but he keeps changing, from lawyer to police chief to night club owner to detective. I know his personality, know much about his private life, but he's elusive. I think he's a detective.

Seshachari: Will he meet any Phelans, Quinns, or Maginn?

Kennedy: He may live next door to one of them. He may know Martin Daugherty, who writes about police matters for the *Times-Union*.

Seshachari: You've often talked of F. Scott Fitzgerald's *The Great Gatsby* in discussing *Legs;* both protagonists are bootleggers and mythic characters. But also you've talked of Marcus Gorman and Nick Carraway as narrators. You say Nick Carraway is boring.

Kennedy: That was an excessive remark. I meant it only in the sense of Nick as a character, as an active figure. His prose is exceptional, and he tells a perfect story. I wanted my narrator to be as vital as Jack Diamond. Marcus really wasn't the equal of Jack as a creation, but I did end up with a living character who has a private life, a fall of his own. And his prose isn't so bad.

Seshachari: In *Gatsby* we see everything through Nick's eyes. The Gorman narrative is exciting because Gorman isn't there all the time. He seems to be, but it's an illusion. Sometimes it's Alice and Jack, or Kiki and Jack, and no Marcus. Yet Bill Kennedy, the author, is kept in the background, and it seems Marcus is telling it all.

Kennedy: That was a case of the matter creating the form. I had this knowledge of Jack's and Kiki's and Alice's interior lives, and I knew Marcus would not have total access to them. But he could get close enough to launch them on their own, let them think privately what was necessary to my story, and then he'd take over again. In *Moby Dick,* Ishmael is the narrator, but Melville doesn't hesitate to go into the mind of Ahab, or Starbuck or Queequeg, when it suits his purpose. Being slavish to form is a foolish consistency. *Legs* went through many changes, a tough book to write.

Seshachari: Didn't you say its manuscript was taller than Brendan?

Kennedy: Right. They were both six years old and the *Legs* pages stood taller than Bren.

Seshachari: The love scenes with Jack and the women are so comic. And the one between Rose and Edward in *Corsage* is both funny and sad. Another one etched in my mind is Daniel Quinn and Maud as adolescents, in *Quinn's Book.* It's screamingly funny. You make this very serious business of love so comic. You poke fun at it.

Kennedy: Sex can be hilarious. So can love. At the end of *Corsage,* Edward is thinking about the last scene in his play, where Katrina dies in his arms. [Kennedy begins to read.] "Edward picked up his whiskey and walked to the front porch. He sat in the chair beside Emmett and decided mockery was a more exalted mode of behavior than was generally assumed." Edward has written a poignant moment of Katrina's death, but she says to him as she dies, "I loved you? Quite likely. I forget." Edward mocks himself, mocks her, mocks death and love. I think it's valuable to be able to do that, and not to die a tragic egoist.

Seshachari: I find your novels are both serious and extraordinarily funny. You said you discovered early on that your fiction was unrelentingly serious, then you infused it with humor. How does one make something funny? Like some painter, you find some hue lacking and you add extra color?

Kennedy: Even when the worst things happen to us, we sometimes find ourselves laughing. My first novel was so excessively downbeat that it was reverse sentimentality: too much death and darkness. Most of my friends constantly try to be funny, and if they miss more than they make it, the effort still counts for something. Francis Phelan in *Ironweed,* a man at the bottom of the world, is constantly cracking jokes, a truly funny man with an ironic sense of his own disaster.

Seshachari: So, you take a serious scene and say, "This looks too serious"?

Kennedy: Not at all. The levity comes when it has to. When it's supposed to be serious it stays that way. In *Very Old Bones,* Billy Phelan and his cousin Orson are in a saloon when a man comes in and tries for the second time to kill a man on crutches whom he's already shot once in the leg. Billy ruins the shooter's aim and he [shooter] succeeds only in shooting his victim in his good leg, and also putting a bullet into a cow's head mounted over the back bar. It's a funny scene, and the conversation reflects that, but the point of the scene is not funny at all. It's Billy explaining to Orson that he's broke and lost and doesn't know what to do with himself, for the world he knew has been taken away from him. But Billy is as witty as he's always been, and why not? That's his personality, even in desolation. My German agent told me a few years ago that some German readers have a problem with my writing because of this mix of humor and high seriousness. This is a bewildering criticism.

Seshachari: I like the polyphonic voices in *Ironweed.* They are humorous too, those ghosts talking to Francis. Those polyphonic voices keep appearing in your fiction as when Katrina and Edward are thinking of the ghosts from their past. That perhaps gives your fiction a kind of richness, a connection of the past with the present.

Kennedy: The dead are always talking to me—people I loved or grew up with or worked with. I hear their voices, the cadences of their speech. They're always on call. When I need them, I bring them back and listen to what they have to say. They are witty. They keep me amused.

Seshachari: What about your mother's wit?

Kennedy: She loved to laugh and had a great sense of humor. It wasn't a sharp, quick-tongued wit like Billy Phelan's, but she was a very good storyteller.

Seshachari: I noticed the mother-son relationships in *The Flaming Corsage*: Edward and his mother, and Katrina as a mother herself. She plays a crucial role, intercedes in behalf of Edward with their son Martin. That emphasis I thought was something I'd not seen earlier.

Kennedy: I would argue that Annie's role as mother in *Ironweed* is extremely significant, the way she holds the family together without a father. So is Katherine Phelan's role in *Very Old Bones*. She's present when the demented Malachi burns his wife as a witch, and she is so traumatized that her puritanical mothering of the family becomes a torture to her children and confounds their lives. Her trauma is understandable, but most of her children don't know why she is the way she is until a very late moment, after her death. And some of them die without ever knowing.

Seshachari: You once said that having the Catholic tradition, you didn't need any other religion like Buddhism, for instance.

Kennedy: I meant that Catholic mysticism and ritual gave me the infrastructure on which to build a spiritual life, even now when I'm no longer a practicing Catholic. We all speak to God in one language. We just have different dialects.

Seshachari: But you have said that the *Tibetan Book of the Dead* was a great influence on you. So what kind of influence did that book have?

Kennedy: I was reading Carl Jung's commentary on the *Tibetan Book of the Dead* when I was writing *Legs* and it related directly to what I was writing—the life and death of a criminal who doesn't really die but is resurrected.

Seshachari: Joyce first calls it a monomyth in *Ulysses* and Campbell uses it to denote the cycle of birth, initiation, and return.

Kennedy: I'd read Joseph Campbell on myth early on and the idea of mythic return stayed with me. The *Tibetan Book of the Dead* seemed at first a perfect vehicle for creating the novel's substructure, but as I went along it became cumbersome, intrusive, and I abandoned most of it. I did use it in the final chapter, when Jack Diamond, the gangster, begins his rebirth as a mythic American villain.

Seshachari: When there's a process of mythicizing, there's also what we call magical realism—glorified vision and hyperbolic language with which we mythicize.

Kennedy: Magical realism as a phrase comes in with García Márquez, and Juan Rulfo, but it preexists these writers. It's all over Shakespeare, Dickens, and Kafka. Thornton Wilder and Pirandello used it. So did the Greeks. It was in my head forty years ago, a gift from the surrealists. It came into play when I wrote *The Ink Truck* and *Legs,* but it's in all my books, really. A parallel dimension to daily life.

Seshachari: You have it in abundance in *Quinn's Book.* Everything in it is larger than life, including Daniel Quinn himself and the women of that book. All your women are outstanding, very different from one another. How do you depict them in voice and point of view?

Kennedy: It's the same as I depict the men—discovering what is singular about them, in some way, extremism of behavior. The protagonists of my books are always extremists, and Katrina is no exception. She's unlike all around her, smarter, more intuitive, more candid and openhearted, probably sexier, and very brave.

Seshachari: And more obstinate?

Kennedy: And more obstinate. She knows what she wants and won't let anything interfere with it. That's a rare quality. So much of what is represented as female in fiction has been the submissive, the subordinate relationship to males and more to society in general. That's not what I saw in Katrina. I didn't see it in Helen Archer [in *Ironweed*] either. Helen knows exactly who she is. She's lived her life on her own terms, and she dies on her own terms.

Seshachari: I read your *Quinn's Book* first and was taken by its two women and also by Molly in *Bones,* who is especially self-directed. Later I read critics who say you give only the male point of view.

Kennedy: I don't see how any serious critic could read *Ironweed* and *Bones* and *The Flaming Corsage* and say that. But not all critics are serious. Some are not even critics.

Seshachari: Think of Maud Fallon or Magdalena Cólon—you give the same freedom to the women as many men appropriate to themselves. Quinn was Maud's seventh lover.

Kennedy: The idea that I either make them Madonnas or prostitutes, or projections of the male protagonists is literary slander. It often comes from male critics who wish they were feminists.

Seshachari: I'm very sensitive to the way writers treat women. Surely there's a view of women as men want them to be, as men fantasize them to be. But there's also another view of women as they think for themselves. I find you represent both. The men may fantasize endlessly about women, as Maginn does in the opening of *Corsage,* but your women characterize themselves through their articulated thoughts and actions.

Kennedy: I'm delighted to hear you say that. That opening in *Corsage*—

Edward and Maginn among the whores—one student implied that this was misogyny on my part. Obviously Maginn is a misogynist. He's a whoremonger who becomes a whoremaster, a total exploiter of women who lives off them eventually. But Edward is no misogynist and neither is his author. On the contrary.

Seshachari: Do you ever answer your critics?

Kennedy: I've never answered a critic in my life that I can remember. Books will live or they won't live. Maybe they won't even outlast the criticism, but so far that's not the case with me. If critics are a problem for you, you shouldn't have been a writer in the first place.

Seshachari: For the first time in your books, you refer to Giselle [in *Very Old Bones*] as a feminist.

Kennedy: She was one, and so, in a peculiar way, was Molly, though she wouldn't have suspected it. Some women in the earlier books were not, by choice. Helen Archer was the exception. Katrina was a nineteenth-century feminist, though she did not proclaim herself as such. Her mother was a proclaimed anti-suffragist. I'm not interested in these labels, only in behavior. If you start thinking in labels, you'll turn into a critic, or a literary cop.

Seshachari: Is there any chance you might write a novel where the woman is the central character?

Kennedy: It's possible. I don't have it on my plate at the moment. I don't know what I have on the plate, to tell you the truth. In the novel I'm thinking about, there's a major woman character, unlike any I've ever imagined. I look forward to hanging out with her.

Seshachari: In this new novel, what direction will you take in terms of narrative technique? I'm not talking of content so much as what you will do with the narrative structure, point of view, polyphonic voices, semi-surrealistic, semi-metaphysical approach.

Kennedy: I always want the surreal, and I'll probably have at least two voices. I'd like a linear narrative too, but I doubt I'll get it. Nothing ever comes out the way you plan it. One unexpected paragraph can change the form of the whole novel.

Seshachari: You have said to write a novel with film in mind is a "sin."

Kennedy: It's also impossible if you are serious about the novel. The novel is the interior life, a film is the exterior—action and talk. The novel is motivation, interpretation, and complexity. A film can suggest these things in screen imagery and bits of talk, and action can be profound, but together at their best they can't explain life the way a serious novel can.

Seshachari: It's particularly true for a writer like you, who uses so much of the metaphysical and the otherworldly. When you see Francis Phelan in the cemetery in the film of *Ironweed,* there is no way the richness of his thoughts and the interaction of the ghosts can be depicted with full impact on the screen. So critics say the film is not as good as the book.

Kennedy: It's different from the book, but it's a fine film. I love the film, and so do a lot of people. But so much of the book is the life of the mind—of Francis, Helen, Katrina. Katrina is hardly there in the film. Michael Ondaatje's *The English Patient,* widely praised as a novel, made an enormously successful film, artistically and commercially. But the director, Anthony Minghella, used only a portion of the novel's complex story, even though it's a very long film.

Seshachari: *The Great Gatsby* was another exception because Fitzgerald did not have this mystical, internalized dimension in his book.

Kennedy: What he had was remarkable prose, which is perfect for observation of Gatsby's life and life in America. It is some of the most beautiful writing in American literature and lends itself to voice-over narration. It's more usable than the interior monologue that Joyce made so popular—the voices of characters who talk to themselves in complex ways and whose lives move backward and forward through pure language and abstraction. You can't get that on screen without destroying the medium. Either medium. It becomes a recording of the novel, not a viable work of film art. But we've all learned from films. The pacing of literature in our age is far more rapid than it was in the age of Henry James. Film editing, storytelling speed, they've transformed literary work and the way we see the world.

Seshachari: In the introduction to *Riding the Yellow Trolley Car* you say, "This book is a writer's oblique autobiography, of his taste if nothing else. It is a tracking of writing style as it develops." Now that you have the collection of your selected writings culled from a couple of decades, how do feel your writing style has changed? There's obviously an evolution.

Kennedy: In the *Trolley Car,* I was talking about the evolution of a newspaperman's writing style, beginning in an anecdotal narrative and growing serious as it moves, and as it confronts literature. I learned the liability of purple prose, and I learned to value concision. I suppose the same applies to my fiction, for I've also learned how to write fictional narrative more complexly, more densely, yet without verbiage, I hope. Get your story in the first paragraph. Get to the point. Advice I've come to live by.

Seshachari: Now that you are not a nobody, where do you place yourself in the tradition of Irish-American writers and the American literary pantheon of the 20th century?

Kennedy: The pantheon isn't my business. You can't join it, and if you could, it wouldn't be a pantheon; it'd be a hippodrome. As to the Irish aspect, I've written enough about Irish-America that I've been ethnicized. Yet I don't write much about Ireland. I've touched on it in *Quinn's Book* and *Corsage,* mainly to talk about the immigrant antecedents of my family, my city [Albany]. My books are about characters who have intense private lives, and sometimes there's an Irish element to them. Albany has been an Irish-American city, in spades, but that's not all it's been. I'm a writer, I'm an American. Calling me anything more is typecasting and I resent it.

Seshachari: You've also been influenced by Joyce.

Kennedy: Who hasn't?

Seshachari: When Joyce was in exile in Europe, he would write to his friends, Now tell me exactly how far this location is from that street. You don't have to do that. You are right here in Albany.

Kennedy: I played that long-distance game when I was living in Puerto Rico writing my first book. I didn't know how to write about Albany, didn't understand the city's power structure. I knew some history, knew a bit about my family, but not enough. The gaps in what I knew made my writing seem tentative. Coming home and discovering the trove of history in the local libraries was stupendous. Some writers, like Hemingway, Robert Stone, Richard Ford, are constantly traveling to give themselves new contexts for their fiction. I lucked out finding I could stay put in Albany.

Seshachari: What about language?

Kennedy: Literature is all about language, not about plot. Best-sellers always have plot but rarely language. There are exceptions.

Seshachari: We think in words, rarely in images. Language creates our worlds and gives them verity and direction. Each one has one's own private world and these worlds coexist, coalesce, or overlap. The world that we all share is the world that overlaps.

Kennedy: That's my experience, all right. Each character has his own language. Billy Phelan doesn't speak the same language as his father, Francis Phelan. When you clearly hear a character's voice speaking to you, you know you have something to write about. When you hear two voices you declare a dividend.

Seshachari: How did you find your fictional voice?

Kennedy: In the early days, I was trying to become all the writers I revered, accumulating elements of their sentences, cadences. Moving between Faulkner and Hemingway, Joyce, Graham Greene and Nathanael West—it turns you schizophrenic. Eventually I peeled away one influence after the other and began to see that what was left over was me. My voice, my cadence. Nobody can tell you how to write a sentence, but they can tell you how not to: Don't do it like anybody else.

Seshachari: Yet for a novelist, while each character has a singular voice, there is also the totality of a projected voice—the writer's voice. That's pretty complicated, is it not?

Kennedy: It is. But the language can take on a life of its own for the writer. In *Ironweed,* for instance, I started writing what I thought was my voice, but it turned out to be Francis Phelan's. I kept reverting to my voice but ultimately, the bulk of the book exists in the spoken mind of Francis, the narrative of the life of his soul. I still believe that's Francis contemplating the most complex matters a human being can confront, in the most eloquent possible language that could be delivered through me. Being unable to express such thought in conversation doesn't mean Francis couldn't have that thought. He's aware of more than he knows. I think we're all born with talent and intuitive knowledge we don't consciously use; and then one day we do, and we discover what we know.

Seshachari: Do you ever look at a book and say, How did I write this? This looks pretty neat. Have you ever felt that?

Kennedy: Often. Especially in the early days. It didn't seem to have come out of my head. But when you write, you tap into that talent and intuition I was talking about, the intensity of actually creating something, bringing it out of your fingertips. It's truly joyous, and then you discover you can do it again. You're communicating with an element of yourself you don't usually reach, even in your most serious conversation. You're inventing out of a

confluence of known facts and random ideas, juxtaposing reality and abstractions, and then—wham! You've got something brand new in your head, and
on the page. You're functioning on a plane of existence you didn't know was
possible. That's creation, and it's profound pleasure. It's what you live for.

Index

Agee, James, 186, 213, 214, 220
Alger, Horatio, 122
Algren, Nelson, 242
Anderson, Sherwood, 136, 147
Armstrong, Louis, 29
Atkinson, Brooks, 21
Atlantic Monthly, The, 4, 9
Auchincloss, Louis, 6

Babenco, Hector, 108, 118, 119, 120, 124, 190
Bakker, Jim, 165
Baldwin, James, 6, 7, 185
Barish, Keith, 108, 120
Barrow, Clyde, 15, 45
Batista y Zaldivar, Fulgencio, 18
Beatty, Warren, 15
Beckett, Samuel, 36, 39, 42, 64, 65, 88, 169
Beiderbecke, Bix, 29
Bellow, Saul, 1, 5, 6, 19, 21, 37, 56, 107, 110, 114, 115, 122, 123, 127, 147, 163, 172, 175, 177, 178, 202, 204, 205, 218, 229
Beowulf, 200
Bergman, Ingmar, 42, 92, 100
Bicileta, Tono, 15
Bierce, Ambrose, 6
Billy the Kid, 102
Boccaccio, Giovanni, 89
Bogart, Humphrey, 60, 102, 200
Bonnie and Clyde. *See* Barrow, Clyde; Parker, Bonnie
Borges, Jorge Luis, 7, 252, 253
Braun, Eva, 102
Breslin, Jimmy, 5, 6
Broun, Heywood, 237
Buckley, William, 49
Buddhism, 85, 198, 221, 258
Buñuel, Luis, 42, 66, 101, 231
Burgoyne, Gen. John, 144
Burr, Aaron, 144
Byron, George Gordon, 200

Cagney, James, 60, 94, 102
Cain, James M., 97
Campbell, Joseph, 110, 258
Camus, Albert, 6, 229
Capone, Al "Scarface," 15, 102, 135, 180

Capote, Truman, 10
Capra, Frank, 74
Carver, Raymond, 96, 137, 165
Castro, Fidel, 17, 116, 177, 240
Chandler, Raymond, 37, 97
Chaucer, Geoffrey, 89
Cheever, John, 1, 6, 65, 68, 136, 137, 165, 185
Chekhov, Anton, 229
Chopin, Kate, 165
Coles, Robert, 19
Coll, Vincent, "Mad Dog," 13, 15
Coover, Robert, 44
Coppola, Francis Ford, 29, 97, 100, 105, 106, 116, 120, 123, 124, 134, 144, 150, 156, 157, 166, 171, 190
Corning, Edwin, 62
Corning, Mayor Erastus, II, 27, 57, 62, 130, 131
Costello, Frank, 15
Coward, McCann and Geoghegan, 12
Cowles, Gardner, 201
Crane, Stephen, 6, 38, 186
Cuomo, Governor Mario, 19, 68, 105, 157, 171

Daily Mirror, 44
Daily News, The, 44
Dali, Salvador, 115, 231
Dalton Brothers, 10
Dante Alighieri, 84
Davis, Miles, 29
De Niro, Robert, 103, 120
Dewey, Governor Thomas E., 62, 80, 140, 225, 251
Dial Press, 78
Diamond, Jack "Legs," 1–3, 7, 10, 12–17, 20, 23, 25, 35, 40, 42–46, 48, 51, 55, 57, 60–62, 67, 71, 77, 80–81, 93–94, 96, 101–03, 105, 106, 111, 114–15, 122, 127–28, 130, 135, 139, 146, 147, 149, 155–56, 162, 168, 179–81, 187, 217, 218, 222, 235, 243, 246, 250, 255, 258
Dickens, Charles, 42, 168, 258
Dickinson, Emily, 232
Doctorow, E. L., 78
Donoso, José, 68
Dorvillier, William J., 31, 201
Dos Passos, John, 48, 49, 50, 136